Antony Wynn

Antony Wynn read Persian and Turkish at Balliol, studying Persian literature, and spent a year at Shiraz University in Iran.

In the 1970s he worked first in Hamadan (western Iran) as resident carpet buyer for Oriental Carpet Manufacturers of London, travelling widely over much of the country covered by Sykes, and then in north-east Iran where he managed a country racecourse. Here he introduced Jockey Club rules to the local Turkoman horsemen, who were not used to any kind of rules.

He still travels regularly to Iran and is a friend of some of the descendants of those who worked with or fought against Sykes, in particular of the tribal chief who gave him the most trouble and of Prince Farman Farma, who was of such assistance to him.

PERSIA

IN THE

GREAT

GAME

Sir Percy Sykes
Explorer, Consul, Soldier, Spy

Antony Wynn

JOHN MURRAY

© Antony Wynn 2003

First published in 2003 by John Murray (Publishers)
A divison of Hodder Headline

Paperback edition 2004

1 3 5 7 9 10 8 6 4 2

The moral right of the author has been asserted

A CIP catalogue record for this title is available from the British Library

ISBN 0–7195–6415–8

Typeset in Monotype Bembo by Servis Filmsetting Ltd, Manchester
Printed and bound in Great Britain by Clays Ltd, St Ives plc

John Murray (Publishers)
338 Euston Road
London
NW1 3BH

To the memory of Kal Heidar
and with grateful thanks to all those
Persians who offered the author their
generous hospitality over the years

Contents

Contents

Illustrations

The author and publishers would like to thank the following for permission to reproduce illustrations: Plates 1, 6, 9, 11, 16, 21, 27 and 32, the Sykes family; 2, 13, 28 and 30, Royal Geographical Society; 3, 4, 5, 7, 8, 10, 12, 15, 17 and 20, Department of Oriental Antiquities, The British Museum; 14 and 19, Oriental & India Office Collection, The British Library; 18, from Frederick O'Connor, *On the Frontiers and Beyond*, London, 1931; 22, 23, 24, 25, 26, 29 and 31, Trustees of the Imperial War Museum, London.

Foreword

I am indebted for their help to Jonathan and Tristram Sykes, who lent me Sir Percy's albums and photographs; to Bill Sykes, who lent me his books by Sir Percy; to Sir Percy's youngest daughter Elinor Sinclair and his grandchildren Mark and Margaret Sinclair, who gave generous material help with the illustrations; to their sister Vicky Austerfield, who at the last moment found the memoir of Elinor's early life with Sir Percy; to Sir Denis Wright, formerly HM Ambassador to Iran and author of *The English amongst the Persians*, for access to his copious notes on Sykes and Farman Farma; to Clare Brown, erstwhile curator of the Middle East Centre Private Papers Collection at St Antony's College, Oxford; to John Fisher at the Public Record Office for his painstaking help in finding documents; to David McLean, Professor of History at King's College, London; to Floreeda Safiri for the loan of her thesis on the South Persia Rifles; to Farugh Farman Farmaian for information about Prince Farman Farma's family connections; to Kaveh Bayat, the Iranian historian and grandson of Saulat ud-Dowleh, for copies of Persian documents; to Dr John Gurney of the Oriental Institute, Oxford, for revising the manuscript; to Dr Homa Katouzian; to the military historian Gordon Corrigan for his information about nappy pins; to the London Library for providing so many source books, old and new; to Kate Paice, who has been an enthusiastic and constructive editor; to Andrew Lownie, my tireless agent; to Matthew Taylor for his final revisions of the text and to Anna Enayat and Caroline Knox for their very helpful guidance and comments in the early days. I am particularly indebted to Dr Sheila Canby and Dr Venetia Porter of the British Museum, who discovered the long-lost photographs and medieval Persian tiles donated by Sir Percy. Most of all, I am indebted to Sir Percy's son-in-law the late Sir Patrick Reilly, who not only gave me all his unpublished notes on Sir Percy and Lady Sykes but spent hours with me and replied at length and by return, with great courtesy and detail, to all my written queries. Finally, I am grateful to my wife, Victoria, for her ruthless comments on my prose and for all her support over the elephantine gestation of this book. Any errors that have entered the book in spite of all the advice from the above are my own responsibility alone.

This book is intended for the general reader with no specialist knowledge of Persia. I beg forgiveness from the experts for my attempts at simplifying the complicated history of Persia and from the non-experts for the detail contained in the Meshed chapters, which tell a story that no one has ever told before and say much about Russian duplicity and scorn for treaties.

Persia or Iran? Herodotus gave the name of Persia to the country, after Pars,[1] the principal province of the empire of Iran, which in those days extended from the Mediterranean and the Black Sea far up into Central Asia. Ever since, Europeans referred to Iran as Persia until Reza Shah, who founded the Pahlavi dynasty in 1925, insisted that the proper name of Iran be used. However, Europeans could never bring themselves to refer to Iranian carpets, miniatures, pottery, poetry – or even the language – and they stuck to the old word for these.

Iran is populated by Persians, Turks, Turkomans, Kurds, Lurs, Arabs, Armenians and Baluchis – all speaking different languages; but it is from the Persians, the people of the central plateau, that Persian culture has come down. So what should we call their country? There is a tendency nowadays, when talking of politics or oil, to refer to Iran; and when talking of the culture or the country before the Pahlavi reforms to use Persia. Percy Sykes was aware of

[1] Modern Fars, centred on the city of Shiraz in the south of Iran, close to Persepolis.

Iranian sensitivities in this regard and, when he wrote his *Ten Thousand Miles in Persia*, he gave it the subtitle of *Eight Years in Iran*. I hope that my Iranian friends will forgive me for following Sir Percy's contemporaries and calling their country Persia.

Maps

PERSIA IN T[...]
GREAT GAM[...]

ANS
SPIA

Geok Tapa
Askabad
Bujnurd
Dareh Gaz
Kuchan
Kelat 1 Naderi
MESHED
Sabzawar
Nishapur
Keshef Rud
Khushk
Amu Daria or Oxus
Torbat
TURSHIZ
Gunabad
Khaf
HERAT
KHORASAN
Kain
Tabas
BIRJAND
AFGHANISTAN
Naiband
KANDAHAR
Khabis
Nosratabad
Kuh-i-Khoja ▲ SISTAN
KERMAN
Hamun
Mahun
Helmand River
QUETTA
▲ Kuh-i-Shah
Bam
▲ *Kuh-i-Malik Siah*
KALAT
NARMASHIR
Rigan
Kuh-i-Taftan
Jiroft
Kuh-i-Bazman
Khwash
Mashkel Date Groves
B A L U C H I S T A N
Fahraj
Magas
Kuhak
Minab
Ramishk
Bampur
Lashar
Fanoj
PANJGUR
Geh
JASK
CHAHBAHAR
GWADAR
Karwan

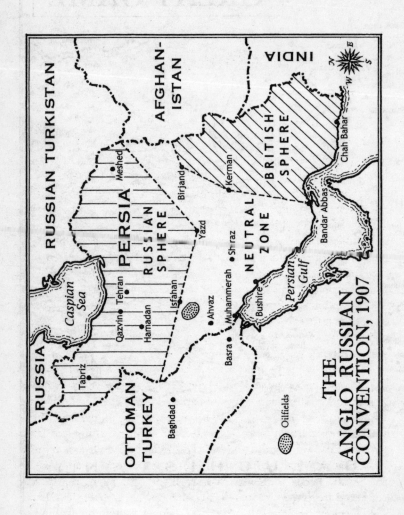

THE
ANGLO RUSSIAN
CONVENTION, 1907

RUSSIA

RUSSIAN TURKISTAN

AFGHAN-
ISTAN

INDIA

OTTOMAN
TURKEY

Caspian
Sea

PERSIA

RUSSIAN
SPHERE

BRITISH
SPHERE

NEUTRAL
ZONE

Persian
Gulf

Baghdad

Tabriz

Qazvin
Hamadan

Tehran

Isfahan

Ahvaz

Muhammerah

Basra

Bushire

Shiraz

Yazd

Birjand

Kerman

Meshed

Bandar Abbas

Chah Bahar

Oilfields

N
E
W
S

Prologue

A S I CAME out of the barber's shop in Shiraz, an old man of sol-
dierly bearing stepped out into the narrow street from the tiny
shop next door and snapped smartly to attention. From between a
full set of gold teeth gleaming through his massive waxed moustaches he barked out, 'Troop ready for inspection, Sahib'. He continued: 'Troop: Order lance . . . Trail lance.' When I asked him
where he had learned these commands from the British cavalry, he
drew himself up and said, with great pride: 'With the South Persia
Rifles, under Sir Percy Sykes, Sahib'. That was all the English that
he could remember. His name was Kal Heidar and in his retirement he was earning his living by pressing suits with a set of flat
irons heated with charcoal.

The year was 1970 and Sir Percy Sykes had been dead for nearly
twenty-five years. I was studying Persian at the University of
Shiraz and was lodging with the barber and his family. Kal Heidar
(Kal is short for *Kerbela'i*, one who has made the pilgrimage to the
holy city of Kerbela in Iraq) greeted me every morning and from
time to time we chatted and he told me his story. He was a jovial
old rascal who had had a colourful military career: in addition to
the South Persia Rifles he had served in and been successively
cashiered from the Ottoman army, the Abadan police, the Persian
Gendarmerie and even the Persian Cossacks, where he claimed to
have been the sergeant who had taught the future Reza Shah to
hold a rifle and to march straight.

There are few left today in Iran who remember Sir Percy Sykes but his legend, over a hundred years after his arrival in what was then called Persia, is still very much alive. Sir Percy had a conventional enough start to his life. At the age of ten he heard Sir Samuel Baker, the great African explorer, speak on his travels. That fired his imagination and he decided to follow the same kind of career. He went to school at Rugby in 1882 and, after going to Sandhurst, joined a cavalry regiment in India. There he spent as much of his time as he could exploring the mountains of Kashmir and Ladakh in pursuit of big game. He soon came to the notice of Army Intelligence and was sent on a mission in disguise into Russian Turkistan. He had joined the Great Game.

What followed was a series of journeys of exploration in the most deserted and unmapped areas of eastern Persia, conducting surveys for the Government of India, which was concerned about the threat to its security posed by the Russian advances into Central Asia. He was then sent to found a consulate in the oasis town of Kerman in south eastern Persia, as an outpost against these Russian moves southward. There, first with his sister and later with his wife, he spent ten years acquiring an encyclopaedic knowledge of the people, language, history, geography, religion, archaeology and folklore of Persia, making many local friends in the process. Astonishingly, he was paid no salary during all this time.

In 1905 Sykes was sent north to take over the consulate at Meshed, which, being close to the Russian border, was the most sensitive of all the British posts in Persia and was vital for gathering intelligence about Russian military activity. During the eight years he spent there he witnessed the drama of the Anglo-Russian Convention, which divided Persia into zones of Russian and British influence; this was followed by the turmoil of the Constitutional Revolution and the Russian-backed counter-revolution. With great skill, tact and patience he cultivated relations with the local Persian government and stiffened its resistance to the Russian attempts to turn the north of Persia into a Russian province and a springboard into India.

By way of an interlude, in 1915 he was sent to Chinese Turkistan to act as Consul-General at Kashgar, taking over from the famous Sir George Macartney, who had been there with his wife since 1898. With his sister Ella, Sykes explored and mapped the Pamir mountains by horse and yak, taking some remarkable photographs.

With the outbreak of the First World War the enemy had changed; Britain and Russia were now making common cause against Germany, Austria and Turkey. In 1915 German agents led by Wilhelm Wassmuss – the German Lawrence – were inciting the southern tribes against the British presence in Persia, threatening the oilfields on which the Royal Navy depended. The Germans were also plotting to raise a revolt of the Muslims in India against British rule and were sending agents through Persia to Afghanistan to descend on India and put a light to the tinderbox. All British troops were fully committed on the Western Front and in Mesopotamia and there were none available to meet this threat. Backed by no more than a handful of Indian soldiers, Sykes was sent to Persia to deal with the problem by raising a force of local levies, which came to be known as the South Persia Rifles. This caused great controversy among the nationalistic Persians, but despite opposition from the Persian government he succeeded in neutralizing the Germans and their agents and in eliminating the menace of the robber tribes, which had brought commerce to a halt. At the end of the war he fell foul of Lord Curzon over his misguided plan to turn Persia into a British protectorate, and Curzon made sure that he was never offered another job.

Sykes was a remarkable man. A young cavalry officer, a good horseman and polo player, an excellent and almost an obsessive shot, he might have been expected to be a non-intellectual, essentially out-of-doors man. Yet he was immensely erudite, with a great breadth of interests and even scholarship. He was astonishingly well read in the literature of travel and exploration, the European classics, and the major English poets. He read both Persian and Arabic, had studied the Qoran and commanded much respect among academic Orientalists throughout Europe. He bequeathed to the British Museum some remarkable examples of prehistoric bronzes, tilework and pottery which he had found in the remotest parts of Persia. And in the playing of the last moves of the Great Game he used his talents to the full.

I

Into the Great Game

'Syke' is an old Viking word for a moorland stream marking a land boundary. It appears from genetic research that nearly all Sykeses today share descent from a single common ancestor in the West Riding of Yorkshire. Percy Sykes's family first appeared there as yeoman farmers. In about 1750 Edmund Sykes left the land to become a linen draper and cloth manufacturer near Wakefield. His only son, William, moved to Cheshire and founded a muslin spinning factory and the Edgeley Bleach Works at Stockport. The business thrived and by 1869 Sykes was among the largest bleachers in the country. The family soon became prominent in public life and acquired a country estate. Between 1822 and 1910 four members of the family, one from each generation, served as mayor of Stockport. Others became involved in the local regiment and served as High Sheriff and Deputy Lieutenant of Cheshire. Another was chairman of the *Stockport Advertiser*. The family contributed generously to the building of three churches. There was money and there was land.

As with many such families, the money stuck more to one branch than the others. Three of Edmund's grandsons had no connection with the bleach works, nor did they benefit to the same extent as the others from the family fortune. One of them, William Sykes (1829–1893), took Holy Orders and spent his entire career as an army chaplain. He saw service in the Crimea and for a time was honorary chaplain to Queen Victoria. He married Mary

Molesworth, the daughter of an artillery officer, and in 1867, while he was chaplain to the Queen's Bays (2nd Dragoon Guards) at Canterbury, their son Percy was born. He had two older sisters: Ethel, who was not greatly loved in the family and was suspected of being 'delicate', and the redoubtable Ella, who later accompanied Percy on many of his travels. Neither of the sisters ever married.

Percy, who in his early life used the surname of Molesworth Sykes, was sent to school at Rugby. Solidly built but not tall, he was strong and athletic; he won several school cups and played racquets for the school. He also received a good grounding in Latin and Greek, those two underpinnings of a gentleman. Coming from the relatively unmoneyed branch of the family, he took the traditional course for younger sons without a large private fortune and joined the army. In due course he went to Sandhurst, where his father was by now chaplain. His conduct there was recorded as being 'exemplary'. After passing out of Sandhurst in 1888 he was commissioned into the 16th Lancers but quickly transferred to the Queen's Bays, who were then serving in India. As his father had been their chaplain, Percy could regard the Bays as the family regiment. Thus far his career had followed a perfectly conventional pattern.

The Bays were a cavalry regiment based at that time at Sialkot, whose officers spent their spare time, of which they had plenty in peacetime, playing polo, pig-sticking and 'poodle-faking', or idling about in an agreeably sociable way. They had a small pack of hounds and hunted jackal. In those days army officers were poorly paid and were expected to live off their private means and, since they were drawing little pay from the Exchequer and were easily bored when there was not much to do, in peacetime they were granted extensive periods of leave; these they were expected to spend engaged in 'important' activities such as polo or hunting, which would improve their military skills and horsemanship. These long periods of leave also allowed junior officers to take command in the absence of their seniors, at a time when promotion was slow, and thus gain useful experience. The Queen's Bays took their polo seriously and for three years in a row while Sykes was with them they were the inter-regimental champions.

In the hot weather the regimental day started at 5 a.m. Adjutant's Parade lasted from 5.30 until 7, followed by Stables until 8 and then Orderly Room, after which the officers took a sharp ride to the swimming baths before returning to the mess for a breakfast at 10.15 of porridge, quails or curry. At 6 p.m. they emerged to play polo or tennis, followed by billiards and cards. The keen young intellectual Francis Younghusband, who was later to lead the invasion of Tibet, spent some time with the Bays and described the life:

> The art of warfare was the last topic of conversation I found that was likely to rise. I found that these same men, as soon as there was any active service in sight, would move heaven and earth to get there. Keenness for sport did not mean indifference to service in the field. All it meant was disinclination to the monotony of preparation . . . To my surprise I found my brother officers excellent fellows; and in my heart of hearts I envied them their good nature. They never went to church except when paraded for service. Their talk was of little else than ponies or dogs. Their language was coarse. And yet they were a cheery lot, always ready to do each other a good turn and secretly possessing an ideal of their own to which I would have been thankful to attain: it was simply to be 'a good fellow', and a good fellow in their eyes was above a good Christian or even a good soldier.[1]

Sykes was remembered as one of the more dashing of the young officers. Although a keen polo player, he was not, according to his younger daughter, Elinor, interested in the 'poodle-faking' and he used to take himself off to Kashmir and Ladakh in the high Himalaya, where for three years he pursued big game and explored the wilder corners before coming to the attention of Army Intelligence, who recruited him.

An indication of the unusual course that his career subsequently took comes in the form of a document found in a scrapbook stored in a tin trunk in the grain room of one of Sykes's grandsons.

---

[1] Patrick French, *Younghusband* (London, 1994).

It was a certificate, written in English and Latin, from the United Grand Lodge of Freemasons, whose Grand Master was the Prince of Wales, and it showed that Sykes had been received into Freemasonry in October 1889 and been admitted to the Third Degree of Freemasonry in the Lodge *Nahab* (Benevolent) No. 988 at Sealkote [Sialkot] on 3rd February 1890. Membership of the masonry proved very useful to Sykes during his later years in Persia, and enabled him to gain the confidence of many of the leading men of the country, who were also Masons.

It was often said of Army Intelligence that officers of the Indian Army joined it because they got better shooting. Freed from the monotonous social round and from the dull parade-ground routine of the sociable dimwits, they were able to take to the mountains of the Pamirs, the Tian Shan and the Hindu Kush, where, as they stalked ibex and the rare Marco Polo sheep and pursued the elusive snow leopard, they gathered information about the local tribes, mapped the mountain passes and spied on Russian military activity on the other side. More riskily, they disguised themselves as Hindu horse-traders and penetrated deep into the enemy camps beyond the passes to spy on Russian movements. Away from the stifling life on the hot and dusty plains, they sought glory and promotion in the clean, clear mountain air and, although they roughed it, living off bully beef and Bovril in their thin canvas tents, they felt as if they lived like kings.

British policy in India at the time was concerned with countering the threat from the Russians, who had been making rapid advances eastward into Central Asia, occupying Tashkent in 1865, Samarqand and Bokhara in 1868, Khiva in 1873, Khokand in 1875, Ashgabad in 1881, and Merv and the Murghab river up to the Afghan border in 1884. Government policy was divided between the 'forward school' under Disraeli's Tories, who advocated pushing out the frontiers of India, and the school of 'masterly inactivity' under Gladstone's Liberals, who believed that the Russians were a civilizing influence on the slave-raiding Turkoman and that they posed no threat to India. The forward school had received a bloody nose with the disastrous defeat of the British in the Afghan War, while the proponents of inactivity pointed out the enormous and unjustifiable expense of maintaining any forward presence.

The Army of India was divided in its views, but one glance at the map showed that the Russians were now poised to fall on India, should they choose to do so, from a number of directions. From their new base at Ashgabad, next to the Persian frontier, they could cross into Afghanistan, with an easy route through Herat and Kandahar to Quetta; from Samarqand they could make their way, albeit with difficulty, across the Hindu Kush to Kabul and the Khyber Pass; from Khokand and Murghab they could drop down from the Tian Shan mountains into Chinese Kashgar and thence, with more difficulty, into India across the Himalayas. What appeared to be the easiest route lay directly south through eastern Persia, an undefended region practically unsurveyed by the British or the Russians. Since the Afghans could be expected to put up some stout resistance to an invasion by the Russians, the British became increasingly concerned that the invasion would come through Persia.

In the autumn of 1891 Sykes took home leave from India and spent some months, in his own words, 'in Eastern Europe, in an attempt to gain some insight into the various problems that would, within the next thirty years, call for solution'. There appears to be no record of what he was doing but, having been recruited by Army Intelligence, he was probably 'getting to know the enemy' so that he could play his part in the Great Game or, as the Russians called it, the Tournament of Shadows.

2

In disguise to Samarqand

IN JULY 1891 news reached London that the Russians were sending a force of four hundred Cossacks with a battery of mountain guns into the Pamirs, the mountains at the roof of Asia where the disputed borders of India, Russia, China and Afghanistan met. Captain Francis Younghusband, also now of Army Intelligence, set out from Kashgar to investigate. After a strenuous journey into the mountains he camped at a lonely spot a hundred and fifty miles south of the Russian border, well inside Afghan territory, and was soon startled by the approach of a party of Russian Cossacks. He offered to share his spartan dry rations with them and in return the Russian officers entertained him to a convivial and copious dinner under canvas with meat, fresh fruit and vegetables, washed down with wine and brandy from the Caucasus. Over the drinks they informed him that they had just returned from a raid across the Indian watershed into Chitral and that they were annexing a large part of the Pamirs extending into Chinese and Indian territory. Three days later they arrested him, declaring that he was on Russian territory, and, with great courtesy and expressions of personal regret, escorted him to the Chinese border. For some time he was unable to communicate with India and rumours began to circulate that he had been shot by the Russians. Whitehall was incensed and the Prime Minister, Lord Salisbury, ordered the British ambassador at St Petersburg to deliver a strong official protest to the Russian government. The British policy of masterly inactivity had received something of a knock and General Roberts, Commander-in-Chief India, mobilized a division in readiness for a pre-emptive invasion of Afghanistan.

In the summer of 1892 Sykes applied to the army for leave to go to Afghanistan to pursue the coveted Marco Polo sheep. The Intelligence Department, however, concerned that the Russians might be planning further expeditions towards India, had other plans for him and sent him to discover whether their fears were well founded. With another young officer, Lieutenant Coningham, he made his way to Odessa, that cosmopolitan Russian port on the Black Sea, and reported for briefing to Colonel Stewart, the British Consul. Stewart had been a famous player of the Great Game who had spent many lonely years on the north-eastern borders of Persia, sometimes openly and once travelling in the Turkoman country disguised as an Armenian horse dealer. In fact he was reporting on the Russian advance into the Turkoman country and he witnessed the famous battle of Gök Tepe, where the Russians slaughtered 15,000 of the Turkoman at their last stand against the invaders. On a later journey through Afghanistan he came across local government troops at Herat wearing Mackenzie tartan over their baggy trousers. The kilts had been taken from the Seaforth Highlanders in battle a short time before. He was later greatly responsible for persuading the Royal Navy to change from coal fuel to oil, having reported on the Russian navy's use of oil by the Caspian Fleet, based at Baku.

From Odessa, Sykes and Coningham took a steamer for another Black Sea port, Batumi, which turned out to be closed because of an outbreak of cholera. They disembarked at the Turkish port of Trebizond and took a rowing boat all the way up the coast, which dropped them off at a beach near Batumi. There they were immediately put into quarantine by the police, who believed that they might be Russian nihilists disguised as Englishmen and intent on assassinating the Tsarevich, who was due to arrive shortly on a visit. After three days of open arrest on the beach they succeeded in persuading the Russians that they were just a pair of mad but harmless Englishmen and they were allowed to make their way inland by train to the Georgian capital of Tiflis, on the road to the Caspian port of Baku.

Their object was to see whether it was possible to travel undetected by ferry across the Caspian from Baku to Uzun Ada in
Turkistan and from there by the new Transcaspian military railway
which the Russians had just built to Samarqand. They were also to
report on any military activity in the area. Neither officer spoke
more than a word or two of Russian and the expedition was
frighteningly amateurish, relying for its success entirely on the
ability of the participants to get themselves out of a scrape.

When they heard that the ferry sailing from Baku had been
delayed, they decided to go to ground for a few days in Tiflis rather
than wait for it in Baku, where they were more likely to be spotted.
The German consul helped them to find a safe hotel, where they
remained undetected. Sportingly, he bet them £1,000 that their
mission was impossible and that they would be caught by the
Russians. With the help of an Armenian dragoman, or interpreter–courier, they bought Russian clothes and, leaving all their
belongings except their hand luggage with another Armenian, went
on down the line in disguise to Baku, where, with the help of the by
now thoroughly frightened dragoman, they boarded the ferry.

Once aboard they locked themselves into their cabin but, since
the crossing was rough and many of the passengers were seasick,
nobody suspected them, and on 19th November they disembarked
on the other side of the Caspian at the railhead of Uzun Ada. After
telling their dragoman to tell anyone who inquired that they were
foreign merchants in the cotton business, they boarded the train
separately and, as if by chance, took seats in the same compart-
ment. They spoke to each other only occasionally, and that in
schoolboy French, until a Frenchman unfortunately joined them,
at which point they switched to monosyllabic German. To avoid
attracting attention they took their meals in the restaurant car after
all the other passengers had finished. At nightfall the conductor
turned them out of their cabin to make room for a Russian officer
but they nevertheless remained undetected. Three days later they
arrived at Samarqand and, to avoid a customs inspection, sent
ahead the Armenian dragoman, who was by now in a state of total
funk, to 'rouble his way through' with the luggage. He rented a
filthy room for all three of them, from which they emerged only at
dusk, to take short drives to look around.

In this game of grandmother's footsteps they realized that they were unlikely to be able to gather much useful information, so they sent for two nephews of the Tiflis Armenian with whom they had left their baggage, one of whom turned out to be a steward in the Russian Officers' Club, and spoke only Russian and Armenian. This was an advantage, because they were able to persuade him that they were French, which Sykes spoke adequately, though with an execrable accent.

The steward provided them with the somewhat thin information that there was a garrison of 3,000 men in six regiments at Tashkent, who did duty for two years before being relieved from Siberia and Ekaterinburg – not by the Transcaspian railway. The troops in the Pamirs came from Osh, close to the Chinese border, and there were three hundred men in winter quarters at Murghab, two marches from the border, with a larger Chinese force camped near by. Murghab was due to be fortified in the following year and the Russians were indeed planning to substantiate their claim to the Pamirs by establishing a base on the plateau.

Other snippets of information were that there was a gun foundry at Tashkent which had produced sixteen field pieces of unknown calibre; that there were some large storehouses and several new factories, one of which was run by an Englishman; and that only one of the Russian officers could speak French fluently. Since French was the language of the Court at St Petersburg, this suggested that the other officers were not of the highest social standing. The railway was due to be extended eastwards to Khokand in 1893. There was also news that the Russians had ordered all Indian traders to leave Tashkent by the end of the year, since they were accused of also being 'newswriters' for the British. This was a setback for the Indian intelligence service, which did indeed employ some of these traders more or less openly as reporters.

Encouraged by the dragoman to leave as soon as possible, Sykes and Coningham had to decide how to get home. They could have carried on east to Kashgar and then headed back to India by crossing the Himalayan passes, but with winter approaching they decided instead to return by the way they had come and check once more on the possibility of travelling incognito on the

Transcaspian railway. After a fright at the Uzun Ada customs, where they were nearly discovered, they succeeded in boarding the ferry unchecked and after a stormy crossing to Baku they finally reached Odessa. Sykes did not record in his report whether he paused in Tiflis to claim his winnings from the German consul.

At Odessa they reported on their mission to Colonel Stewart, who congratulated them on having achieved the impossible. They attributed their success to the fact that they were never asked to produce their passports and that their unshaven appearance 'did not present us as persons whose acquaintance it would be desirable to make'.

Well into his old age Sykes would recount the bare outlines of this adventure to his family but, even fifty years later, he never spoke about the military information that he had acquired, saying rather pompously that it was 'still secret'. It was in fact relatively low-grade intelligence that he had gathered, and in any case the Imperial Russian army that he had been observing all those years ago had long since been swept away by the Bolsheviks, so there was hardly any need to maintain secrecy about his adventure.

A year after this escapade Sykes's companion Lieutenant Coningham was sent on another mission to spy out the land in the mountains of the Russo–Persian border near Ashgabad, where the British had heard that the Russians were trying to persuade the Shah to cede them the village of Firuzeh. He set out from Meshed by horse, carefully avoiding any towns with a telegraph or a Russian agent who might report his presence and discovered that Firuzeh, of which the Shah had never heard, lay across a pass that the Russians could use to invade Persia, which was why they wanted it. This information was duly reported back to Lord Salisbury and to the Shah, who, his spine stiffened by British encouragement, refused to let the Russians have Firuzeh. Russian pressure was such, however, that he was later forced to yield it, in return for a piece of Russian territory on the border of Azerbaijan.

3

Meeting the Prince

AFTER A SHORT home leave following this escapade Sykes was, as he states somewhat disingenuously in the introduction to his book *Ten Thousand Miles in Persia*, 'given leave' to rejoin his regiment in India by travelling overland via Persia instead of taking the normal sea route by steamer. In January 1893 he took the train to Vienna and Odessa, where, with the help of Colonel Stewart, he hired an educated and well-travelled Persian named Yusef Abbas to act as his guide and factotum on the journey. Preceded out of the frozen harbour by an icebreaker, they took the steamer to Batumi. In Tiflis they put up at the Hôtel de Londres, otherwise known as Madame Richter's, the last decent hotel between Europe and India, where all eastward-bound Englishmen liked to spend a few days before going on to Baku. There the oil industry was in its infancy, with new refineries built by the Nobel brothers. Oil was cheaply and easily extracted by hand-digging from shallow wells and taken in drums by camel down to the port, where at any time up to six vessels would be waiting to take the cargo up the Caspian to the European market via Astrakhan and the Volga river. Oil leaked out of the ground all round the city, and one of the entertainments on a calm evening was to set light to the oil floating on the sea off the main promenade.

Instead of taking the usual ferry down the west coast of the Caspian to the Persian port of Enzeli, they took one going across to Uzun Ada and then down to the island of Ashurada, at the mouth of a lagoon off the Persian coast, which the Russians had occupied on the pretext of setting up a naval station to suppress the Turkoman pirates. The Persian port at Ashurada was nothing more than a hulk anchored a mile offshore in the lagoon; to get ashore passengers had to be rowed in small boats to a rickety pier sticking out from the muddy and desolate settlement of Bandar Gaz. There was no hotel, but the resourceful Yusef Abbas persuaded the Persian telegraph operator to put them up. This lonely man was only too pleased to have their company and gave Sykes his first introduction to the Persian way of cooking steamed *chelo* rice with meat and vegetables. It was so good that Sykes wrote down the recipe, with the recommendation that it should be given to Indian army cooks to improve their dismal curries.

When they found that horses could not be hired for a fair price they telegraphed to the local British agent at Astarabad, an Indian trader, who sent up some sturdy little Caspian ponies, on which they started their journey inland. Astarabad (now Gorgan) was a town set close to the sea in very fertile country at the foot of the forested Alborz mountains on the southern edge of the Turkoman steppe and it frequently suffered from tribal raids. Napoleon and Tsar Paul had once planned together to invade India through here and the scheme had been revived during the Crimean War, but its strategic importance had been removed with the construction of the Transcaspian railway.

After spending a fruitless week in the wooded hills looking for stag to shoot, Sykes rode a short way north of the town to the camp of Musa Khan, chief of the Aq Atabai tribe of the Turkoman, to whom he carried a letter of introduction from Colonel Stewart, who had previously served as consul at Astarabad. In spite of this introduction, the Khan refused to allow Sykes to proceed off the main road to travel to Meshed through Turkoman country, for fear that he would be held responsible should Sykes be attacked, robbed or kidnapped. He was not in the least impressed when Sykes told him that he was a member of the Royal Geographical Society, the very purpose of whose existence was to explore the unknown, nor was he won over when Sykes offered him a revolver as a present. The Khan had been to Moscow and had already acquired a collection of good revolvers. However,

Sykes finally struck the right vein by observing that the Khan enjoyed a good name in Europe for hospitality, which he would lose if he persisted in blocking his progress. Musa Khan gave in and provided three of his relatives to accompany Sykes to the edge of his tribal territory and to arrange for his onward escort.

As a guide they were given a mulla called Haq Nafas, who turned out to be an outlaw wanted by the authorities in both Astarabad and Bojnurd, which was on their way to Meshed. At one point he threatened to seize the mules, which caused much weeping from the muleteers and led to a fierce shouting match in the *alachik* with Yusef Abbas, who yelled to Sykes, 'They mean to kill us, Sah, so let us shoot first.' This was clearly out of the question but Haq Nafas had to be got rid of and Sykes, combining charm with brute force, told Yusef to inform the mulla that he loved him as a son and so forth and, while this was being translated, slapped him violently on the back, both to show his affection and to prevent him from replying. Finally, to the delighted laughter of the rest of the Turkoman, Sykes chased the mulla away.

The group carried on through the rolling grassy hills along the Atrak valley to Bojnurd, which was populated by the tribe of Shahdillu Kurds, moved there in the seventeenth century by Shah Abbas, the builder of Isfahan, to act as wardens of the marches and to keep the Turkoman from raiding the road to Meshed. With the recent defeat of the Turkoman by the Russians at Gök Tepe their life had become more peaceful. At Bojnurd, Sykes met the Il-Khan of the Shahdillu, who was also the hereditary governor of Bojnurd and very well informed about India. At first, not surprisingly, he refused to believe Sykes's story that he was travelling in a private capacity for his own amusement. After finally being reassured, however, the Il-Khan warmed to him. The resulting friendship proved very useful to Sykes when he became Consul-General at Meshed twelve years later.

Moving on from Bojnurd, they rode up one of the most fertile valleys in the country to Quchan, another Kurdish town. Protocol required that they call on the governor, but since this dignitary was known to be in a continual stupor from opium[1] and they were in a

---

[1] Curzon had had the same problem with him; see *Persia and the Persian Question*, vol. I, p. 94.

hurry to reach Meshed, Sykes decided to press on, although the usual form was to give three days' notice of one's intention to leave. A few miles out of Quchan, however, they were held up when one of his horses had an attack of colic. Sykes's servants refused to apply the standard Indian army cures that he suggested and insisted on using their own methods. They cut the horse in the tongue and at the root of its tail and then poured mutton grease down its throat. Then a passing holy man appeared and offered to effect a cure by weeping into the horse's eye, but this was refused by the waggoners, who said that he was asking spectacularly more than the going rate for this particular piece of magic.

Three days later, at the end of February, still some miles out of the holy city of Meshed, they saw a man standing on the top of a caravansaray waving to them. This was a *sowar* (outrider) sent by the British Consul at Meshed to meet him. Sykes left Yusef Abbas to follow with the baggage wagon and 'cantered mile after mile towards the city, with the beautiful golden dome of the shrine shining like a flame in the rays of the setting sun. We hardly drew rein until we reached the city gate.' He spent a few days in the British Consulate with the famous Ney Elias. The consulate was then in a battered caravansaray in the bazaar quarter, but the Consul was busy constructing the new and imposing building that Curzon had ordered.

Ney Elias had been born to a family of Jewish merchants of Bristol who had given up their faith. From an early posting to the branch of the family firm at Shanghai he had started exploring the Yellow River, which was a mere overture to the most astonishing series of journeys in the unexplored parts of Mongolia, Yunnan and Tibet. After abandoning commerce for government service in Ladakh and Chinese Turkistan, he took seventeen months to explore no fewer than forty of the Himalayan passes, covering three thousand miles in the process and gathering detailed intelligence about Russian activity in the mountains to the north of India. He was a mysterious, enigmatic and ascetic character and he gave Sykes a detailed briefing about the affairs of Meshed, this sensitive city close to the borders of Russian Turkistan and Afghanistan which teemed with priests, pilgrims, spies and agents.

As the capital of the fertile province of Khorasan it was of vital interest to the Russians, who depended on it as a source of supply for their new colony over on the north side of the mountains at Ashgabad, which was otherwise surrounded by desert. Elias suggested that Sykes cross the desert of the Lut, which was unmapped, and visit Kerman and, seeing that Sykes had finished the last of his supply of Bovril, solicitously insisted that he stock up with sufficient stores for his journey. He himself would have done without.

Still with Yusef Abbas as his factotum, Sykes hired a Turkoman muleteer for the baggage and set off southwards across the cold, rolling, snow-covered country. On the first day out they entered a steep valley and were soon in deep snow. At the top of the pass at the valley head they came to a very narrow ledge with a cliff above it and a bottomless snowdrift on the other. Sykes told the muleteer to let the animals go through one by one on their own, but the muleteer insisted on keeping them tied together. The first one stopped to sniff and test its footing; the second one pushed into it and shoved it, baggage and all, so that it tumbled into the snowdrift below, and was then itself dragged down with the leader. Sykes just managed to stop the third mule from meeting the same fate. It took them four hours to find the boxes and haul them up to the ledge with ropes and then to find a way to bring the mules that had disappeared into the snowdrift back up to the track. When they reached the top of the pass at 6,500 feet and began their descent to the little town of Torbat-i Haidari, they met a heavy sleet storm. After crossing another pass to Gonabad they entered the desert of the Kavir-i Lut and made for Naiband, an isolated village perched on rocks in the centre of the desert, which had been founded as an outpost against the raiding Baluchis. This village is so remote and the people consequently so inbred that today most of them are born with cleft palates and many of them are blind.

The central Persian desert is not a flat expanse of sand like the Arabian desert; most of it is above 3,000 feet high and, except for the central part, is broken up by several ranges of sharp and barren mountains, some of which reach over 10,000 feet. Here and there, wherever there is water, there are small villages with gardens protected by mud-brick walls to keep out the wind-blown sand.

Persian travellers believed the desert to be inhabited by all manner of terrifying *djinns* and ghouls, and even the normally prosaic Sykes admitted to seeing visions of towers, houses and figures of men in the moonlit, fantastically sculpted rocks near Naiband.

European travellers in Persia took their own camps with them if they could. There were caravansarays along the road, which were used by Persian travellers, but they were usually crowded, filthy and crawling with bugs and lice. Not only that, but there was no privacy within as Europeans were considered objects of communal curiosity. Passing one of these caravansarays, Sykes came across a party of wayfarers who had been robbed by a gang of Arabs that he had just met on the road and, seeing that he was armed, asked for his help. Sykes rode off with Yusef Abbas and caught up with the Arabs, who threatened them with their knives until the sight of revolvers made them hand over their loot.

Instead of following the known road to Kerman, Sykes made an exploratory detour to the east to Khabis (now Shahdad), a little oasis town on the edge of the Lut, which still produces excellent dates, oranges and henna. To reach it they had to go through a very narrow valley in the mountains which ended at the *Khar-Shikan* or 'Donkey-Breaker' defile, which was so narrow that all donkeys had to be unloaded, and their loads carried through by hand, before they could pass. By the time he finally reached Kerman, he had compiled an extensive array of maps and notes for Indian Army Intelligence and for the Royal Geographical Society.

Kerman was known territory, with a small British community of missionaries and a branch of the British-owned Imperial Bank of Persia,[2] so Sykes pushed on south-west in the direction of Shiraz, seeking out unexplored routes through the rolling uplands and eventually reaching the fertile district of Pariz at the edge of the province of Kerman, lying at 7,500 feet and surrounded by orchards. It would have been a prosperous place but for constant raiding by the Baharlu tribe coming from the province of Fars to the west. So great was the fear of the Baharlu that Sykes's muleteers all deserted and it was only when the governor of Pariz

---

[2] Later the Bank of Iran and the Middle East, subsequently the British Bank of the Middle East, now subsumed into HSBC.

explained to the men that they would have more to fear from him than from the Baharlu if they refused to move that they agreed to carry on.

That evening there was a thunder of hoofs at the door of the house where Sykes was staying and there appeared a messenger from Prince Farman Farma [Issuer of Edicts], the Governor-General of Kerman, who was camped a little way behind him and, having heard that Sykes was travelling through his province, wished to meet him. Sykes was reluctant to retrace his steps but decided that it would be discourteous to ignore this summons. It was as well that he did so. He described his meeting with the Prince as follows:

Abdul Hussein Mirza Farman Farma was about thirty-three years of age. He was slight, rather below the middle height, and somewhat short-sighted. Educated by officers of the Austrian military mission, he had acquired a smattering of the military art and was, generally speaking, well informed for a Persian and spoke French well. His thirst for knowledge was a passion, and his quickness in picking up facts was quite Gallic. Indeed, Persians with their polite manners and vivacity closely resemble the Latin races, being more polite than Frenchmen and also wittier, but there is an absolute want of system and no idea of thrashing out a question in the way so dear to the soul of an Englishman. At night I had a chair and a table set for me and thoroughly enjoyed a luxurious Persian meal, at the conclusion of which Her Majesty was toasted by my courteous host.

During my stay with His Highness two points struck me in particular; firstly that all Farman Farma's inferiors were his servants, with generals and majors acting as waiters, like mediaeval Europe. The second point was the want of proportion displayed, the smallest and least important case generally occupying the longest time, while everything, even to a dispute among the suite, was settled by His Highness himself, whose whole day was thus occupied.

The Prince invited Sykes to stay with him for the next two days while he made his semi-royal progress towards Rafsenjan.

Realizing that this was an opportunity for a rare and privileged insight into Persian life, Sykes accepted and the next morning he was initiated into the royal sport of gazelle shooting. His description of it shows that the Persian miniaturists were not completely fanciful in their depiction of the hunt:

The two hundred *sowars* accompanying His Highness formed up in groups of two or three, four hundred yards apart, and we swept the plain in the form of a crescent, the flanking groups being thrown forward to prevent the quarry escaping into the hills. In time we sighted a herd of seven gazelle, which at first moved slowly away, but kept looking round, as if desirous of breaking back. At last they made up their minds and trotted towards one of the intervals, which slowly lessened in width as the group closed in. When about a hundred yards distant from us the gazelle raced along at top speed, and we galloped to cut them off, arriving within forty yards of them, whereupon His Highness fired both barrels of a 10-bore, which was loaded with slugs. On more than one occasion I have seen the Farman Farma bag a right and left. Of course, the sport is risky and I have been peppered by the group on either side of me. If the horse falls the gun generally goes off without doing any harm, although two men had their hats blown away on one occasion. The sport is excellent and the finest training for man and beast and is the only way to get on level terms with the gazelle.

We spent two days in a walled garden near Bahramabad, the chief town of Rafsenjan and, after being royally entertained, I said good-bye to His Highness, who warmly invited me to join him in Baluchistan during the winter.

Persians say that to become friends with someone one must go on a journey with him; Sykes had not only travelled with Farman Farma, he had galloped with him in the hunt and, more than that, had won his respect by keeping up with him. This was practically the first time that any Englishman had met a high Persian official or a member of the royal family on any other than a purely formal footing. Such was the predilection of the Qajar dynasty for forging alliances through marriage within the family that Farman Farma was uncle, brother-in-law and son-in-law to the Crown Prince, the future Muzaffar ud-Din Shah.[3] The friendship that was formed from the chance meeting of these two men set their careers on a parallel course and created a mould for Anglo-Persian relations that was to endure for twenty-five years, with echoes that continued up to the reign of the last Shah.

Crossing the salt flats to the west, Sykes hurried on towards Shiraz and fell in for a few days on the way with a New Zealander whom he found prospecting for borax. Nearing Shiraz he met a line inspector from the Indo-European Telegraph, who informed him that there was rioting in the city. The company at that time had a line which went underwater up the Persian Gulf, calling in at Gwadur, Jask, Qeshm Island, Bandar Abbas and Bushire, from where it went overland to Baghdad and eventually reached London. Within Persia there were overland lines connecting Shiraz, Kerman and Tehran to the system. It was maintained by lonely British engineers whose job was often made more difficult by the local tribesmen or villagers who, in a treeless country where timber was valuable, had the vexing habit of helping themselves to the wooden telegraph poles for roof beams or fuel. Dedicated as they were to their duty, many of these men went mad through drink or died of disease and their monuments are to be found in the Christian churchyards of Persia.

A curiosity of Persian life was that a telegraph office was one of the places considered to be *bast* or sanctuary, in that it was supposed to be connected directly to the Peacock Throne of the Shah, to whom one could thus appeal directly for a wrong to be righted. Other places of *bast* were the royal stables, some of the holy shrines and foreign legations or consulates.

In Shiraz, Sykes found that the rioters had taken *bast* in the British telegraph office and were demanding the dismissal of the Qavam ul-Molk, the Governor-General, whose exactions and

---

[3] He was Muzaffar ud-Din Shah's second cousin and first cousin to his father, Nasir ud-Din Shah. His sister was married to Muzaffar ud-Din Shah. Furthermore, he was married to a daughter of the Shah from a different wife. Strictly speaking, he was not uncle to Muzaffar ud-Din Shah. However, his father was uncle to Naser ud-Din Shah. Any reference to 'FF' as 'uncle' is correct but it should be understood that this would be in fact his father. Customarily an uncle to a first generation would also be referred to as 'uncle' by the following generation.

depredations had become intolerable. The Shah at first refused to dismiss Qavam, who was also the head of the most powerful and influential local family, and telegraphed to him that he would hold him responsible for keeping order. At this point the rioters, despairing of seeing satisfaction from the British and their telegraph, began to threaten them and forced them to leave the office and take refuge in their walled garden outside the city. In the morning shooting broke out between the opposing parties and a group of Baharlu tribesmen arrived to support the Governor. Savage fighting continued until finally a telegram arrived from the Shah summoning the Governor to Tehran to account for himself. He left the city in disgrace, accompanied by the wishes of the populace that he should meet the same fate as his great-grandfather, who had been boiled alive for similar behaviour.

Having seen how the people of Persia, when pushed, could force changes on their despotic government, which lacked any democratic institutions, Sykes set out from Shiraz over the mountain passes to the south-west, down to the Gulf port of Bushire, from where he could take ship back to India. He completed his journey to the coast in a leisurely five days and embarked for Karachi to rejoin his regiment in Rawalpindi, but first he had to report to the Foreign Department of the Army at Simla to submit an account of his travels. His report, particularly his account of meeting Farman Farma, was duly noted and passed back to London, where it was eventually shown to Lord Salisbury himself. Sykes had made his mark in Persia.

4

Terriers in Baluchistan

IN OCTOBER 1893 the Army Foreign Department at Simla, now more concerned than ever about the possibility of Russian invasion through Persia, sent Sykes on a journey of reconnaissance through Persian Baluchistan to survey the possible routes down which the invasion might come and to decide where best to establish military outposts to give warning and act as a deterrent. They needed to discover where animal transport, fodder and supplies could be secured, and to acquire information about the tribes along the way and their attitude to the British, the Persians and the Russians. Since Baluchistan was divided between Persia and India and the Persians had only very recently annexed their part of it, on which they had only a tenuous hold, the question was of some importance. The party, which embarked on the SS *Pemba* from Karachi, as shown in the official record,[1] was made up of the following:

2nd Lt P.M. Sykes (Queen's Bays)
Surgeon Major Brazier Creagh (Army Medical Service)
Duffadar Sultan Shukru (3rd Punjab Cavalry)
2 *sowars* of the Corps of Guides (Cavalry)
2 personal servants each

---

[1] The more entertaining parts of the account of this expedition come from Brazier Creagh's report, lodged with the Sykes papers at St Antony's College, Oxford.

2 *syces* (grooms)
6 horses
2 Irish terriers

On 15th October the *Pemba* put in to the bay of Chahbahar, just inside the Persian border in the district of Makran. The Makran coast is almost totally barren and was described by the chroniclers of Alexander the Great as the land of the *Ichthyophagi*, or fish-eaters, for there is so little grazing that even the camels are fed on dried fish.

Chahbahar, which is now an important naval base, was a deep natural anchorage, with no surf. After the ship had dropped anchor, the horses and baggage were winched overboard onto a local wooden *bughala* to be taken ashore but, since this vessel could get no closer than two hundred yards from the beach, the animals would have to swim for it. However, the high-sided *bughala* was not equipped with slings to lift the horses over the side, so while Sykes went ashore to make arrangements for the onward journey, Brazier Creagh (whose report, lodged with the Sykes papers at St Antony's College, Oxford, provides the most entertaining account of the expedition) busily piled up all the cargo against the bulwarks on one side and covered it with grain bags, old sails and bits of matting to make a ramp. Then he plugged the horses' ears with cotton wool and vaseline to keep the water out and persuaded the reluctant beasts to go up his ramp and jump over the side into the sea. His own two horses were used to swimming the River Jumna or crossing it in boats when out pig-sticking and managed easily, but the other four, which had enjoyed no such training, were more awkward. Once they were in the water, instead of making for the shore, they aimed straight for the nearest boats and tried to scramble back aboard. It took three and a half hours to get the animals ashore and the expedition under way.

First, however, they needed baggage camels. The manager of the telegraph office, glad of unaccustomed English company, was happy to help and, since he knew the district well, was able to produce twenty-three camels with Baluchi drivers. The camels were fine, but the drivers were another matter. They spent the next day 'wrangling like jackals' over the distribution of the loads, complaining that they were too heavy for their beasts. Sykes solved the problem – a perennial one with Baluchi camel-men – by giving them an empty box to load. When they complained about that one as well, he opened it up and that was the last complaint they made. A day later the noisy *bandobast* of loading was completed and the caravan moved off inland.

On the second day one of the Irish terriers, which was unwell, got lost. Two Baluchis were sent back to look for it, but said that they could not find it. The expedition halted and spent a day searching for it, and eventually it was discovered back at the site of their first camp. The two Baluchis, who had not appreciated the sentimental value to a large burly Englishman of a small sick dog, had not bothered to go back and search for it at all.

There were no roads of any kind in this part of the country and the way led across a lava plain, broken by lines of jagged cliffs, to the village of Geh, the old capital of Makran, which had a small river running by it. Here they halted while Sykes's soldier escorts used their mosquito nets to catch fish.

At the next village, when the head man, 'black-bearded, swivel-eyed and evil of countenance', tried to prevent the villagers from answering their questions or producing any supplies, Sykes caught him by the shoulder and chucked him into the stream, after which they had no problem getting what they needed. The questions, which the head man did not want answered, concerned routes, local agricultural production and a detailed list of tribes and their headmen. In Persia unknown outsiders were – and often still are – regarded as tax collectors or government agents in search of plunder, and the safest policy was always silence. It was only when Brazier Creagh opened his medicine chest and offered to treat the villagers for their various maladies and festering wounds that they lost their inhibitions, for this man who offered cures for their ailments without demanding payment was clearly no rapacious tax-gatherer.

Sykes went for a walk in the hills and caused some merriment when he returned carrying a bag of some strange wood ash that he had found when searching for geological samples. The villagers told him that it came from a bush that grew only near Mokht, and that it was traditionally ground into a paste and shaped into balls which were strung together and worn round the arm as a fertility charm. Women wore it on the left arm and men on the right. Thin stuff was very famous and sold all over Persia, as far away as Meshed.

The group proceeded on down the Fanoj gorge towards Fahraj. At one very narrow point in the gorge they came across a striking, round-pointed pillar-like red rock guarding the way. The locals told Sykes that its name was Kiri, but they were too embarrassed to tell him what this meant; it translates as 'phallic'.

The track ran through the cliffs along the river, sometimes disappearing and forcing the travellers to swim across, and sometimes soaring precipitately into the rocks, with barely space for a goat to pass. Brazier Creagh's horse fell into the river, to the merriment of the chief camel-man, who shortly got a ducking himself when his own donkey slipped off a high part of the track and crashed into the water. The local Lashari camels, astonishingly, were able to cope with this very rough terrain, which would have brought any Indian camel to a halt, but their lurching movement gave the Indian servants such camel-sickness that for some days, until they got used to it, they preferred to walk.

At each village they stopped to talk and take note of the *khabar* or local news. The Baluchis, living in this desolate and God-forsaken part of the country, were practically independent of the Persians, for whom they had no love at all. Being warlike Sunni Muslims, they regarded the Shia Persians as effete heretics who did nothing but tax them unjustly. Wherever Sykes went in Persian Baluchistan he was told that the Baluchis in British India were much better treated and that the Persian Baluchis wanted British protection from Persian rule.

At the end of November Sykes reached Fahraj, a small town of some three hundred houses at an altitude of 1,900 feet and surrounded by date groves, guarded by a newly built mud-walled fort. Sykes was unwell with a fever for some days and caused Brazier Creagh some concern by frequently wandering off on his own. When he recovered they turned east into the cold uplands of the lawless Sarhad (frontier) district, where border raiding was the norm. The people of the village of Magas, where they made a halt, were occupied in nothing else but said that, given the choice, they would have preferred to have been taken over by British India rather than by Persia because, although the British dealt firmly with lawbreakers such as themselves, they did so with justice and fairness.

In mid-December Sykes's group reached the town of Khash, where they spent some time in conversation with the Sartip, or brigadier, who rejoiced in the splendid title of Zein ul-Abedin Khan, As'ad ud-Dowleh ('Adornment of the Devout, The Most Felicitous of the State'). He told them that he knew that, on the death of the Shah, the Russians would take Persia if they could but that Britain would not permit it. Given the choice, he would far prefer British rule to Russian and he felt, he said, that his district would prosper under British protection. One of the local problems was that the date groves at Mashkil straddled the unmarked frontier between Persia and India. This led to much trouble, with both sides demanding payment of taxes. Although he never paid any of the taxes demanded of him, he felt that the British taxes were fairer and he preferred not to pay those. He went on to say that he was assuming that Sykes was on the way to Kerman and Tehran to negotiate the transfer of the province to British rule and that, now that he could see security and prosperity coming, he felt he could at last die in peace. As'ad ud-Dowleh's friendship proved useful to Sykes when he came back two years later as adviser to the Perso-Baluch boundary commission.

The expedition moved on northwards towards the smoking mountain of Kuh-i Taftan, which stands out in splendour from the plain like Mount Ararat. On the way they passed small camps of wild Sarhadi nomads, living in mean goat hair tents. They had nothing to offer and practically no possessions, not even a *qalyan*, or water pipe, although when Brazier Creagh produced some tobacco they fashioned a pipe for him out of a brick of wet clay. And while there were no provisions to be had, there were plenty of partridge, sandgrouse and the occasional snipe to make up the pot.

The horses were tired from lack of proper feed, and Sykes decided to rest them for a day while he set off on foot to climb the Panj Angosht (Five Fingers) mountain. Although he took a local guide, a second man insisted on accompanying him. It was not until four hours later, when they reached the top, that this man explained his purpose. 'Sahib,' he began, 'we have all heard of British justice, and I wish to lay my case before you.' He was a poor man who had been betrothed two years previously, but could not marry until he had provided the bride price of a quantity of cooking pots and clothes. A rich man now wanted the girl and she was to be handed over to him, regardless of her previous engagement. The unfortunate young man said that he had followed Sykes all the way from Khash to hear his decision and swore to abide by it. Sykes told him to go to the Governor, but as the young man begged him to decide then and there, Sykes asked him whether he had paid any of the due bride price since the betrothal, which he confessed he had not. Sykes pointed out that, at that rate, he could never marry the girl, and as it seemed unfair for her to be kept tied, he thought he had better accept the position. This decision was rather a blow to the young man, but he accepted it and set off to release the girl from her engagement. To be ordered to break it off by the English sahib was much less of a disgrace than to be forced to do so by his richer and more powerful compatriot.

On 29th December, riding through a snowstorm, the party reached the 13,000 foot volcano of Kuh-i Taftan. At sunset they pitched their tents at a tiny village at an altitude of 6,500 feet, where they were found a cave in the side of the mountain to stable the horses in for the night. Early the next morning, as it was too cold to ride the horses, Sykes set off for the mountain on foot, accompanied by some most unwilling guides. Brazier Creagh was lame and had to stay behind.

For the first seven miles the track lay up the valley. We then reached a most extraordinary fissure, known as the Gelu-band or Necklace, up which we scrambled, to find ourselves in quite a new country, which recalled *Jack and the Beanstalk* to my mind. At 10,000 feet the actual climb began. Huge boulders had to be surmounted for some distance, but the last thousand feet were covered with deep white ash, which has given rise to the belief in the existence of eternal snow on the top.

The crater was belching out blinding clouds of sulphurous smoke. There was no fresh lava stream and there is no record of the volcano ever having been in eruption. It was with considerable difficulty that we collected samples of the sulphur and sal ammoniac,[2] which form part of the revenue paid by the Sarhad.

The view was the finest that I have ever enjoyed in Persia, every peak within a hundred miles standing out distinctly.

The mountain carries many legends and is known locally as the Kuh–i Chehel Tan, or Mountain of the Forty Spirits. The inhabitants of the valley below, only partially converted to Islam, had worshipped the volcano for centuries and made periodic sacrifices to it. The valley showed signs of habitation from prehistoric times, with many ruined forts and caves cut into the cliff. The natives believed that there was much buried treasure to be found and assumed that Sykes and Brazier Creagh were searching for it.

Brazier Creagh's diary shows the true purpose of the expedition: it is full of great detail as to the names of the tribes and their chiefs, their attitude to the Persian government, the numbers of men at their disposal and the availability of water and fodder for an army on the march. As they left the Sarhad he wrote:

For some time now our military authories have been considering the advisability of establishing a firm footing in East Persia by permanently occupying a portion of the country. Sistan [some way to the north, at the junction of the frontiers of Persia, Afghanistan and India], with its unhealthy climate, is not practical in that one could not conduct military operations there between November and March. The Sarhad is high, with a good water supply and has a healthy climate. The Baluchis and Sarhadis are pro-British and therefore the boundary must be clearly delimited, especially at Mashkil.

Five years previously Russia was pressing the Shah to give them Chahbahar, which makes it imperative that we should occupy the Sarhad. With a permanent occupation of the healthy Sarhad plateau on a line running to Sistan we should undoubtedly be in a position to check a Russian advance through Persia by threatening the flank of a force marching eastwards, and we

---

[2] Samples were given to the British Museum.

should be supported by the tribes. This would be the first move towards the inevitable division of Persia between Russia and Britain, which is generally expected throughout the country.

Farman Farma has assured us that Baluchistan is a useless appendage of Persia. It costs him 30,000 tomans to maintain an army to control it and it gives only 17,000 tomans in revenue.

Brazier Creagh was right about partition. Persia was divided along these lines in 1907.

Farman Farma was travelling near by at the time, touring his province, and had been generously sending Sykes's group supplies and spare mules, with friendly messages inviting them to join him at Bampur. On the way there they climbed another extinct volcano at Bazman, known as Kuh-i Khizr-i Zendeh, or Mountain of the Living Khizr. There was a legend that the prophet Khizr, who had drunk the water of eternal life and was the patron saint of travellers in distress, lay buried at the heart of the mountain. With Brazier Creagh leading the way, they floundered through the snow to reach the top, exhausted, at 11,200 feet. Sykes impressed Brazier Creagh with his toughness. His feet had become too blistered and swollen for him to wear boots and he had made the climb wearing only tennis shoes and rags bound round his feet. From the top they could see in one direction the peak of Kuh-i Taftan, while in the other the flat expanse of the Lut desert gave an impression of boundless distance that Sykes had previously experienced only at sea.

On 9th February at Bampur they finally met up with the young Prince Farman Farma, with his entourage of two hundred armed horsemen. His arrival was greeted with a salute from the fortress cannon and dancing by the Baluchi women, who were suitably rewarded with money. Brazier Creagh recorded: 'He gave us a most warm welcome and was particularly demonstrative towards Lt Sykes, kissing him. This performance from horseback before the entire crowd was singularly trying to Sykes, who was quite unprepared for such an outburst of feeling.' After this exuberant performance Farman Farma gave them an exhibition of shooting from horseback at francolin (black partridge), taking rights and lefts at them at the gallop.

That evening the Prince invited his guests to dinner at his camp. Brazier Creagh described the occasion:

At 8 p.m. two *farrashes* appeared with immense lanterns to guide us to the Prince's *shamianeh*[3] for dinner. The camp presented a lively appearance by night, lit up by lamps and camp fires. Prince Abdul Hussein Mirza Salar-i Lashkar, Farman Farma is a young man of genial and agreeable manners. HH's style and manner are French; there is none of the staid and formal Persian officialese about him. He is very proud of being a soldier and of having gone through all the grades from private. We dined in English style at tables, with candelabra, knives and forks. The menu was: –

Potage	Consommé
Entrées	Côtelettes de gazelle, rillettes en brochette
Relevées	Selle de gazelle aux épinards, sauce piquante, pilau de perdrix noires aux navets indiens frits
Fromages	Laitue, cresson à la moutarde
Entremets	Gâteaux, oranges, pistaches, manna nougat-muscat
Vins	Vin de Shiraz, sherbet

A band played Persian music throughout. The Prince regretted that he was not at home, where he would have been able to entertain us properly!

The next day Farman Farma paid the Sykes camp a state visit. He was given some Lee Metford rifles as a present, with which he promptly began to shoot at coins thrown into the air, shooting alternately from the right and left shoulder and missing very few. Sykes took advantage of the Prince's good humour to send his Indian surveyor, who had joined the expedition, to sound him out unofficially and discreetly on the idea of the British opening a consulate at Kerman. Two letters to Curzon on this subject, written in gushing schoolboy style, survive among Curzon's papers,[4] which show that Sykes was already hoping to be appointed Consul.

---

[3] An open-fronted and embroidered tent for entertaining, much illustrated in Persian miniatures.
[4] MS Eur. F 111/69 in the OIOC.

Later that day Farman Farma, who had not yet replied to Sykes's overture, gave an open-air durbar, to which he invited all the Baluchi chiefs. His band struck up 'God Save the Queen' before playing the Persian anthem and he strolled round ostentatiously arm in arm with Sykes and Brazier Creagh in a show of informal intimacy that was meant to impress on the Baluchis that the British were also friends of his. The two groups of travellers now combined and moved together towards Fahraj. With Farman Farma providing all necessary stores and provisions, their progress was much easier. On the way Brazier Creagh gave a demonstration of jumping with his horse, something that the Persians, living in a country where hedges and fences were unknown, had never seen. On arriving at Fahraj they

found the troops drawn up in a long line near the fort and a tremendous crowd of Sardars of Baluch, Lashari, Bashakird, Kurd and other tribes. As we rode along, inspecting the line of troops, we were preceded by *farrashes* on foot clearing the way. The guns boomed out a salute and a deafening roar of huzzas in strange tongues greeted us. Preceded by the bands, we rode into camp; all along the route rams and calves were being sacrificed and the bleeding heads thrown on the ground before us . . . The Prince has not been down here amongst these tribes before.

The Persian troops were of poor aspect until Farman Farma commanded them. He pulled them up wonderfully. HH is an ardent soldier and has a powerful word of command.

The Prince then called in all the chiefs and told them to answer any questions that the English might put to them and to provide them with any supplies that they might need on their travels. As Sykes admitted, with the benefit of this introduction they gathered more information in a week than less favoured travellers would have collected in many months.

They made their way along the Fahraj valley towards Kerman, shooting and hawking as they went. If they saw gazelle, Farman Farma, who was in good form and great good humour, would gallop after them with eighty or a hundred of his men fanning out in a big semicircle, to shoot them from the saddle. One morning, however, the Prince appeared looking seedy and weak, and announced that he had just discovered that he would have to give up the Governorship of Kerman at the next annual round, since the Shah had raised the annual prepayment from 60,000 to 70,000 tomans. He refused to pay the extra 10,000 tomans, as he was not prepared to screw the peasantry and lose his popularity to recoup this extra outlay. He remarked that he had not had to execute or severely punish anyone (by which he meant cutting off a man's fingers, ears or nose) for over a year.

Everywhere that Farman Farma went he would ostentatiously perform his prayers in public. He told Sykes that he did this because, with his European manners and his drinking of wine, he would otherwise be taken for a freethinker and be hounded out by the mullas. He also confided that he felt that his property would be insecure when his cousin the Shah died, and secretly handed Sykes 25,000 rupees in cash (then equivalent to about £1,700) to invest for him in India. He also said that he had a further £60,000 (equivalent to about £3 million today) in the Imperial Bank of Persia, which he also wished Sykes to invest for him. He clearly had a remarkable degree of trust in Sykes, whom he had met only very recently and clearly judged to be completely honest and trust-worthy. After this conversation they were escorted back to their tents by 'a long, lanky, cadaverous-looking *farrash* who, on inquiry, turned out to be the Prince's head executioner'.

Camp life began at 5 a.m. with the firing of a cannon. The party shot game all day on the march and arrived at the next camp at sundown to find the tents already pitched. Dinner was enlivened by music and the arrival of various guests. After dinner coffee and *qalyan* were served as they reclined on rolls of felt *namad* rugs and rich carpets. One of the Persian generals, who was also the prince's physician, played the *santûr* (or zither) and the Chef de Musique played the xylophone, while a young tenor chanted love poems, with Farman Farma often joining in for the most intense of the verses. However, to the irritation of Sykes and Brazier Creagh, the Persians had no sense of privacy while on the march and were always dropping in and out of their tents.

On 21st March, the Persian New Year, they all exchanged pre-sents and went on one last shoot before the end of the season. As the party travelled north-west towards Kerman, there had been much discussion about the relative merits of the neat and sure-footed Persian horses, with their Arab blood, and the big, lean Australian-bred 'walers' used by the Indian cavalry. Farman Farma bet Brazier Creagh 1,000 tomans that his best horse could beat Sykes's Cotmore over a mile. Not willing to be entangled in the potentially embarrassing consequences of a lost cash bet, Brazier Creagh changed it to a wager of his hammerless shotgun against a Kerman carpet. Sykes repeated the bet and, so confident was Farman Farma as to the outcome, he publicly promised to give the gun to his page. What none of the Persians knew was that Cotmore, despite being as long and skinny as a camel, had won many races in India.

A difficult course was laid out through rough wormwood scrub and Farman Farma's horse, caparisoned in scarlet and gold trappings about its saddle and bridle, was led down to the start. Sykes got Brazier Creagh, who was lighter, to ride Cotmore, while the Prince's jockey rode the challenger. Farman Farma acted as judge and Sykes as starter. Sykes cannily took a native horse down to the start rather than one of his own, in case Cotmore should refuse to be parted from his stable companion at the off. Cotmore led from the beginning and even though Brazier Creagh pulled him up a bit, won by a furlong. To compound the Prince's discomfiture, the heavyweight Sykes came in second, riding his little starter's pony and carrying two saddlebags full of feed. After much good-natured ribaldry Farman Farma immediately took up a serious interest in English bloodstock and saddlery, especially when it was pointed out to him that the high-pommelled saddles and the heavy and vicious high-ported Persian bits, which made the horses raise their heads and 'star-gaze', were a serious hindrance.

On 1st April the party reached the large village of Mahan, a short way south-east of Kerman. There, on a hillside at the foot of the mountains, Farman Farma's elder brother had built the famous walled Bagh-i Shahzdeh, or Prince's Garden, which, well restored, still stands today as a popular public monument. They proceeded on to Kerman but did not stay there more than ten days because, with the change of governor in the new year, the Prince had to leave. Before doing so Farman Farma asked Brazier Creagh, who was returning to India, to inform the Viceroy (Lord Elgin) that he would always be a supporter of the British cause.[5] He was replaced as Governor by the 84-year-old Sahib Divan, who was married to the sister of the Shah's father. This old man had previously been Governor at Meshed, which was under Russian domination, and he was therefore expected to be pro-Russian in his sympathies, which disturbed the British. He came with the reputation of being wealthy and therefore willing and able to buy up grain and fix its price at a reasonable level. He was also interested in establishing a proper water supply and in introducing some basic sanitation to the city. He was what the Persians call 'a very good man', often a polite way of describing a weak man of whom they are not afraid.

Sykes made his way home on leave via Yazd and Tehran, while Brazier Creagh returned to India. The tribes, having heard that Farman Farma had been replaced by an old and weak man, had resumed their traditional occupation of raiding and robbery, which meant that he could not go back the way they had come but had to take a long detour in the opposite direction via Shiraz and Bushire. Brazier Creagh's report on the expedition concludes: 'Kerman must be a strategically important point in our defence of the sea-board and gulf against attacks from the north. Kerman–Bam–Narmashir–Sarhad must be the line of defence, because Russia will surely not face the waterless desert of the Kavir-i Lut.'

Sykes made his way swiftly towards Yazd, making long marches each day across fertile country which provided so much fodder that his horses, for the first time on this journey, at last began to put weight back on. At Yazd he stayed with the manager of the Imperial Bank of Persia, to find the atmosphere tense. The town's tiny community of Europeans was living in dread of the Yazdis, who were known for their fanaticism and xenophobia. There was no governor to keep order and an anonymous notice had gone up in the bazaar warning that Europeans who rode on horseback in the city would be shot. Riding inside the city was a privilege reserved for Muslims and denied to Jews and Zoroastrians. The

---

[5] Farman Farma remained a highly valued supporter of the British until the end of the First World War and was awarded the GCMG. He more than anyone maintained British interests in Persia at a very dangerous time for them, and it was largely due to Sykes that this was so.

atmosphere was so threatening that the bank had decided to close its branch in the bazaar. Sykes remarked with unusual humility that it required much more courage for European civilians, isolated and unsupported as they were, to live in such places than for soldiers such as himself, who were never alone or without an escort, to do so.

In Tehran Sykes stayed at the Legation and was introduced to Nasir ud-Din Shah, who questioned him closely about the country that he had been travelling through. In early June he set off home on the metalled road to Qazvin by carriage. This luxury did not last long, however, because the carriage soon lost a wheel and he had to take to horse again. Then, soon after leaving Qazvin, the post horses all lay down and refused to move, so the party had to continue on foot carrying their saddles on their shoulders to the end of the stage.

Crossing the mountain range that divides the arid Persian plateau from the fertile Caspian coastal belt, Sykes descended through the steep green and forested mountain slopes to Rasht. From there he was rowed across the lagoon to the port of Enzeli, where he took ship for Baku. Although part of Persia, Enzeli was to all intents and purposes a Russian colony. The only entertainment for the bored Russian officers and their wives was the weekly arrival of the ferry, and Sykes reflected that at least the British in their colonies had cricket and polo to keep tedium at bay. From Baku the ferry continued up the coast to the spectacular Daghestani fortress city of Derbend, from where Sykes took the train to Moscow, Berlin and Flushing before finally reaching home after nine months of constant travel.

5

Side-saddle to Kerman

IN THE AUTUMN of 1893 the Imperial Bank of Persia suffered two indignities. At Sirjan, to the west of Kerman, the bank's caravans carrying silver were robbed and its Mining Rights Corporation engineer was beaten up and put in stocks, with an iron collar round his neck. When Sir Mortimer Durand, who had previously been Foreign Secretary in India, became the new British Minister to Tehran the following summer he favoured a more active policy than that of the somnolent Liberals and recommended bringing in Indian Army officers to provide intelligence and establish a more effective presence on the lawless eastern frontiers. Then, in the autumn of 1894, London was alarmed by more reports of Russian moves against India and Lieutenant Sykes was urgently seconded from his regiment and ordered to go and found a British vice-consulate at Kerman as an outpost from which to observe matters, reporting to the Foreign Office.

Aged only twenty-seven, Sykes was to be posted as a Vice-Consul, with an allowance for expenses but no extra salary. His private means gave him an income at that time of £400 a year – sufficient for his needs but not enough for any extravagance. In a letter to the Foreign Office he admitted that he was 'fool enough to take the post from pure love of the work' but requested that he should be gazetted with the local rank of captain or major and that he should also be made a full Consul. The Foreign Office agreed to his being raised to captain, a matter that impinged on nobody else in their system, but making him a full Consul did upset things. They jibbed at the idea until he pointed out that to make him a Vice-Consul would lower his prestige with the Governor of Kerman, Prince Farman Farma – whose good relationship with Sykes had already been noted and approved in London – by putting him on the same footing as that inferior person of trade the British bank manager at Yazd.

The Foreign Office was not at all sure what to make of Sykes. When he wrote to the Earl of Kimberley to apply for £60 to buy tents for his travelling, the Earl minuted: 'He was on the list of trading consuls, even though he was not a trader. Is there any precedent? – I cannot find one.' The chief clerk at the FO replied, 'Mr Sykes, who though nominally a Consul is really an Intelligence officer, ought in my opinion to be supplied with what he asks.' Kimberley responded, 'Treasury sanction will be required.' Sykes's mission must have been given the highest sanction, since the normally frugal Treasury came straight back with the minute 'Strongly recommend.'

He was given ten days to prepare for the journey. Since he would be living in a solid building for the first time in Persia and had no wife, he recruited his sister Ella to travel out with him and keep house for him. She later described her experiences in *Through Persia on a Sidesaddle*. According to Sykes's son-in-law the late Sir Patrick Reilly, Ella was not interested in men or in settling down to a conventional married life, but was interested in travel – the more adventurous the better. With her sister Ethel, Ella Sykes was among the first women to go to Oxford in 1882 and was one of the original blue stockings. The men in her circle found her intimidating and she found most of them dull. In those days of heavily circumscribed social life she did not have good enough family connections to introduce her to interesting young men and so, being a woman of spirit with independent means, she preferred to go without. Using a rather delicious expression, Sir Patrick confided that some of the family thought she might be 'Lebanese'.

She was tough. On 2nd November 1894 she and her brother left London for the Caspian port of Enzeli, travelling by way of Constantinople, Batumi and Baku. At Enzeli they disembarked from the Russian ferry on to a lighter and then in two rowing boats crossed the lagoon to the village of Pir-e Bazaar. There the wooden jetty had collapsed, and they were forced to step out into the mud to get ashore. A Tehrani bride had lost her trousseau when it fell into the water, and a European family's piano, which suffered a similar fate, was for months used as a stepping-stone.

From Pir-e Bazaar, Sykes and his sister took a carriage and drove the six miles inland to Rasht, where they stayed with Harry Churchill, the British Consul, and his wife. When they left they drove 'along a charming road bordered with beeches, oaks, acacias and pollarded willows, its big hedges overgrown with ivy and maidenhair fern, while handsome little humped cattle wandered under the trees. The bridges here were peculiar, going up to a sharp point in the middle, the steep cobbled inclines being very slippery for the horses, which galloped up and down them at a great rate.' As it was too wet to camp on the Caspian coast, they took rooms for the night in a house built on stilts to keep it out of the damp. Ella described the scene in her book:

> Our servants unpacked our belongings, covering the floor with carpets, hanging up curtains before the draughty doors and windows, setting up our folding wrought-iron bedsteads, removing the leather covers from the enamelled basins that contained our washing apparatus and mounting them on tripods. All our bedding was carried in 'Sykes Tent Valises', a handy invention of my brother's, which unrolls ready for use in a couple of minutes. By the time we had used our indiarubber baths the servants had prepared us an excellent dinner of soup, pillau rice, woodcock, stewed fruit and custard. It was served on 'Paragon' tables – an ingenious arrangement of string, laths and oilcloth, which folded into nothing and was easily repaired.

At this point the road ran out and they took to post horses, which had to pick their way along narrow paths through mud and rocks, fording five flooded rivers as they headed to the top of the mountain range dividing the humid and cloudy Caspian coast from the vast, dry Persian plateau. Sykes had to use his hunting whip to fend off baggage mules blocking the path as they came

down in the opposite direction. Near the top of the pass the horses floundered nervously over the ice and it took some hours to reach the top, where a bitter wind sliced through their clothes. Ella was struck by the sparkling clear mountain air on the other side, which gave a very false impression of distance. Their destination of Qazvin was visible thirty miles away but, as they rode wearily towards it, never seemed to get any nearer. When they finally reached Qazvin they left their post horses and took carriages for the rest of the journey into Tehran on one of the only two level roads in the country. At the city gate they were met by a mounted Legation *gholam*, who led them at a gallop to the Legation building, where they stayed with Sir Mortimer Durand and his wife.

While in Tehran, Ella was invited to visit one of Nasir ud-Din Shah's wives, the mother of the commander-in-chief of the army:

Crowds of carriages were waiting at the gate of her palace as we drove up, and a long carpet-covered palisade had been erected inside the entrance so that no curious eye might penetrate the recesses of the *anderun* [private quarters or harem] garden. A eunuch escorted us past this, and up an avenue of trees to a large building, in front of which women dressed in all colours of the rainbow were squatting on the ground or strolling about. Passing through a hall crammed with women, we made our way up a staircase into a fine room covered with paintings by Persian artists . . . Here were assembled the Shah's many wives, who received us very graciously; and most of the female aristocracy, European and Persian, of Tehran were present.

All the Persian ladies wore loose-sleeved jackets of the richest brocades and velvets, and had short, much-stiffened-out trousers, which did not reach to the knees, the costume being completed with coarse white stockings or socks. Before the Shah went to Europe the Persian ladies all kept to the old national costume of long, loose embroidered trousers, but on the return of the monarch, this present ungraceful costume became the fashion in the royal *anderun* and has spread throughout the whole country; it being, I believe, a fact that the dress of the Parisian ballet girls so greatly fascinated the Oriental potentate that he commanded it to be adopted by his wives . . .

The wives were all very stout, and to European ideas the lengthening of their eyebrows with streaks of *kohl* [collyrium] so as to make them meet, and also to be double their natural breadth, was not becoming; neither did I appreciate the occasional little *kohl* moustaches, nor the thickly rouged and powdered cheeks and the henna-tinted nails. There was a sad lack of intelligence on most of the faces, which however all at once brightened up and there was quite a commotion among the throngs of women as the Shah entered the room. His wives pressed forward smirking and smiling, only to be waved aside by their royal master . . . I observed the splendid rubies and diamonds decorating the front of the Shah's uniform, the well-known diamond aigrette, and his trick of pushing up his spectacles on to the front of his *kolah* [a round, brimless hat, often of astrakhan]. He was accompanied by Sultan Aziz, the youth who is always with him, and whom he regarded as a sort of fetish.[1]

At the end of January 1895, after Sykes had been briefed about his position and had obtained all the stores and equipment needed for the new consulate, he and Ella set off with nine servants and fifty mules on the long road to Kerman. The only accommodation on the way was a series of caravansarays so filthy and verminous that, although it was winter, they decided to camp all the way. The first part of their journey took them, on the only other carriage road in the country, to the holy city of Qom. Out of a sense of propriety Ella always rode on her side-saddle when in public view, although she far preferred to ride astride like a man.

Among the party was Sultan Shukru, the Indian NCO whose job it was to survey and map the unknown country through which they were to pass. An Indian syce (doubling up as cook, saddler, cobbler, carpenter and tailor) saw to the horses. Hashem, the *pish-khedmat*, was in charge of the servants and Seyyid Ali, soon to be sacked, was the cook. He was always galloping and falling off his

---

[1] This village boy had saved the Shah's life from an earthquake and had become quite a pet. He had replaced a previous favourite who, when the Shah was staying in Buckingham Palace in 1889, displeased him in some way and was garrotted there and then with a bowstring. His corpse is said to be still buried in the palace garden. See Ralph Nevill, *Unconventional Memoirs* (London, 1923).

horse, which the other servants said was a punishment for forgetting to say his prayers. Ella's Swiss maid Marie, who could not ride and later had to be sent home as unsuitable for Persian life, together with her dog Diana, travelled in a *takht-i ravan*, a covered litter slung fore and aft between a pair of mules. They averaged fifteen miles a day and, to relieve the boredom and to supplement

the tinned rations, Ella would throw stones down the *qanats*[2] to make the pigeons roosting in them fly up for Sykes to shoot.

When they reached Kashan, Ella bought an old brass bowl, once the stock in trade of a doctor. 'The signs of the zodiac are inscribed all round the outside and inside are engraved descriptions of the different diseases which afflict man, combined with prayers to

---

[2] A line of wells joined at the bottom to bring underground snowmelt water from the mountains to the villages.

Allah. The doctor possesses a small key for each prayer and he would cure his patients thus: he fills the basin with water, drops the key against the prayer suitable for the complaint with which he is dealing, and if the invalid swallows the water in a believing spirit, his recovery from illness will be effected. Women wishing to gain the love of their husbands also use these bowls, repeating an invocation to the Prophet as they pour the water over their heads.'

They passed through the oasis town of Natanz, where Sykes acquired some tiles from the fourteenth-century mosque which he later gave to the Victoria and Albert Museum. The mornings were cold and after breakfasting in the open air they walked for the first two or three miles to warm themselves up, with Sykes killing snakes on the way with his hunting whip. They crossed a plain where herds of camels from Isfahan were feeding on the spring scrub. This part of the country was often raided by the Bakhtiari tribe and Ella was amused to find that the camel herders took them for these bandits, and grabbed their guns when some of the party galloped towards them to inquire the way.

At the small town of Anar 'a guard drew up as we rode towards them, attempting a salute – not a brilliant success, as they persisted in bowing at the same time – and then they marched proudly in front of us towards the town, hopping at intervals to keep step with one another.' Six weeks after setting out they reached Yazd and were put up by Mr Ferguson of the Imperial Bank of Persia, who doubled up as British Vice-Consul. Yazd, although now predominantly Muslim, was the last city to be converted to Islam by the invading Arabs in the seventh century and is the chief city of the Zoroastrian Parsees. The Fergusons took them to have a picnic at the top of a hill beside one of the *dakhmes,* or towers of silence, where the Zoroastrians exposed their dead to the vultures, taking care to check that a corpse was really dead by placing a piece of bread on its breast and calling in a dog. If the dog ate the bread, it was considered a sure sign that life was extinct.

Near Rafsenjan one of the baggage mules fell into a river and dumped the supposedly airtight trunk containing Sykes's new consul's uniform into the water. Then trekking on towards Kerman, they entered the small town of Bahramabad, where they were given a formal reception. 'A loud *salaam* resounded from hundreds of throats, and hundreds of eyes fixed themselves in one concentrated stare upon us, while a huge grey monkey, led with a chain, made obeisance in fine style; and the usual squalid guard presented arms and fell into rank, marching us to our quarters.'

The day before entering Kerman, on 30th March, two months after leaving Tehran, they halted some six miles out to allow the *istiqbal* or reception by the Governor-General to take place. This very ancient Persian custom could be tedious, but had to be submitted to; even Ministers entering Tehran were not spared. Sykes was now no longer a young army officer but a Consul to whom due respect had to be paid. He also firmly believed that it was essential from the beginning to establish his prestige by 'filling the eyes of the Persians' with a good show. His servants accordingly salvaged his sodden uniform and polished his boots and brasses until everything was gleaming. The Governor-General wished the procession to wind round the city walls, but Sykes insisted that it should traverse the whole length of the main bazaar, where it would be seen by everybody. Ella stayed behind to make her entrance privately and avoid embarrassing the Governor-General with the unaccustomed presence of a woman at such a public occasion. When the auspicious day came, Sykes rode to a tent some four miles from the town and was welcomed by a general, who ceremoniously offered him tea. The appearance of a tiny pony of 13 hands 2 inches, covered with gorgeous velvet and gold trappings, on which he was to make his entry, was an unexpected surprise. Sykes, who was large enough to have crushed the pony beneath him, extricated himself from this embarrassing situation with diplomatic aplomb by saying that in full uniform he must ride on a military saddle and, as his saddle obviously would not fit the pony, he would have to ride his own Cotmore. The preliminaries having been thus settled, a medley of riders, some two hundred in number, with numerous led horses, led them at a snail's pace towards the city, the Hindu traders and the Zoroastrian community welcoming them on the road. At the west gate a fanfare was sounded, with a roll of kettledrums, and about a hundred *farrashes* and mace-bearers on foot joined in the procession as it wound through the narrow bazaars. The old Sahib Divan watched it all from his citadel, imagining himself to be unobserved.

Later that afternoon the *syce* turned up and conducted Ella on her horse to the six-acre walled garden outside the town, well away from all its noxious diseases, which was to become the consulate. It was surrounded by high walls of mud and straw and was planted with long avenues of poplars and fruit trees, with barley and lucerne, spinach, beans, onions, vines and herbs. In the middle were four great walnut trees that shaded a mud *takht* or platform, where one could spread rugs and take tea in the summer, or even sleep out. An underground *qanat* brought cool running water from the mountains into the garden, which was enlivened by rose bushes everywhere. It was all very welcome after two months of riding through the desert.

Kerman, famous for its fine carpets and shawls, was one of the most agreeable Persian cities, a pleasant backwater far from the politics of Tehran and, so far, out of reach of the Russians. The climate was bracing in winter, with crisp bright skies, and not too hot in the summer. Outside the walls were pleasant walled gardens irrigated by *qanats*, in which grew pomegranates, pistachios and all manner of fruits, herbs and vegetables, in contrast to the desert beyond. The mud-brick houses were cooled in summer by windtowers, which funnelled the dawn breeze down into the basement, where the family sheltered from the heat.

In addition to the Muslims there was a sizeable community of Zoroastrians – merchants, farmers and landowners – who were noted for their honesty. They were pure Iranians, with none of the blood of the later Arab, Turk and Mongol invaders, and related to the Parsees of Bombay. Although regarded by the Prophet as People of the Book, they suffered much discrimination at the hands of the Muslims, who forbade them to ride in the bazaars or lock their houses, and forced them to wear only sober-coloured clothes. Much worse persecution, however, was directed against the quite numerous community of Bahais, whose religion, full of ideas of tolerance and good works and quite new in Persia, was treated as total heresy by the clerical establishment.

Close to the bottom of the social order was the small Jewish community, who in Sykes's words were 'in a wretched condition and yet, as petty dealers, are absurdly grasping, their ideas of profit being extortion. They are an offshoot of the Yazd colony and are said to have come from Baghdad.' Lower, however, in his estimation were the twenty Hindus, who were British subjects and therefore, under the Capitulations, entitled to his consular protection. 'Their trade flourishes, but as money lenders of the most voracious breed they are unsurpassed.'

Sykes was much impressed by the Nematullahi order of Sufi mystics. Their shrine was at Mahan, where their founder, Shah Nematullah Vali, was buried following his death in 1431. This was the most 'respectable' of the orders of mystics; its followers were not given to piercing their cheeks with skewers or walking on coals, but concentrated on contemplation with music and chanting. The Nematullahis, with their emphasis on tolerance, were very influential in Persia, in a discreet way, and were the repository of classical Persian culture, with its liberal poetry, music and painting, which was suppressed by the puritanical mullas. By no means monks living in seclusion, they drew their membership from all walks of life, from the highest to the lowest in the land. Their structure was similar to that of the Freemasons, with lodges all over the country.

Sykes was a frequent visitor to their *Murshid*, the head of the order, who told him that the religious fanaticism encouraged by the city mullas was the result of ignorance, which should be swept away to make room for universal love. Sykes developed a great respect for him and wished that this doctrine of tolerance had more influence in the Islamic world. The image of the burly Englishman sitting humbly at the feet of the holy man and imbibing his wisdom seems improbable, but it is the key to Sykes's relationship with the Persians. He had discovered the essential individual goodness of the Persians that underlay the corruption and tyranny of public life: 'In no part of the world could we have been treated with more consideration, and in my opinion the abuse heaped on Persians by travellers who have never even learned their language is altogether unmerited.' This sympathy for the Persians did not always endear him to his colleagues and superiors.

While Sykes set about his consular work and established relations with the Kerman notables, Ella occupied herself organizing the household and entertaining the various dignitaries' wives, who were curious to see how this independent woman lived.[3] She, for her part, also took a great interest in her new environment, and she and her brother both set about learning the language, history and literature of Persia. They also treated the Persians with the respect that they deserved, an attitude that was appreciated and recipro- cated. Persia, unlike India, was never a British colony and the Persians often complained about the English who arrived from India with an ignorant caste-based set of mind and treated them disrespectfully, as if they were untouchables.

Ella's first task was to sack her cook, Seyyid Ali. It was normal practice for all shopping to be done by the servants; they were not paid very much but there was an unspoken understanding that they could take about 10 per cent from the purchases for them- selves. Seyyid Ali, who claimed to be a descendant of the Prophet, had decided that his dignity and religious rank entitled him to 50 per cent. The other servants also helped themselves to Ella's stores and, when reproached, replied that it was 'not accounted stealing to take food, as the more of his master's food a servant eats, so much the stronger is he to serve him'. This was too much for the faithful Sultan Shukru, who put Ella straight on all the goings-on in the servants' quarters. Although this initially caused some ill feeling, the servants respected her as someone not to be cheated, and she respected them.

Order was maintained by her head servant, 'Black Akbar', the son of the executioner of Kerman. He was very unpopular with the others and any calamity was said to be due to his presence. He disciplined the servants by allowing them to bastinado each other. This was a traditional Persian form of punishment where the mis- creant had his bare feet lashed to a pole and raised up, to be beaten with a heavy stick on the soles. This caused a lot of pain and bruis- ing but no permanent damage. Black Akbar would afterwards restore mutual respect by giving the offender a *khelat* (robe of honour) and a tip for his pains.

The grand houses of Kerman were served by slaves, usually of East African origin. Ella was quite matter-of-fact about this:

---

[3] She later wrote a very competent book, *Persia and its People*, on Persian customs, as well as a story book for children based on Ferdowsi's *Shah-Nameh, or Book of Kings*.

Persians give their slaves very light work, as they say they are costly articles and must therefore be well treated. All jewellery and money are as a rule confided to their care, for, as they are cut adrift from their own family ties, they are supposed to attach themselves strongly to their masters. An Ethiopian is frequently the confidant of his master, knows all his secrets, and is entrusted with the bringing up of his children. In Persia there does not seem to be the slightest slur attaching to slavery; in fact, as my experience went, it was just the contrary and the negroes appeared to command the whole household.

In her book Ella recounted how processions of curious women with their servants came to see her and look at her possessions, bringing *qalyans* to smoke and small boys to guard the slippers left outside the door. They came all veiled, but uncovered themselves as soon as they were out of public view. At first, she recounted, she spoke no Persian and 'after serving them with tea and sweetmeats I could think only of entertaining my visitors with a dancing clock-work nigger, which nearly sent one of them into a fit, as she thought it was a *sheitan-i farangi* or foreign devil.' Later, when Ella had learned to speak Persian, she heard how the women went to the *hamam*, or public bath, to inspect potential brides for their sons in the flesh, how they were married, how they were pained by their sons being taken from them at an early age to be brought up by *lalas* (tutors), and how their husbands sometimes paid mullas to sleep with these boys, who were afraid of being alone and were frightened of *djinns*.

Ella did not keep purdah and met many of her brother's visitors. Indeed in Persian eyes the situation was much less fraught with potential embarrassment than if she had been his wife. A frequent caller was Haji Muhammad Khan Isfandiari, the son of Vakil ul-Molk, a famous Governor of Kerman, renowned for his probity and public works; many of his buildings survive today. Before the Crimean War Haji Muhammad Khan had been in Paris and London, where, he claimed with a delightful turn of fancy, the Prince of Wales, at Queen Victoria's insistence, had pressed the Order of the Garter on him, although he had refused it. When he came to the house he would, with great ceremony, present Ella with an orange plucked from his garden as if it were a bouquet. More bizarrely, he had decided that Sykes was not only a general but also an admiral, and wanted to know where his fleet was.

Another friend was Haji Zain ul-Abedin, the head of the Sheikhi sect, a heterodox and, theologically at least, relatively liberal and freethinking branch of the Shia Muslims whose founder had been invited to Persia in 1806 by Fath Ali Shah. Socially, however, they were conservative, counting many of the Qajar princes among their number, including the Crown Prince Muzaffar ud-Din himself.[4] The leading landowning families of Kerman were members and Sykes was frequently invited to their houses to dine and afterwards take a pipe or two of opium with them. (None of Sykes's writings gives the slightest hint that he ever smoked it, but the old Kermani families remember fondly that he shared this pleasure with their grandfathers.) Persian gentlemen over the age of about forty took opium after a meal much as English gentlemen might take port and a cigar. In moderation it was a civilized and companionable habit, leading to relaxed conversation; the Persians also believed that it kept the blood flowing in old men's arteries.

According to Sykes, Haji Muhammad Khan was 'a distinguished looking man, possessing charming manners and a knowledge of the outer world which makes his society most agreeable, especially as he is entirely free from fanaticism'. He had a very Persian history. A rich man had left his father a large sum of money. The Shah heard of this and sent soldiers to extort the money from him. They ransacked the house and put the father in gaol for two years, in the hope of getting hold of the money. Eventually, however, the Shah, tired of waiting, released him. The old man returned to his derelict house and found the chest where he had hidden his 10,000 gold coins among the family burial shrouds. Anxious not to show any sign of his recovered wealth, he defaced one of the gold coins and sold it to a Jew for half price, saying that he had dug it up by chance. He lived like this for years, selling one coin at a time. Many villages had been left to him but the Shah's soldiers had taken the deeds. However, bit by bit he

---

[4] See Mangol Bayat, *Mysticism and Dissent: Socioreligious thought in Qajar Iran* (New York, 1982).

retrieved them and his friends interceded with the Shah, who finally allowed him to enjoy his property in peace.

Sykes spent his mornings working and his afternoons riding with Ella, often sweeping visitors off for a ride with him. The townsmen were poor horsemen but the nomad chiefs were very different. One of them, Reza Khan, was taken to the tent-pegging course that Sykes had laid out for his Indian escort to practise on. He acquitted himself well and then invited Sykes to try his hand at some Persian sport. He placed an egg on a tiny mound of sand, unslung his rifle and galloped towards it, looping his reins over the high peak of his saddle. He aimed at the egg on the way, passed it at full tilt, stood up in the saddle, turned round and hit it, a Parthian shot. He was much piqued, however, when Sykes followed suit, but using a shotgun. After this Sykes, who loved nothing better than leading outdoor games and entertainments, organized a weekly gymkhana, with tent-pegging, lemon-cutting and shooting at eggs, while 'the older Khans enjoyed the pastime of galloping past buckets and throwing in stones.' Tent-pegging involved galloping flat out at a wooden tent peg and lifting it from the ground with the point of a lance without stopping. The original idea was to flatten a line of enemy tents while the enemy were still inside them. Lemon-cutting involved galloping at a lemon hanging by a string and slicing it in half with a sabre.

Sykes was interested in the tribal khans, who ruled much of the territory outside the city, and often rode out with Ella to camp with them in the hills. On one of these occasions she was visited in her tent by all the wives of one of these khans, with their servants – fourteen women in all – who, disturbingly, refused to leave until her servant, seeing her distress, announced that Sykes was coming. With a flurry of their many-layered skirts they left her in peace.

In June Sykes and Ella escaped the heat by taking to the hills, retracing Marco Polo's route through the Lalezar mountains. They camped at 11,000 feet to stalk mouflon and climbed to the shrine at the top of the Kuh-i Shah Qotb ud-Din Haidar, at a height of 13,700 feet. On their way down they visited a chief of the Mehni tribe, who told them with glee of a previous Governor who, hearing that he had a good mare of waler blood, had sent his men to steal her and her foal. The chief heard of it and fled with his

mare into the hills, leaving the Governor's myrmidons to be bastinadoed for failing.

In Britain, meanwhile, the Conservatives had returned to office
and Sykes began writing reports on his travels directly to Lord
Salisbury, who was not only Prime Minister but also Foreign
Secretary. Farman Farma, now aged thirty-five, was appointed as
the new Governor of Kerman after the usual court intrigues at
Tehran. He left his wife, the daughter of the Crown Prince,
behind at his home in Tabriz but brought a suite of French speakers with him, who brightened up the provincial society of
Kerman.

One day he took Sykes and Ella on a hunt with him; the scene,
apart from the modern firearms, is straight out of a Persian miniature.

The Prince rode a horse with a gold collar and embroidered
saddlecloth, his English *terai* hat with its flowing *puggaree* being
strikingly out of harmony with the trappings of his mount. He
was followed by some hundreds of wild-looking retainers on
horseback, clad in all kinds of flying-skirted coats, and carrying
guns and hunting knives.

We had hardly left the garden when HH's favourite servant, a
handsome youth in a green silk coat, galloped up, calling out the
magic word *shikar*, at which everyone stopped and the Prince,
dismounting, cautiously approached the game. I was puzzled at
seeing no partridges and my surprise was not lessened when the
Prince fired at a magpie, which flew off unharmed!

Our way led up stony valleys, along dry riverbeds, and the
Persians galloped their ponies over the rough ground with the
greatest dash, men on horseback tearing full tilt up the low hills,
riding along their summits and howling vigorously to frighten
the partridges into the crowded valleys beneath. The unfortunate birds were flushed by mongrel pointers to be dropped at a
few yards' distance by the eager sportsmen, while the falconers
loosed their charges to swoop down on any bird that might try
to escape up the hillside. The Prince was greatly excited and
shouted orders and encouragement without ceasing. He would
gallop half way up a hill on his wiry horse, would dismount, fire,

and remount, and gallop down again . . . Scores of horsemen raced helter-skelter in every direction, shouting in a frenzy of excitement, and so reckless was the firing on all sides that I was surprised that no casualties occurred . . . Lunch was served in a garden of peach trees beside a running stream, the food being spread on a large carpet around which the Persians sat on their heels.

The immediate shift from the violence and excitement of the chase to the poetry of the peach trees is very Persian.

Life passed thus agreeably, with an undemanding social round, relieved by expeditions into the country to show the flag among the tribal chiefs and landlords. With winter approaching, Ella felt that the time had come to light fires in the consulate, but Sykes refused to allow her to do so. They were about to start on a long expedition to Baluchistan and he wanted to toughen her up for it. From her memoirs it seems that she saw his attitude to be perfectly reasonable.

6

Baluchi boundary

Persian Baluchistan had been incorporated into Iran only thirty years previously, by Farman Farma's father and the father of Haji Muhammad Khan. They had sworn peace on the Qoran to the Baluchi chiefs and summoned them to Kerman, where they promptly threw them into chains for the rest of their days. To settle ownership of the land on which the new overland telegraph line to India would run, the frontier with British Baluchistan from Kuhak to the sea had been demarcated at about the same time by Sir Frederic Goldsmid, who had constructed the first telegraph line across Persia in the 1860s, but the border between Kuh-i Malik Siah and Kuhak had never been settled and Kuhak had remained independent of both powers.

This would not have mattered, except that the Baluchi tribes on either side had taken to raiding, particularly in the Panjgur region. British troops had recently been stationed there and needed to know how far they could pursue them before crossing the Persian border. Nasir ud-Din Shah had taken no interest in going to the expense of organizing an expedition to settle it until a Kermani wrote informing him that the date groves of Mashkil, which straddled the border, produced the finest dates in the world, that these date groves therefore belonged to Persia, but that they had just been taken over by a Baluchi khan from the other side. Sykes suggested that Farman Farma should send him an official letter asking him to have the khan evicted, to which Sykes's official reply was that until the border was officially marked, there was not much that could be done. Copies of this correspondence were sent up to the Shah, who finally agreed to form a Persian boundary commission to meet up with a British commission, which would come up from India to settle the matter. The Foreign Office wrote to Durand asking him to tell Sykes that his work in Persia had been very well received.

Durand recommended that his glowing protégé Sykes head up the boundary commission, but the Government of India decided that he was too junior and put Colonel Holdich from India in charge, with Sykes as his assistant. The Durands offered to have Ella to stay with them in Tehran while Sykes was travelling in this particularly barren and wild part of the country, but she insisted on joining the expedition. She was put in charge of the stores, a subject on which she had now become expert.

In January 1896, with fifty camels lent by Farman Farma, Sykes and Ella set off from Kerman to meet Holdich at Kuhak. The weather was blisteringly cold in the high ground; their tents were blown down in a dust storm, which was immediately followed by a downpour of freezing rain. They would have lost their entire camp when the *farrashes* pitched it on the very spot where Alexander the Great had lost his camp in a flash flood, had not Sykes, who was reading an account of Alexander's Persian campaigns, made them move it in time. Worst of all, Sykes's best horse, an Arab given him by Farman Farma, died after falling into a ravine when the track gave way under it. As they descended towards Bam the weather began to warm up and they passed through pleasant country with tamarisks and mimosas, and with plenty of francolin. By the time they reached Bampur the weather was so hot that they could only travel in the hours of dawn, resting in the daytime and going to bed as it got dark. They found it hard to sleep for the rumblings of the malodorous camels couched around them for the night. The job had to be finished before the end of March if they were to have clear enough weather. After that it would be too hazy for surveying since, even in February, the sun was too hot after 10 a.m.

At Fahraj they met up with the Persian boundary commission, which was led from Tehran by Ali Ashraf Khan, the Ihtisham ul-

Vizarah ('Glory of the Ministry'), and locally by the Governor of Persian Baluchistan, the As'ad ud-Dowleh ('Most Felicitous of the State'), who were travelling with a vast retinue. Two days were spent in the required exchange of courtesies before they moved on to Isfandak. There they found 'a charming date grove, a stream of crystal water, but no inhabitants, the fact being that the headman felt uneasy in his mind at the prospect of meeting the As'ad ud-Dowleh, as he had been concerned in various raids and other misdemeanours'. The entire village had decamped to a mountain range to the north in order to watch developments.

Sykes, knowing that the Persian party would strip the country of scarce fodder and provisions, tactfully suggested that his party should go ahead to make arrangements with the party coming up from India for a suitable reception of the Persian dignitaries. He and Ella, after six hundred miles and forty days' march from Kerman, a record for an Englishwoman marching with a caravan, rode down to the welcoming sight of the neat lines of the tents of the British camp pitched by the Mashkil river, with its escort of two companies of Jacob's Rifles and some cavalry *sowars*. The Persian party arrived the next day.

The Ihtisham now became very conscious of his glory and the As'ad of his felicity, for was this not Persian territory that the English were about to tread on? The Persian camp was pitched on the left, Persian, bank of the river, while the English were on the right bank. The question then arose as to which party should pay the first call on the other. The Ihtisham was well versed in European manners and ready to act accordingly throughout, but as he depended on the As'ad for all his supplies he had to be guided to a certain extent by this stubborn Warden of the Marches, who was determined to stand up for what he considered to be his rights. The English view was that, as the first arrivals, it was they who should be called on, but unfortunately the Persian practice was just the reverse. The Persians also held the view that Colonel Holdich represented only the Queen's Viceroy, whereas they represented the King of Kings and the As'ad ud-Dowleh was his Governor. The Colonel stood firm and the As'ad stood on his dignity, while messengers scuttled between the opposing camps.

Although apparently ludicrous, the matter of relative official standing was highly important, not least because the assembled Baluchi chiefs from both sides of the frontier were watching from the sidelines to see which side would draw first blood. The stalemate might have dragged on for days, had not a solution been found when Farman Farma diplomatically sent a letter to the Ihtisham and the As'ad pointing out that since both of them had been the first to call on Sykes at Kerman and at Fahraj, it was only right that they should do the same for his superior officer.

When the day came, the British escort was drawn up in two lines, and as the Persian cortège approached, all possible honours were rendered them. Since neither of the Persians could give precedence to the other without implying acceptance of his seniority, the opening to the meeting tent was widened so that they could enter together. Sykes had thought of everything.

The commission's starting-point was on the Mashkil river, opposite Kuhak, and, to save time while waiting for the others to arrive, the British had already built a decorative cairn on the left, Persian, bank. This was at once questioned by the Persians, but the difficulty was smoothed over by explaining that the opposite bank was lower, and that the next cairn would be on the British side. The astute and prickly As'ad, when invited to have his photograph taken beside the cairn, declined, on the grounds that his presence would imply consent.

The second frontier post was placed on top of a hill and a full meeting of both parties was held beside it. Sykes heard afterwards that, had it not been for the fact that Ella had already reached the top of the hill to take a photograph and the As'ad feared her ridicule, nothing would have induced the portly Governor to make the ascent. He was pulled up from in front by his bandmaster and pushed from behind by a servant until he reached the top, where he collapsed in a heap. Once there, after recovering his breath, he became cantankerous and, looking down, declared that they were robbing him of a valuable and fertile district, which proved, on examination, to be all of half an acre in extent. The fact that the line had already been decided at Tehran counted for nothing, and they had to leave him to be calmed down.

The two parties marched slowly northwards along the valleys, followed by a motley collection of camels, mules and donkeys, with a flock of sheep and goats to provide fresh meat while the markers did their work in a line along the mountain tops. Tempers occasionally flared when the local Baluchis reported to the Persians that frontier posts had been laid on their side, which turned out to be just triangulation stones. At one point the camps were hit by a gale, which split one of the English tents in two and blew all the Persian tents down. To prevent this happening again the As'ad ordered a sentry to sleep next to each of his tent pegs.

After the stark bareness of the mountains they reached the large oasis of Jalk, with its date palms, under which grew barley, wheat, beans, pomegranates, figs and vines, with a marsh in the middle full of wild boar, which provided the English with some sport. There they rested for a fortnight. The Mashkil date groves, which had prompted the commission, were forty miles away; they proved to be of very little value and were thus conceded to the British side. Holdich noticed that they were fed by springs from Jalk, which ran underground all the way to the Hamun marsh.

More trouble came on 21st March, which was Nowruz, the Persian New Year. Holdich's proposal to make a ceremonial call on his counterpart, the Ihtisham, upset the As'ad, who felt that, as Governor of Baluchistan, he was the senior of the two and merited the call. Further offence was taken when the British pointed out that in their eyes the Ihtisham, as Frontier Commissioner, was the representative of the Shah but that, if the As'ad wished, they would pay him a visit later on. The breach between the two Persians grew wider, and when Holdich demanded, as part of the frontier settlement, that the Persian authorities should be responsible for dealing with the raiding Yarahmadzai tribe of Baluchis, the As'ad threatened that if the Ihtisham accepted he would leave him without supplies in the desert on his return journey.

The rest of the border district, apart from some insignificant date groves, was desert and it was agreed to hasten the marking process by sending a flying party to run a line straight down the mountain range from Kuh-i Malik Siah. Sykes had already surveyed the date groves in 1893, which enabled a line to be drawn up in camp and then marked out later.

With the work of the commission finished, Sykes decided to

celebrate the occasion in his usual way by organizing a gymkhana. Ella describes it:

The first event was a display of tent pegging, done by the Indian troopers; then followed horse races, donkey races, foot races and camel races . . . After these diversions a piece of ground was smoothed for wrestling, and the big Persian *pahlavan* [champion] strutted about defiantly, confident that he would beat his opponent, a Sindi man chosen from among the Sepoys. I retired to my tent and a great crowd closed in round the performers. After about ten minutes I heard a mighty shout of '*Ali*' arising and the masses of onlookers began to surge backwards and forwards while, to my surprise, the Indian *sowars* appeared to be galloping into Persians and Baluchis alike. The Ihtisham rushed to my tent and the As'ad galloped off to his own camp, surrounded by a swarm of his own soldiers, who with hearty goodwill were actually belabouring their own general. Stones began to fly and I thought we were in for something unpleasant. The Persians, seeing their champion getting the worst of the fight, began belabouring his opponent. The whole mass of Baluchis who, being Sunnis, hated the Shia Persians anyway, rushed into the English camp offering their services in exterminating the Persians. British officers got badly bruised in the crossfire and Percy, being mounted, chased after the As'ad to persuade him to come back and finish the sports day by distributing the prizes.

The As'ad was much upset at this outcome, and threatened to have every one of his men bastinadoed, whereupon the entire Persian army sought refuge among our horses, as in Persia a royal stable is always *bast*. At Colonel Holdich's suggestion, it was agreed that, to restore peace, two men from each side should be bastinadoed.

A great banquet was the last event to commemorate the fact that the frontier, three hundred miles in length, had been delimited in just a month . . . Fat Haji Khan, the Ihtisham's interpreter, came to the front, and electrified us when he suddenly struck up *Highland Laddie*, which had been taught him, so he said, by an English lady, to whom he had become tenderly attached during his stay in London.

Their mission accomplished, Sykes and his sister rode into British Baluchistan. What should have been an uneventful ride produced some excitement when they reached Panjgur. Ella noticed that a wild-looking man was following them as they rode ahead of their caravan and remembered that, a year before, a local *ghazi* or fanatic had been hanged on the orders of the British commissioner for the attempted murder of a British officer. Sykes bore a strong resemblance to the commissioner and it occurred to Ella that their follower could have been a relation of the hanged man seeking vengeance. Saying nothing, she quietly kept her horse between the two men until the ruffian disappeared as they approached the British camp.

On 30th April 1896, after a total journey of two thousand miles on her side-saddle, Ella rode into the British cantonments at Quetta, where her horse, which had never seen a wheeled vehicle, shied at the prams and nearly unseated her.

The boundary commission had completed its task ahead of time. In his report Sykes attributed its success to the co-operation of Farman Farma, who, he said, had been instrumental not just in the matter of assisting with supplies and transport but, crucially, in dealing with the patriotically obstructive As'ad ud-Dowleh. Sykes mentioned that Farman Farma's greatest ambition was to receive an English decoration and recommended that he should be given one for his services to the British Government. As he said in his report to Sir Mortimer Durand:

> My position as Consul was most enviable, as I merely had to express my wishes for them to be carried out, while so evident was the friendship of His Highness for Her Britannic Majesty's Government that all the district officials and local chiefs came to see me when they visited Kerman and told me that such were their instructions. Furthermore, the fact that HH has invested a considerable sum of money in British securities means that he is bound to our side, as he cannot believe but that HBMG would confiscate his property were he to play us false.

Durand, when he forwarded this report to Lord Salisbury, added his own comment, describing Sykes as a 'capable and manly young officer. He has attached firmly to our interests one of the most important men in Persia, the Farman Farma, and has acquired a great reputation for himself.' In October Salisbury wrote to Durand to congratulate Sykes on his work for the boundary commission. It was unusual for an army captain to be singled out so conspicuously by a prime minister and Sykes was to continue to be picked out for special tasks.

7

Fever and fanatics

ON ARRIVING FROM Quetta, Sykes immediately reported to Army Intelligence at Simla, supplying detailed maps and accounts of the people that he had met on his travels, the tribes and their allegiances. Much of it was completely new material and gave the British an increasingly complete picture of the country that bordered the Empire of India.

In May 1896, as Sykes was riding past a railway station near Simla, he was handed a telegram announcing that Nasir ud-Din Shah had been shot in the Shah Abdul-Azim mosque outside Tehran. The prime minister, fearful of anarchy before the succession could be settled, had had the presence of mind to announce that the Shah was only slightly wounded and, propping the corpse up in his carriage, drove it back to the royal palace. There, to gain more time, he gave out that the Shah was ill and summoned the European doctors. He then got Sir Mortimer Durand to order the Imperial Bank of Persia to advance money for the payment of troops to escort the new Muzaffar ud-Din Shah to Tehran from Tabriz, where, in the tradition of the crown princes of the Qajar dynasty, he had been Governor-General. The new Shah was thus installed before any of his rivals could make a move against him.

Farman Farma was the new Shah's uncle. He was still Governor-General of Kerman and had been very effective in maintaining order there. In the neighbouring province of Fars, however, where the tribes were more powerful and more given to

63

banditry than the Kermani tribes, there was a breakdown of order and much plundering of property from British subjects.

Meanwhile, much debate had been going on between the home government and the Government of India about the wisdom or necessity of fostering trade into south-west Persia from Muhammerah (present-day Khorramshahr) up the Karun river to Ahvaz, Shushtar and then overland to Isfahan. The Foreign Office had noticed that the Russians were building roads from Rasht to Tehran and from Ashgabat to Meshed, which would soon enable them to push out British influence and what little trade there was in the south. Using political rather than commercial arguments, they had persuaded the Government of India to take over half of the subsidy to the British-owned Euphrates and Tigris Steam Navigation Company to run a steamer to carry the mail and any cargo up the Karun river, but trade remained very limited. However, if roads could be built to Isfahan from Ahvaz and Shushtar, the two main towns on the river, the prospects for maintaining British influence would be brighter. The British Consul at Isfahan accordingly wrote to Lynch Brothers, the principal British trading company in southern Persia, to tell them that Britain needed a road to maintain its position with the powerful Bakhtiari khans, whose lands lay along the route and who were traditionally cultivated by the British as a power in their own right. Yet the difficulty remained that neither the Imperial Bank of Persia nor Lynch Brothers could see any commercial sense in the project. With matters now coming to a head, within a fortnight of reaching Simla, Sykes was ordered to go to the Karun to report on the whole situation.

With the ever resourceful Ella, Sykes took a steamer up the Persian Gulf, stopping off at Bahrain, where they watched the pearl fishers at work. (Most of the profits, they noted, appeared to end up with the Hindu moneylenders and traders, who added to their profits by mixing in artificial pearls sent from Paris.) The water was too shallow to allow their ship to berth and they were rowed to the beach, where they found a herd of the famous Bahraini white donkeys, which had pack-saddles but no bridles, and ferried them unbidden to the shore. The British agent came to meet them and took them on a tour of the island on donkey back.

For decorum's sake Ella rode side-saddle, but she found it uncomfortable and insecure and said that if she had been alone with her brother she would certainly have ridden astride. The sights included springs of fresh water which came up under the sea: the native women dropped their water jars upside down on ropes through the salt water and turned them the right way up at the bottom to collect the fresh water below.

In early June the Sykeses were dropped off at Muhammerah, where the Karun debouches into the Shatt al-Arab. Here they stayed for a few days with the British vice-consul before taking a river steamer up to Basrah, the centre of British commerce on the Tigris. The steamer had a British captain and a crew of muscular Chaldean Christians. The captain spoke neither Arabic nor Persian but, such was the British presence in the area, all the passengers and crew understood his English.

A mile upstream from Muhammerah they passed the residence of Sheikh Mizal, chief of the Ka'b tribe of the Arabs.[1] Here the steamer dipped its ensign in salute, in memory of the assistance that the Sheikh's father had given to a company ship that was being attacked by pirates. The salute was punctually returned, as it always was.

Basrah, despite being in Ottoman Turkish territory, was then the British centre for the trade in dates, which were shipped off to America and Britain, where they were used for making hot sauces and vinegar. There was some friction among the various companies during harvest and packing time, but 'with sterling common sense, when it is all over and the last load of dates is disposed of, they hold a dinner which wipes out all disputes of the past'. It was always hot and humid, 'no place for a man with a short neck'.

Ella found it all charming:

The broad Shatt al-Arab might pass as a much magnified Grand Canal, and branches off on either side into dozens of fairy creeks stretching far inland and fringed with palms, willows, broad-leaved bananas and shady vines. The river is always alive

---

[1] His brother Sheikh Khazal was later the custodian of British oil interests in Persia until Reza Shah deposed him.

with *bellums*, not unlike gondolas in appearance, with passengers sitting on cushions at the bottom of the boat under an awning to keep off the glare of the sun – as much conducive to the *dolce far niente* as the gondola itself.

Sykes, however, after his life in the bracing climate and open spaces of Kerman, saw it differently:

> Although it could be called the Venice of the East, it is not an ideal place of residence, as riding is almost impossible, the right bank consisting largely of squalid malodorous lanes and ill-kept cemeteries; further, between every house is a creek, which necessitates the use of a raft. At the time of our visit floods had converted the lawn-tennis courts into miniature lakes, and when they subsided, the smells from dead animals and decaying fish were appalling.

After receiving a briefing in Basrah from the local Lynch Brothers manager, Sykes set off up the Karun river into the fertile Persian province of Arabistan (now known as Khuzistan), where he knew were many of the archaeological sites of classical Persia. He called on Sheikh Mizal, who, after showing him his beloved stud of Arab mares,[2] told him that, although he had nothing against the British, he was against opening trade into Persia, as he would then be overrun with Persian troops and officials. To emphasize his point he had acquired two steam launches to run his own service up the river, and ensured custom for them by organizing a very effective boycott against the Lynch boats.

Curzon, who was now Parliamentary Under-Secretary at the Foreign Office under Lord Salisbury, had travelled in the area only six years earlier and reported on it, but Sykes found that the Foreign Office had a very confused picture of the situation. He pointed out, first, that there were rapids at Ahvaz, which made it necessary to trans-ship any cargo destined up river for Shushtar and destroyed the point of building a road from Shushtar to Isfahan; second, it was only 117 miles from Muhammerah to

---

[2] At that time all stallions not wanted for breeding were killed. Only mares were ridden.

Ahvaz, or five easy stages overland, so that a steamer service in fact made little difference. He sent ahead his faithful surveyor Sultan Shukru, who established that there was a far easier overland route to Isfahan direct from Ahvaz, which would shorten the usual journey from Bushire to Isfahan by some two hundred miles and avoid the need to pass through the fanatical city of Shushtar, where the Lynch manager had only recently been viciously attacked in his own house.

Leaving Ella in Ahvaz, Sykes and Sultan Shukru took the Lynch boat up the Karun to Shushtar, with its spectacular river gorge and third-century dams built by Roman prisoners of the Sassanians. They had hoped to see a lion on the way, since Curzon had heard one roaring, but all they saw was a dead one floating down the river, and a number of sharks. At Shushtar they hired horses and rode through the narrow stinking streets to the Lynch house, which was surrounded by a high wall. They barricaded themselves in, for the blood of the Lynch manager was still visible on the floor. He had recently been attacked by his servant, who had stabbed him in the face and cut off one of his hands, and he had only just managed to escape with his life. The brother of the attacker, who had been arrested and sent to Tehran, had vowed to take vengeance on Sykes. Shots whistled over the house every night for the three weeks that Sykes stayed there making his investigations, and he found the Shushtaris, who were Shiite Muslims, to be not only fanatically opposed to foreigners but also ignorant. He was cursed in the street, not so much for being British as for being, as they imagined, a Sunni.

At Shushtar, Sykes called on the Governor-General, who was the only one in Persia who failed to treat him with the proper courtesy, even though he had come with all the proper letters of introduction. Part of Sykes's business was to claim compensation for an assault by some Persian soldiers on two British officers and other British subjects at Ahvaz. The Governor refused to discuss the subject, saying that the soldiers would not obey him and had nearly thrashed their general to death. Sykes eventually took the case to Tehran, where the Prime Minister sent a telegram via Sykes to the Governor, ordering him to make payment of £300 to the injured parties.

Much of the hostility in Shushtar was stirred up by the mullas, who were in the pay of a merchant from Bushire who had obtained some land with a trading concession in Muhammerah, Ahvaz and Shushtar and had no wish to see the British taking his business away. One of the leading mullas, who had been black-mailing the Lynch brothers, asked to see Sykes, who reluctantly rode through the muddy bazaars, being spat at as he passed, to find the mulla in the middle of a great gathering. Sykes began the con-versation by complimenting the Shushtaris on being so God-fearing and obedient to their mullas. This remark having been approved with much stroking of beards and mutterings of thanks to Allah for such a satisfactory state of affairs, he then asked how was it that the mulla's flock had stoned the severely wounded Lynch man, whom they had never dared touch when he was well, as he was struggling on his way to get a boat down to Ahvaz. For a moment they were embarrassed.

Hearing that an attack was expected on the launch carrying him back down river, Sykes had the wheelhouse barricaded with bales of wool. A few shots went over their heads as they dined on board, but the passengers replied with their Martini rifles. The attackers made off, but the passengers were kept awake all night with war dances, cries and more shots from the shore. It may just have been a wedding party.

In his report Sykes recommended that Lynch should finance two bridges over the Karun on the Isfahan road and allow the Bakhtiari khans to take a toll to repay the cost of building them. The tribes were losing twenty or thirty men and hundreds of live-stock as they crossed the flooded Karun during the spring migra-tions from the plains up to the mountains. This was agreed later in 1896, after discussions in Tehran with Durand and Farman Farma, who persuaded the Shah of the value of the project, and the road became one of the safest routes in the country. Sykes also recom-mended moving the vice-consulate at Muhammerah up to a full consulate at Ahvaz, to cover Arabistan and Luristan, the moun-tainous province in the hinterland on the way to Isfahan.

The steaming humidity of Shushtar had given Sykes a bad case of pleurisy, which he was unable to shake off. Ella had to look after him for three weeks in Ahvaz before he could move, with nothing but mutton, rice and onions to feed him on, plus a little of the Bovril that they always took with them. Since he was in no condition to ride across the mountains up to Tehran, he and Ella took passage on a ship going from Basrah to Karachi with a cargo of Arab horses and Persian opium. On their way home on leave via Suez they stopped off at Constantinople before taking the Orient Express via Budapest. There they called on Professor Vambéry, the celebrated oriental scholar and traveller in Central Asia, with whom Sykes was to keep up a correspondence to the end of his life.[3]

One duty that Sykes enjoyed during this home leave was to act as escort to Abul Qasim Khan, Nasir ul-Molk, who had been sent to Britain to announce to Queen Victoria the accession of the new king, Muzaffar ud-Din Shah. Nasir ul-Molk was chief of the Qaragozlu tribe, a great landowner in the Hamadan region, and had been the first Persian to go to Oxford, where at Balliol he had made friends with the young Curzon, Sir Edward Grey and Cecil Spring Rice (later Minister at the Tehran Legislation). The Queen was at Balmoral, where the Persian khan proceeded to pay his respects. Whether he enjoyed crawling through bogs and wet heather to stalk a stag is not recorded.

---

[3] See Fitzroy Maclean, *A Person from England* (London, 1958).

8

Murder on the coast

B Y NOVEMBER 1896 Sykes and Ella were back in Tehran, where they spent the three months of winter at the Legation while he wrote up his report on the Karun expedition and studied Persian politics. Sykes's pioneering work in Kerman and Baluchistan, along with his excellent relationship with Farman Farma, who was both cousin and brother-in-law to the new Shah, had earned him much approval from Sir Mortimer Durand, who had already reported his friendly relationship with Farman Farma and good reputation among the country people.

Indeed, Farman Farma was at Tehran at the time and introduced Sykes to many high officials. Such was the convoluted web of Qajar marriages that most of them were his relations and also fellow Freemasons.[1] Sykes's introduction to these people by the Prince as 'one of us' meant that they were able, after the initial formal courtesies, to relax and open up in his presence, speaking in Persian without the inhibiting presence of an interpreter and discussing all sorts of congenial subjects, far removed from the disagreeable matters which the Minister, in his official capacity, was obliged to press them into addressing. So by the time Sykes came to have official business with these people, they were already his friends.

It was not so much from the 'country people' that Durand had

---

[1] The first Masonic lodge was formally established in Iran in 1906.

heard of Sykes's good reputation as from the latter's blowing his own trumpet. His reports extolled his own successes in establishing or maintaining British prestige wherever he went, but in Persia people are taken at their own valuation, and given the relatively weak standing there of the British (compared with the Russians), it was important that he should play the prestige game.

Durand had been Foreign Secretary in India and spoke Persian well, although with an accent that the Persians looked down on as 'Afghani'. He not only saw through the Persian courtesy and politeness but also made it clear that he knew what they were up to, particularly with the Russians, and he was never swayed by their blandishments. But Charles Hardinge, a secretary at the Legation who later became Viceroy, also found him to be 'a very idle man. He spent the whole morning in his bath reading French novels and never appeared until lunchtime.' Perhaps this was why Durand appreciated Sykes's energy.

Sykes, who felt indebted to him, wrote a biography of Durand later and said. 'The Persians generally regarded him with more respect than affection, owing to his stiff manner, but I recollect a grandee saying to me many years after his departure: "Durand was your great Minister".' He made a great impression, not because of any power of incisive intellect, but because he was 'thoroughly imbued with pride of race, as every Briton ought to be.'[2] Sykes's youngest daughter, Elinor, gleaned a different impression from the book: 'Durand, who fixed somewhat arbitrarily the border between India and Afghanistan, was my father's hero, yet his biography showed him to be a vain, uninteresting man who did not take sufficient trouble over his Line and this caused continuing bloodshed.'

In his biography of Durand, Sykes told the story of the chief eunuch to the uxorious Nasir ud-Din Shah who came galloping into the Legation in a state of high excitement. He explained that the Shah's wives were upset because His Majesty was about to marry a sister of one of them, a gardener's daughter. He had been sent to ask whether Durand would allow the affronted women to come into the Legation and take *bast*, or sanctuary. Durand said

[2] Sykes to Curzon, 3 April 1903, Curzon Papers, BL OIOC, MS Eur. F111/162.

that he would be honoured to be of service to the Shah's ladies but was staggered when the eunuch told him that there were three hundred of them. The eunuch galloped off; when he came back two hours later, he had had tents pitched on the lawn and sheep and charcoal brought in, as well as the entire contents of a bakery. Satisfied with his arrangements, he told Durand that the ladies were now getting into their carriages and the Shah was furious. With that, he galloped back to the palace, while the Legation staff awaited the arrival of the harem. After a while the eunuch appeared like a whirlwind once more, this time to announce that the Shah had given way and that the ladies had got out of their carriages and wished to send Durand an expression of their thanks. The tents were packed up and the sheep lived for another day.

Sykes's work had come to the attention of Lord Salisbury. While on his surveying expeditions Sykes had been sending him long, rambling, almost schoolboyish, hand-written despatches from his tent. Curzon, whom Salisbury was grooming to succeed him as Foreign Secretary, had also spotted Sykes as a useful person whom he could use in his own grand design to beef up activity in Persia, but Salisbury, as ever reluctant to engage in anything other than masterly inactivity in the region, was frustrating Curzon in his designs.

Bored by the lack of entertainment in Tehran, which offered nothing more exciting than billiards, Sykes organized tent-pegging and paper chases for the younger members of the Legation as well as reviving the game of polo, which, although invented by the Persians had not been played in the country since Safavid times in the seventeenth century. He was assisted in this by Horace Rumbold of the Bays, who had played in Cairo and was now a junior secretary at the Legation. By Christmas the British were able to put on a polo match in the Tupkhaneh Meidan [Artillery Square], the main square of Tehran, the first of many games that were played every week for years.[3] The young diplomats who learned at Tehran later went on to start the game in Vienna and Constantinople while, down in Kerman, young boys started playing it on donkeys.

---

[3] The Moghuls had brought the game to India, where the British changed the Persian scoop into a mallet. 'Polo' is the Tibetan word for a ball made from willow.

Sykes's energy and efficiency, however, were not generally appreciated at the Legation, except by Sir Mortimer Durand, whose staff were mainly languid young bloods from well-connected families. They were totally uninterested in the Persians, whom they regarded as the lowest form of humanity and irredeemably corrupt. Into their company strode the bumptious Sykes, who was not even a Foreign Office man; he had the presumption to know the country intimately and spoke the language fluently, and he hobnobbed freely with Prince Farman Farma, who treated him like a brother. Some of this might have been forgiven, but Sykes was unable to conceal his lack of esteem for his colleagues' abilities. Some of them, unfortunately for him, went on to achieve high office. Charles Hardinge wrote of him:

There is a queer fellow here, Captain Sykes, HM's Consul in Kerman, who has been staying in the Legation for the last three months drawing up a report on the Karun, which he visited last autumn. He is a young man of 29, of great energy, very moderate ability and absolutely tactless. He never leaves the Chief [Durand], and has acquired great influence over him, not always of the best kind. I found on arrival that he was the cause of a good deal of friction with the staff owing to the position that he had assumed in the Legation, but I think that he has at last begun to realise that he is not the proper person to run this show. His aspirations amuse me as he told me that he hopes to be made a Consul-General at once or be put into the Diplomatic Service, but I could not gather whether as Ambassador or merely as Minister![4]

And he wrote in his memoirs much later:

Sir Mortimer Durand was completely under the domination of a certain Captain Sykes, whom he had picked up somewhere, a terrible bounder, who was the source of much friction at the

---

[4] At that time the only ambassadorial posts were Paris, Berlin, Constantinople, St Petersburg and Vienna. Tehran was raised from a Legation to an Embassy for the Tehran Conference between Stalin, Roosevelt and Churchill in 1943.

Legation. Sykes's one good point was that he introduced polo at Tehran and it was thanks to his energy that a beginning was made. I could not bear him, and as he left with Sir Mortimer when the latter went home on leave, I took care that he should not return to Tehran so long as I was in the Legation.

When Durand wanted to appoint Sykes to a senior post at the Legation, Horace Rumbold warned that there would be trouble and the idea was dropped. The young Rumbold wrote to his father: 'We none of us can stand Sykes, who is an intriguing brute.' In his journal he noted: 'Sykes had unbounded energy and was in many ways worthy of admiration but we none of us liked him. He was too self-assertive and seemed to think that he could order us about as he liked. His great sin was a complete lack of tact. He did one thing for which we blessed him. He practically started polo in Tehran, with me helping him. The Persians came in crowds to watch.'

It is easy to imagine that Sykes, after four years of constant travel over vast areas of Persia, did not show much respect for these career diplomats in Tehran and that they did not relish the knowledge that Durand, their chief, found more of a kindred spirit in him than in any of them. Sykes was better at handling his superiors and Persians than he was at dealing with compatriots of his own age. Part of his difficulty resulted from the long isolation from his own kind.

Persian society is essentially formal and conversation is guided by the rules of *ta'arof*, according to which the parties can express themselves through a ritualized exchange of elaborate courtesies for hours without engaging in the slightest intimacy and yet establish a clear understanding of each other's views. Everything that a Persian says in formal conversation, however disagreeable, must be framed in such a way as to flatter and please the hearer. No word is uttered without the speaker first minutely considering every possible way in which it might be interpreted, in case it should cause offence or give rise to misunderstanding. The hearer, equally, examines every utterance for its nuances before responding. Directness of speech is frowned on as being crude and indelicate; things are said obliquely and through subtle suggestion, for it is only to donkeys that one should have to spell out the truth. The effort of constantly treading carefully through this minefield is exhausting for a naturally direct and outspoken Englishman, and it is not surprising that, when with his own kind, Sykes felt that he could relax and tell them just what he thought of them. He forgot that the English were just as conscious of their own dignity and self-importance as the Persians.

Sykes's subsequent career suffered as a result of these early impressions on his colleagues who, with their better connections in London, were able later to confine him to the periphery of empire. This, in fact, was to suit Curzon very well, because that was just where he later needed men of Sykes's stamp.

Meanwhile, however, Sykes was seeing something of the rottenness at the centre of Persia. The country was financed by a series of large loans from Russia and smaller ones from Britain, which were squandered by the grasping Shah and his parasitic court. There was no money for public works; neither the army nor the civil servants were properly paid. Provincial governors paid the Shah in advance for their posts, which they then used to extort as much as possible in the short time given to them before rivals outbid them for their positions. This state of affairs was well illustrated when Muzaffar ud-Din Shah reviewed the army. After the parade he summoned the regimental commanders to his presence to receive a small bag of gold from each of them. The gold had, of course, come from the money provided for the half-starved, undrilled, ragged and ill-armed troops, who had to make their living by looting what they could.

Sykes heard the now legendary story of Zill us-Sultan ('Shadow of the Sultan') the Shah's half-brother, who was the Governor-General of Isfahan and notorious for his rapacity:

He summoned a local governor whose revenue was in arrears. He discussed the matter with him in a friendly manner while, in accordance with Persian custom, three cups of tea were served. To signify that the meeting was concluded, he sent for the coffee. Now Qajar princes were accustomed to poison those of their subjects whom they wished to put out of the way in this beverage, so much so that 'Qajar coffee' became proverbial. The Governor then, fearing to drink his coffee, tried to excuse himself on the grounds of feeling ill but, as this excuse was not accepted, he turned green with fright and began to offer sums of money for his life. Zill us-Sultan said never a word until the bidding had reached a figure representing the entire fortune of the man, when he signified that he would accept the sum. The wretched Governor wrote a bill for the amount, which his host pocketed. The Zill us-Sultan then, with grim humour, stretched out his hand, took his unwilling guest's coffee – and drank it himself.[5]

At the beginning of February Sykes and Ella returned home. They hit foul weather on the road and had to fight their way through blizzards and deep snow over the Kharzan pass, which turned into deep mud on the Caspian side. Arriving at Rasht, they found the consulate closed but, rather than face a doubtful hostelry, Sykes broke his way in. To make matters worse, he then set the chimney on fire while cooking supper. The next day they took the steamer to Baku and were home by March for six months' leave, some of which he spent writing up his reports.

At the end of October 1897 Sykes returned to Persia via India with official instructions to visit the ports of the Persian Gulf and produce a report for the Government of India on the extent to which British–Indian trade had been affected by the plague in India, and to comment on the proposed revision to the rates charged by the Indo-European Telegraph Company. The trade mentioned in these instructions was actually of less concern to the government, however, than the rumours of modern arms being smuggled from Europe via the little Gulf ports and the lawless southern parts of Persia into Afghanistan. It was suspected that a big Persian merchant at Bushire, the Malik ul-Tujjar, who had been behind the trouble along the Karun, was also behind this business. He was also thought to be supplying the local Persian tribes with these weapons, making them much better armed than the Persian army itself.

---

[5] Some years later Haji Muhammad Hussein Kazeruni, the richest merchant of Isfahan and a Constitutionalist, had Zill us-Sultan recalled to Tehran. When Zill us-Sultan returned to his post he recouped the 10,000 tomans it had cost him to do so with the same trick.

In the Political and Secret archives of the India Office Library lies a small folder of correspondence, which tells a tale that could have come straight out of John Buchan. It begins with a hand-written letter from Sir Mortimer Durand, now living in Brighton, to Sir William Lee-Warner of the Intelligence Department of the India Office in London, who had asked him for his opinion on the arms rumours. Durand suspected that the rifles were destined for the Afridis on the North-West Frontier, who were always resisting British rule, but he advised Lee-Warner not to confide any of his suspicions to Colonel Meade, the new Resident at Bushire, who was the obvious person to take charge of the investigation:

He knows nothing of Persia and he is, though an excellent fellow, a man of very ordinary intelligence. He will most probably blunder and find out nothing, while putting the people concerned on their guard.

The man who ought to be able to find out everything is Sykes, the Consul at Kerman, through whose territory the whole trade probably passes. He is keen and energetic and knows the province well. Just now he is in England . . . If he went back to Persia as consul in Kerman entrusted with the whole inquiry this would be your best chance of working the matter out . . . But Sykes's appointment is in jeopardy and he can hardly be expected to return to Kerman without pay. He has had nothing hitherto but a temporary appointment and his military pay as a Lieutenant of Cavalry. He can be trusted and he knows more about Persia than any official under me . . . Hardinge has unfortunately taken a dislike to him on account of his manner and you must allow for this.

Intelligence were worried that these guns were for more than the sporting purpose of taking pot shots at passing British officers. A big Indian merchant in Muscat had ordered five tons of blank copper discs an inch in diameter from a firm in London. Since the Royal Mint had advised that they were not of suitable size or metal to be die-stamped to make counterfeit coins, Intelligence had concluded that they would be stamped and issued as badges of allegiance to members of a secret army of agitators in India, as had happened once before. The news of the copper tokens, which suggested an invisible enemy, combined with the news of the arms shipments, gave rise to serious alarm, and Sykes was accordingly summoned by Lee-Warner and given his real instructions.

The Royal Navy had ships patrolling the Persian Gulf and Sykes was given a free hand to make use of them. The Navy was concerned about the danger of loose talk spoiling the operation and Evan MacGregor at the Admiralty wrote to Lee-Warner with great secrecy:

> As the officers in the Persian Gulf usually work on the instructions of the Residents I suggest that Captain Sykes should have a hint to warn the Captain of any ship referred to <u>not</u> to mention anything to the Resident and to so manage that the movement of the ship does not attract notice as far as possible.
>
> PS I have written and press-copied[6] this letter myself so that it does not pass out of my room or my hands.

By the end of November 1897 Sykes was at Bandar Abbas and reporting back to Lee-Warner. He had pinpointed one Abraham Ben-Messulam, a Gibraltarian Jew in Muscat, supposedly importing cotton piece goods from Manchester, as the prime mover in the arms trade. His principal customer was the Sultan of Muscat, who was making a lot of money shipping the arms across to the inaccessible little Persian port of Lengeh. Sykes also reported that eight Afghans from Kabul pretending to be merchants had gone over to Muscat to await the arrival of the SS *Tresco* and that they had a large number of camels and drivers waiting for their return. He had paid a local man in the bazaar to find out who the rifles were for and by what routes the camel caravan would travel. He intended, he said, to seize the arms on arrival and expel the Gibraltarian Jew.

Sykes then went up the coast to Bushire, where he discovered that there was a vast traffic in arms, which he assumed to be destined for the inland tribes. At this point he was distracted by news

---

[6] This would have been done on a tray of gelatine.

that a Mr Graves of the Indo-European Telegraph had been mur
dered in Baluchistan. Graves had been carrying money to pay the
wages of the linemen and had been killed by a band of Karwani
Baluchis. He was also supplying intelligence and it was thought
that he might have found out something about the arms traffickers.

Meanwhile, Lee-Warner's agents had discovered that, although
most of the arms were made in England, some of them were being
supplied by a Russian firm. Moreover, the bore of the rifles was
exactly the same as that of the rifles used by the Army in India,
which meant that the final users must be planning to use stolen
government ammunition. The affair had now taken a serious turn
and was brought to the attention of Lord Salisbury himself, who
tried to get the Persian government to stop the trade. However,
since the Bushire governor habitually defied the orders of the
Persian government and protected anyone who bribed him, other
means had to be found.

Sykes's enthusiasm and bounding energy had displeased Lee-
Warner, who sent him a long, irritated cable from London.
Reading between the lines, it appears that he was not impressed by
Sykes's arrest of the arms-carrying *Tresco* and his expulsion of Ben-
Messulam from Muscat. Lee-Warner wearily pointed out that
most of Sykes's information merely confirmed what he already
knew from other sources and that he had expected him to let the
Tresco shipment through so that it could be followed, in order to
find out the routes that the smugglers were using. He also told him
that it was pointless to expel Ben-Messulam, who would only be
replaced by a new agent; it made more sense to let him alone and
keep a good watch on him. Sykes had acted impetuously when he
should have waited for orders.

Graves's murder required immediate punitive measures and
Sykes was called off his investigations to deal with it. The province
of Baluchistan had become virtually ungoverned by the Persians
and was being stirred up by one of their khans, who was doing his
best to fulfil the prophecy made over four hundred years earlier by
the Sheikh Nematullah of Mahan that the last Shah of Persia
would be called Nasir ud-Din – the name of the Shah who had
been assassinated the previous year. The British decided to send a
gunboat and persuade the Persian authorities that it was time to

reassert their rule over the Baluchis. A joint Anglo-Persian naval punitive raid was planned and Sykes was ordered to join it.

The Governor of Bushire, the Darya Begi (Sea Lord) embarked on the *Persepolis* with sixty soldiers, including thirty wild Tangistani[7] hillmen that he had recruited from the hinterland of Bushire, who were well suited to pursuing the equally wild Baluchis. Sykes embarked on the gunboat HMS *Pigeon*, which came up from Muscat, and set off for the Makran coast, where HM Cable Ship *Patrick Stewart* and the *Persepolis* were anchored and waiting for him off the desolate fishing village of Galag, about fifty miles east of Jask. They immediately encountered a difficulty: the Baluchis had driven off all the camels from the village and there was no transport to be had until the sailors and the Tangistanis succeeded in rounding some up.

The Bluejackets were delighted at the prospect of a scrap ashore. With their usual versatility, they started loading the camels as if it were their daily occupation, taking no notice of the protests of the camel-drivers. When however, the first 'Ship of the Desert' arose, its load fell off astern, after which the Baluchis were given a greater share in the proceedings. The crew included half a dozen Arab Sidi boys who revelled in such names as Ropeyarn, Hammock and Bilgewater, who acted as the stretcher party.

With camels carrying a light Krupp cannon in sections, which the Baluchis regarded as a somewhat unsporting weapon, the incongruous party set off inland in search of the murderers, threatening to burn the villages and date palms of any who obstructed them. This was a serious threat for, while village huts could be rebuilt in a day, it took seven years for a date palm to bear fruit. The map was a blank and they were totally dependent on local guides, who were naturally reluctant to take them anywhere near the gang of murderers and tried to lead them in circles for a long time. The country was densely covered with tamarisk – perfect for ambush – but they found a safe place to camp overlooking a wide dry river bed which

---

[7] These hillmen were well known to the British, having given them a very bloody nose in the Anglo-Persian War of 1857.

gave a wide field of fire against attackers. The escort cut down a swathe of tamarisk behind them, twisted it into a barricade and they settled down for the night. After Sykes had offered a reward, villagers began to come in bearing Graves's watch, pocket book and other belongings, and led them to the site of a camp freshly abandoned by the murderers. The raiding party set off, soon caught up with the Karwanis and had a number of running skirmishes with them before they escaped into the desert. The Darya Begi fired a number of villages until the Baluchi elders agreed to hand over the murderers if their date palms were spared, but it was too late and they had gone. The expedition had by now gone too far inland for the sailors, who returned to their ships, and Sykes called off the chase and returned to his investigations into the arms smuggling.

The murder could not, however, be left unresolved after all this and shortly afterwards Sykes was ordered up to Bandar Abbas to ride inland and join an attack coming from the north with a force provided by the governor of Baluchistan at Fahraj. Again there were no camels for hire and he was obliged to buy some. Neither could the consulate spare him an escort. Alone, with only some local camel-drivers and suffering from sun-fever, he rode east of Minab for a hundred miles across the unknown desert country north of the Bashakird range to the oasis of Ramishk. Horses could not survive in this country, so he took a fast riding camel for the journey, but such was his fever that he was almost unable to stay on it. It also rained every day, which gave them water to drink but made the ground slippery. There was nothing to feed the camels on except dates.

At Ramishk, Sykes's situation began to look difficult. There was no sign of the expected Persian force and the Baluchis believed that the British force on the coast had been wiped out in a *shab-i khun* ('night of bloodshed'), which meant that they would not be shy about cutting his throat as well. Then a deputation of elders came to inform Sykes baldly that the Karwanis had taken refuge with them and that, as the British had killed one of their number, they, as fellow Muslims, intended to avenge their kinsman by killing him. Without an escort of Indian cavalry to protect him, and in a fit of recklessness brought on by the fever that he had caught on the coast, Sykes resorted to bluff.

He politely informed the elders that not only was a large Persian force on its way to meet him but also that the British had a treaty with the Persian government whereby, if a Consul was killed, the Persians were obliged to provide a hundred heads from the guilty tribe, on top of any that had also been killed by the English. These heads were to be taken to Tehran and built into a tower at the gate of the British Legation. Sykes was hoisted on to his camel and allowed to make his fevered way towards Fanoj, avoiding another band of Karwanis who he had heard were waiting in ambush for him in the hills. There he met the Persian force led by his friend the Asaf ud-Dowleh, who announced to the Karwanis that he was coming from the north to meet a second force coming from the south and that they were surrounded. The elders capitulated and handed over the chief of the murderers, who was taken down to Jask, near the scene of his crime, and hanged from the tallest tele- graph pole they could find.

This first joint Anglo-Persian military operation had not only been very good for relations between the two countries, but had also forced the Persians to stir themselves sufficiently to take back control of this 'lost' and lawless corner of their land.

The whole expedition had taken Sykes two months. To get back to Bushire he went down to Chahbahar to catch the mail ship to take him across to Muscat and up the Persian Gulf. While waiting for his ship in this barren place he had to live on fish and turtle eggs, which were so plentiful that, since nothing grew there, the Baluchis fed their camels on them.

Meanwhile, the SS *Baluchistan*, laden with a much bigger cargo of arms declared on its manifest as 'merchandise' or 'machinery', was heading from England for Bushire. There was some discussion with London as to whether the Royal Navy ships based at Muscat should stop her on the high seas or whether Sykes should 'employ a stratagem' to get the Persian authorities at Bushire to arrest her and seize the arms. It was decided that more trust could be put in action by the Navy than in a 'stratagem' that depended on the co- operation of Persian officialdom, and the *Baluchistan* was duly stopped at the mouth of the Gulf before she could discharge her cargo. This caused uproar among both the local traders and the English suppliers, who demanded compensation for their loss. The

India Office blandly suggested that they would be compensated, but only if they could produce proof that they had obtained official import permits for the arms from the Persian government. This put an end to their complaints and, for a while, to the trade.

Back in London on leave, Sykes gave one of many lectures that he was to give to the Royal Geographical Society, bound copies of which, well illustrated with photographs and maps and with very detailed topographical descriptions, are in the society's library. His lecture on the deserts and mountains that he had explored was followed by fulsome and complimentary remarks from Sir Frederic Goldsmid. Other compliments came from Sir Mortimer Durand and Colonel Stewart. Finally Nasir ul-Molk rose to his feet and, after congratulating Sykes on his lecture, politely reminded the society's members that they should not form the impression that Persia consisted only of rocks and sand, but that there were also areas of cultivation and highly civilized cities. To this day urban Persians find it hard to comprehend why the British should prefer the deserts and mountains of their country, which the British romantically call 'the real Persia', to the cities.

9

The race to Sistan

EARLY IN 1898 Sykes was ordered to proceed from Bushire at the head of the Persian Gulf, with its British Residency – the most important British post in the Persian Gulf – up to Shiraz, in the heart of southern Persia. The road led from the marshy coastal plain up through the dangerous mountain territory of the Tangistanis and then through the craggy passes in the series of serrated Zagros mountain ranges that run north-west to south-east and divide the central Persian plateau from the coast. The passes were controlled in the summer by the nomad Qashqai tribe, who supplemented their income from rearing sheep by exacting tolls from travellers and merchants bringing their caravans of imported goods up to Shiraz and Isfahan. If times were hard, or the tolls were unpaid, they robbed them of their merchandise. As elsewhere in Persia, the term 'road' meant no more than a track worn down over the years by the passage of travellers. In mountain country these 'roads' were frequently blocked by snow or rock falls; they were never maintained and were certainly not passable for wheeled vehicles. They were neither safe nor secure for travellers without a substantial armed escort.

At Shiraz, Sykes halted and waited for orders to go to western Persia and open the road from Borujerd to Dezful, which had been blocked by the tribes of Luristan (where oil was shortly to be discovered). Here, in the city of wine and poets, he had a pleasant stay among the small British community of the consulate, bank and missionary hospital. He also spent many hours in pleasant conversation with Farman Farma, who, having been Minister of War, had just been appointed Governor-General of the province of Fars and the Gulf Ports. A lucrative function of this position was the collection of customs duties.

From Shiraz, Sykes took the well-worn road up to Isfahan, accompanied by Mr Wood, of the Indo-European Telegraph, who was surveying a route for a new line to India and had been travelling up from Bushire with him. As they passed the village of Gorgab, where the best watermelons were grown, they were told that in the summer mornings the gardeners would stop any speeding riders, offer them a melon and ask them to ride at a walk, since ripe melons burst if a horse galloped near them. At Isfahan, Sykes waited for further instructions but in September the plan was suddenly changed and he was ordered to go east and found a new consulate in Sistan (present-day Zabol), the well-watered and fertile region at the meeting point of the frontiers of Persia, Afghanistan and India.

Sistan, with its plentiful water and supplies, was the point through which the Russians would have to pass on their way to India, and word had come in the autumn of 1898 that they were about to open a consulate and establish a presence there which had nothing to do with their legitimate interests in Persia and could be seen only as a threat to India. While Lord Salisbury felt that for the British to open a new consulate in Sistan would be 'like thrusting a poker into a dull fire', Curzon, who had just been appointed Viceroy (although he did not take up the position until early 1899) and was himself burning to pursue his forward policy against Russian advances, took a different view. The race was on to get to Sistan and raise the flag before the Russians did.

The plan was for Sykes to travel the long way round the central desert via Kerman and the Indian border, where he would pick up supplies for the journey. At Nain, a small town on the edge of the desert famous for its very finely knotted carpets, Sykes and Wood stopped and met the extraordinarily well-read and well-travelled dervish Haji Agha Hasan. Sykes's Persian secretary mentioned that he had been pained to see from the 2,000-year-old sculptures at Persepolis that in those days Persians sat on chairs, while now they were sitting on the floor. The sage tried to cheer him up: 'In those days we cared only for material progress, but we have now abandoned that for higher things, whereas the backward Europeans have only just reached the stage of enjoying material objects.'

Wood fell into conversation with a mulla on the way and said proudly that the English, unlike the Persians, were known throughout Asia for being truthful. 'Agreed,' replied the mulla, 'but why is it so? The devil has got the English in his claws and so does not object to their speaking the truth, but he has not yet got the Persians, and so he is trying to corrupt the true religion.' The mulla's perverse remark reflected the Persian view that speaking the plain truth is crude and unmannerly; a polite and educated man should merely hint subtly at the truth, leaving his hearer to catch his meaning. Truth is a commodity of great value and should be used as sparingly as possible.

Sykes and Wood rode to Kerman, some three hundred miles away, and spent three weeks there mustering riding camels and supplies for the journey up to Sistan. From Kerman they took the long route south and east, down by Bam and Narmashir, where they had some good shooting at partridge, francolin and snipe. From there they rode across towards Rigan, on the border, where they were to meet up with their consular escort. Although it was December, it was very hot as they came off the high central plateau down into the true desert at the lower altitude of 2,000 feet. This was unmapped country, which urgently needed to be surveyed in case the Russians came down the Sarhad frontier.

Before them stood the smoking peak of Kuh-i Taftan, which they climbed; Sykes's thermometer burst when he put it into a jet of steam from one of the vents at the summit. Christmas was spent at a nearby village, which was surprisingly green and provided them with some woodcock to go with their partridges. At Rigan they were joined by a troop of the 6th Bombay Cavalry who had ridden hard for three hundred miles from Quetta across a totally barren desert, carrying the forage for their camels and horses with them in the newly invented bales of compressed hay, without which they could never have done a desert journey of that length. Now on the Indian side, they went up to the Afghan border together and crossed into Sistan from the east, travelling over a monotonous series of broken nullas dotted with tamarisk, before coming out suddenly into a great flat, watery plain.

Sistan[1] stands to the east of the Hamun, a shallow lake about a hundred miles long into which the Helmand river debouches, after rising in the Hindu Kush in Afghanistan and making its way along the north of the Helmand desert. The river splits into a number of channels as it nears its end, irrigating the area all around and flooding it with snow melt in the spring. The Helmand at this point formed the boundary with Afghanistan, as Sir Frederic Goldsmid had settled it some thirty years previously, but the water course had changed through successive floods, leaving the Afghan side high and dry.

The capital of Sistan was the fortified village of Nosratabad, which had been built only thirty years previously. It was a quarter of a mile square and protected by thick mud-brick walls thirty feet high, with a number of towers along its length and a moat around it which could be flooded. The governor of Sistan was a lad of nineteen who wore blue-tinted sunglasses, the son of the governor of the adjoining province of Qaen. Under his command were a regiment of soldiery armed with ancient guns which 'looked like gas-pipes' and a small detachment of Tabrizi gunners manning some equally ancient artillery, who made up for the non-payment of their wages by lending money to the villagers at 500 per cent interest, and dealt very firmly with any defaulters.

A site outside Nosratabad was agreed with the youthful governor for the consular post and Sykes duly raised his flag over his camp to signify its establishment. This immediately caused an uproar, encouraged by the mullas in the village who, not knowing what a consulate was, took exception to what they saw as an annexation of Persian territory. Sykes stood firm, pointing out that both the British and Russian consulates in Meshed flew a flag, but neither side backed down until the son of the chief mulla sagely suggested to the mob that if and when the consular flags of Meshed were ever torn down, they could also tear down Sykes's flag in Nosratabad. Honour was thus satisfied and the consulate

---

[1] The area known as Sistan at this time was much smaller than the modern province of the same name.

was duly recognized with the Russians having not yet arrived. Sir Mortimer Durand, in his report on the affair to Lord Salisbury, noted: 'Captain Sykes seems to have behaved with his usual resolution in the matter of the flag. It is very important to have in Persia officers who are not easily frightened.' Indeed, Curzon had selected Sykes for his swagger and self-assurance; as he put in his recommendation, 'Sykes swells himself out a little, and struts before the world.'

His mission accomplished, Sykes set off on the serious business of duck shooting on the Hamun. He was taken by one of the *seyyads* or netters, who made their living from the Hamun by catching duck and selling their feathers for stuffing cushions. They got about the lake on *tutins*, rafts made out of reeds, similar to the ones on Lake Titicaca, and set sprung traps of underwater nets laid at the end of funnels of reeds, down which they drove the duck. When the duck were on top of the net the *seyyad* pulled a string and the net snapped shut. By way of tax, these fowlers sent half a ton of feathers a year to the governor of the province.

After shooting some duck Sykes was ready to explore further east. Heavy rain had turned the camp into a lake and left the camels unable to move on the slippery ground for a day. Anxious to get out before the approaching floods marooned them for weeks, they pressed on, crossing the fast-flowing main channel of the Hamun, a quarter of a mile wide, which came six inches above Sykes's saddle flaps as he forded it. They landed in a tamarisk swamp, which turned out to be only an island, with another branch of the river beyond it. When Sykes's fox terrier saw that there was more water to cross, it sat down and howled. A few miles after reaching dry land they found themselves in a dense forest of more tamarisk, twenty feet high, which was so impenetrable that they had to march for miles up the river itself, which by now was shallower.

Much of the country was cultivated, but it was also the site of many ruins of substantial villages destroyed by the Mongol hordes who, by wrecking the ancient irrigation systems, had turned Persia from a fertile and prosperous country into a desert. Sistan, which in the old days had extended well into modern Afghanistan, had been the heart of the Persia of legend, where the hero Rustam – the Persian Hercules – rode his mighty black stallion Rakhsh, slaying devils, monsters and the enemies of civilized Iran. He wrestled with the tomboy Gord-Aferid, loved the smouldering Tahmineh and slew his unrecognized son Sohrab in battle, but survived to the age of 120. Sykes recounted these stories at length in his political and geographical reports. He seemed to feel bound to share his knowledge of Persian literature with his masters who, while they may have known the stories, needed to know where they had taken place.

To get back to Nosratabad they had to cross another river, which was three hundred yards wide and unfordable in the middle. The baggage was unloaded from the camels and put on to *tutins*, while the horses were swum across. The camels, however, were not natural swimmers so, once they had been unsaddled, six big gourds were strapped around each one to act as floats and the drivers, with gourds under their arms, led them into the water. One driver hauled from the front, while another sat on the camel's rump to balance it for, being heavier in front than behind, camels would drown without a counterweight astern to keep their heads above water. The camels made no attempt to swim but, with expressions of dignified melancholy, allowed themselves to be towed across the river like logs. It took them a day to get all the beasts across, whereupon they were hit by a sandstorm. This would have blinded them all had not Sykes provided goggles for all hands except for his terrier, which could not see for a day afterwards and had a very raw face.

April had brought hot weather and with it the mosquitoes, snakes and the searing blasts of the *bâd-i sad-o-bist ruz*, or the Wind of a Hundred and Twenty Days, which blows down from the Kara Kum desert in Turkistan and makes Sistan almost uninhabitable, were about to appear. It was time for them to move north to the province of Qaen.[2] Knowing that forage would be two and a half times as expensive up there, Sykes collected a hundred camels to carry two months' supplies for his journey to Birjand, the capital of Qaen. Two marches across bare desert and three long marches through the hills took them up to a pleasant village four thousand

---

[2] In those days spelt as Kain and also known as Kainat. Confusingly, the provincial capital was not the town of Kain but Birjand.

feet up, above the heat and the mosquitoes. Here, where there was grazing, they discharged most of the camels and used the remainder to carry the baggage in relays for the rest of the journey. To the delight of Sykes's terrier the country here swarmed with tortoises, which it learned to turn over, forcing whoever was nearest to dismount and right them.

The power of the hot north wind, which in Sistan blows throughout the summer, was harnessed by huge numbers of primitive windmills, which had been there for thousands of years (some of these are still standing today). The wind funnels its way between pairs of thirty-foot high mud-brick walls to meet sets of reed sails, each mounted on a long vertical pole, which turns the upper millstone against the lower one to grind the corn. Grain was brought in from a great distance and the millers made a good living, for there were no rivers to power water mills for hundreds of miles.

After passing over some high country Sykes's party came down to the treeless valley of Birjand, ruled by the tough Amir Shaukat ul Mulk ('Glory of the Kingdom'), whose father had successfully rid the province of Turkoman, Baluch and Afghan raiders and turned it into a peaceful and fertile place. The Shaukat took an informed interest in politics and his younger brother and heir, the eighteen-year-old Ibrahim Khan, already came across as a 'pleasant, gentlemanly young fellow'. He asked Sykes to start polo at Birjand, but all his polo sticks were broken and it was impossible. Ibrahim Khan went on to become one of the most progressive and enlightened landlords in the country, starting schools for girls and ensuring grain supplies throughout periods of shortage, while other landowners turned to hoarding and profiteering. Although courted by the Russians, he became a very hospitable friend to successive British consuls in the area, right up to the Second World War. Here, in this strategic and fertile province bordering on the Afghan and Russian frontiers, Sykes settled in camp for two months to take stock of the district and survey the passes through which the Russians might come south. There was some discussion between London and India as to what to do about the consulate that he had founded until, at the end of September, he was ordered back to Kerman.

Sykes's movements, which appear from *Ten Thousand Miles in*

Persia to have been those of a freewheeling explorer, had been controlled from afar. Throughout 1899 he was sending long reports directly to Lord Salisbury. They were full of detail about his findings but were over-long and larded in high Victorian fashion with rambling references to ancient Persian history, the travels of Marco Polo and the eastern campaigns of Alexander the Great. They made heavy reading but, for all that, there were many sixpences in the pudding. The political situation in Persia and the state of the game with the Russians were like constantly shifting mirages and, as they shifted, so did Sykes's views.

The territory of Qaen and Sistan rightfully fell within the purlieu of the British Consulate to the north at Meshed, where Colonel Temple took a poor view of Sykes's coming up from Kerman to poach on his land. This, too, had a bearing on the new Consulate. The first whiff of awkwardness came with a telegram from Durand to Curzon in July 1899, which said, 'Temple is evidently most jealous of Sykes.' Durand went on to write:

> Colonel Temple advocates the return of Captain Sykes to Kerman and the appointment of a medical officer to do medical and political work in Sistan. This may be a good solution to the difficulty. Colonel Temple, fearing the diminution of his charge, is anxious to get rid of Captain Sykes and Captain Sykes, who thinks a resident consul is unnecessary, is anxious to go.

At the same time the Russian Legation, which had been beaten to the post in Sistan, was inquiring as to whether Sykes would be staying there or returning to Kerman. Durand told Curzon that he thought that the Russians would not appoint a consul of their own in Sistan unless the British also did so and asked Curzon what he wanted him to do. Curzon replied that he wanted Sykes back in Kerman, but Durand had been wrong. A few days later the Russians said that they were going to send a consul to Sistan, but that he would remain only a short time, like Sykes. Durand asked Curzon whether he still wanted Sykes to leave Birjand. The immediate reply from Curzon, who was touring under canvas and taking a rare break from Viceregal Lodge, read:

Sykes to return to Kerman but via Sistan for a few weeks. Wait and see what Russia does. If they keep a consul, we shall appoint one directly from India or appoint a Native Agent.

I have not been impressed by Sykes's writing from Meshed or Birjand. He entered Sistan with his mind made up and has contradicted himself several times since. He has also shown an unseemly independence of Meshed;[3] for if one thing is clear, it is that no Agency in Sistan can be independent of the Consul-General in Khorasan. I agree with you in thinking that Meshed is over-officered, overstaffed and overpaid; and I propose to cut it down. As for the newswriting for which we pay so much, it seems to me to be contemptible.

In October Sykes duly set off south with a caravan of fifty camels, leaving an Indian medical assistant to look after the post in Birjand. Always looking for unmapped routes, he came across the village of Cheneshk, perched among boulders on a steep hillside, where a deformed dwarf took him scrambling up to a cave. This, he said, was a shrine and he was its guardian. They squeezed through a hole, down some steps cut in the rock which led to a vast catacomb full of skeletons. The dwarf told Sykes that these were the remains of pilgrims on their way eleven hundred years previously to visit the Imam Reza at Meshed, who on hearing that the Imam had been poisoned, had decided to end their days in the cave. In reality they were probably villagers who had taken refuge in the cave against later Afghan or Mongol invaders and had been suffocated by smoke. This version, however, would have given no sanctity to the place, nor made it a profitable place of pilgrimage for the dwarf and the headman of the village.

Sykes then called in at Sistan, where this time he received a cordial welcome, as a result of the presence of a very efficient Indian medical officer who had been doing good work in his absence. All was in good order for Sykes's successor to take the consulate over, for indeed the Russians duly established their temporary presence permanently and the British followed suit. (At its height the consulate had a staff of 137, including Indian medicals;

---

[3] The Consulate at Meshed came not under the Foreign Office but under the Government of India.

there was even a vice-consulate attached to it at Kuh-i Malik Siah, a hut on the border staffed by one very lonely Indian keeping an eye on the Afghan post opposite.[4])

On his way back to Kerman Sykes passed through Yazd, where he found that the anti-European feeling that he had encountered on his first visit five years previously had gone, partly because of the work of the hospital established in an old caravansaray given to the Church Missionary Society by a Parsee merchant. Indeed three of the leading Muslim clerics, who had previously put all *farangis* [Europeans] under anathema, came to call on him. The British community amounted to two bankers, five medical missionaries, including a lady doctor, and the carpet buyer from Ziegler's of Manchester. Their only entertainment had been tennis, but Sykes wasted no time in getting a gymkhana going and teaching several Persians the arts of tent-pegging and jumping.

In December 1899, after sixteen months on the march, Sykes returned to Kerman. His first act, in an effort to encourage trade with India, which at that time hardly existed, was to send a trial caravan of Persian carpets to Quetta, the first time that this had been done overland. The consignment comprised one silk carpet, 880 wool carpets, pistachio nuts, saffron, fine Kermani shawls and silks, and some homespun cloth, to a value of £500. He had written to Lord Salisbury on the subject, pointing out that for eighteen months not only had he had no salary, but his office expenses had not been paid and he had had to use his private means to finance the entirety of his activities. It was the recent payment of his arrears that had enabled him to put this caravan together. He worked with the Parsees and one of the leading Muslim merchants, who planned a return load of tea and indigo for carpet dyeing. The Governor-General was made responsible for the safety of the caravan, which made the 500-mile trip to Quetta in thirty stages. The timing was good, since the Viceroy was in Quetta at the time. Curzon bought well, setting an example to his compatriots. The venture was a success and brought home to the Kermanis the nearness of British India. By way of making further agricultural improvements, Sykes showed the farmers how

---

[4] See Frederick O'Connor, *On The Frontiers and Beyond* (London, 1931).

to dig artesian wells, which were much easier to maintain than the traditional *qanats*.

In the spring of 1900 Sykes set off with a team of Indian surveyors on a lengthy tour of exploration south-west of Kerman, mapping and gathering information as he went. At Nagar he found the ruins of a Nestorian Christian church which had been converted to a mosque in the early thirteenth century. On his way he sought out the routes taken through Persia by Alexander the Great and Marco Polo, collecting archaeological artefacts and recording the inscriptions on any ancient monuments that he found. He later published his finds in academic journals.

At a place that Sykes decided must have been Marco Polo's Camadi he discovered the remains of a city which appeared to have been washed away in a flood. A curiosity was that a number of carnelians were found in the remains of a graveyard. The Muslims of Kerman also buried their dead with a carnelian, engraved with the names of the Twelve Imams, in their mouths but this find showed that it was a much more ancient practice.

Near Jiroft a villager appeared with an eight-inch tall alabaster pot. Although it was almost as broad as it was tall, the space inside was drilled out to just a two-inch cylinder, indicating that it was probably used for storing precious ointment. The villager offered to exchange the pot for a pair of Sykes's cast-off trousers, now worn by one of his servants. The servant was reluctant until Sykes, who had decided that the pot had been left behind by Alexander the Great himself in the fourth century BC, promised to give him another pair – together with a generous tip – and duly bagged the artefact. After his return the British Museum confirmed his attribution, but in 1984 the Ashmolean Museum in Oxford dated it much earlier, to about 2000 BC.

On the day that Sykes reached Sirjan, on the border of the lawless province of Fars, where the Bandar Abbas road split to Yazd or Kerman, it was raided by a gang of tribesmen under Qavam ul-Molk, the former Governor-General of Shiraz. Just before he had left Kerman a party of British Indian Muslim pilgrims had been attacked and robbed by Afshar tribesmen and Sykes had forced the Governor-General, who declared himself to be impotent against these brigands, to compensate the Indians for their loss. When

Sykes went with his Indian cavalry escort to visit these tribes, who scoffed at Persian authority, he was treated with respect.

The Hindu moneylenders of Kerman were a different matter and caused Sykes some embarrassment since, as British subjects, they were under his official protection. They had begun lending money at extortionate rates, then falsifying the accounts and bribing the new Governor to seize the property of their victims. This man was replaced by Hissam ul-Molk, a cousin of Nasir ul-Molk, who was not only immensely wealthy but also proved a capable and just ruler of the province for the short term of his tenure.

In his last despatch to Lord Salisbury in May 1900 Sykes reported: 'A party of three Russians, stated to be surveyors, who are of course accompanied by Cossacks, has just reached Kerman. In reply to the Governor-General's polite query as to their object, they answered that Russia had territory in this direction and they wished to visit it. Comment is superfluous.' He went on to say that this was one of six Russian parties mapping their way towards Jask and Chahbahar on the coast of Baluchistan. He recommended putting a British garrison into Persia to defend the Indian frontier, saying that 'British troops would thrive splendidly in the cool plateau of Iran'. This plan delighted Curzon, who for years had been trying to convince Lord Salisbury of the real threat of a Russian advance towards India, and he determined to attach Sykes to his camp. Curzon had spent 1889 and 1890 travelling the length and breadth of Persia by post horse, with only a servant as escort, and had written a monumental two-volume work, *Persia and the Persian Question*. He was the only member of the government with any experience of Persia, which he later came to regard as belonging to him personally. He had to wait for a while, though, to obtain Sykes's services, because Salisbury was distracted by the outbreak of the Boer War.

In the late summer of 1900 Sykes received a message from a khan at Khinaman, about forty miles west of Kerman, saying that he had been laying out a new garden and his men had dug up a great number of bronze artefacts. Sykes rode out at once to investigate and was given a number of bronze spearheads, cloak pins, bracelets, some metal bowls and two very striking ceremonial axe heads. This collection is now in the British Museum, where the pieces have recently been dated to about 2000 BC, matching the date of the 'trouser' pot.

In his report to the Foreign Secretary, Lord Lansdowne (who had been Viceroy until 1894), Sykes remarked that this was a district full of potential; although now inhabited by nomads, it had flourished once under the Arabs and again under the Seljuks in the eleventh century. He was right, for now it flourishes again with citrus fruit groves and light industry. He was joined on this trip by Lieutenant Crookshank of the Indian Survey Department, but he and his Indian followers fell ill and their baggage animals collapsed, to Sykes's irritation. Sykes left Crookshank to recuperate while he continued his own survey, heading west towards the province of Fars, following Marco Polo's route (which Alexander the Great had also followed). In Fars he decided to wait for an escort as there were reports that the Russians were establishing consulates all over south Persia. However, hearing that the luckless Crookshank was unable to move, he headed back to look after him and to deal with a group of British artesian well engineers visiting Kerman. He then headed down to the coast at Jask to take some leave.

IO

Boer War and marriage

IN 1900 THE British went to war with the Boers in South Africa. Sykes, although he was acting as Consul in Kerman, was still a serving soldier and keen to see active service, not least because his standing in his regiment would have suffered if it were thought that he had not heeded the bugle call to war. He approached the Tehran Legation to see whether he could rejoin his regiment, but was informed that the Bays had not been ordered to South Africa. Not deterred, in the autumn of 1900 he applied for home leave, which was granted and, taking his charger with him, he sailed to Karachi. There General Craigie, the GOC, talked of stopping him but, when Sykes pleaded that he was a Consul and therefore not under his jurisdiction, he allowed him to sail on the first ship bound for East Africa, which was carrying Indian labourers for the sugar plantations. When Sykes landed at the Seychelles, the appearance of his enormous sixteen-hand charger created some excitement; many years later he heard that children born at that time were referred to as 'the children of the year of the horse'. From the Seychelles he took a series of ships to Mauritius, then on to Port Elizabeth and Cape Town. On the voyage he wrote his best book, *Ten Thousand Miles in Persia*, an account of all his travels in Persia to date, which was published by John Murray and went into several editions, establishing Sykes as a popular expert on Persia.

Sykes was more or less absent without leave, and to regularize his position he sent a cable to General Sir John Ardagh, Chief of the Army Intelligence Department in India, under whom he had compiled the record of his second journey in Persia. The cable ran, 'Proceeding South Africa. Hope you approve.' The reply was, 'Strongly advise you proceed South Africa.' However, when Sykes reported to the base commandant in Cape Town, nobody had heard of him. Nevertheless, General Ardagh's cable worked its charm and Sykes was sent off to join the Intelligence Department.

Before long Sir Hely Hutchinson, the Governor, heard that Sykes was a Consul. He sent for him and asked him to go on a mission to the authorities in the German colony of South West Africa to complain of the encouragement they had given to the Boers at Warmbad, in allowing them to cross the frontier and refit. Sykes immediately saw that to get to Warmbad he would first have to cross a desert where the Boers would easily find and arrest him. Fortunately, his demand for a £500 advance for his expenses required a reference to Lord Kitchener, who turned down the scheme and ordered him to Pretoria. Here Sykes met up with the officers of the Intelligence Department and was put in command of the Montgomeryshire Yeomanry at Bulawayo in Rhodesia. Many of the men were farmers, already able both to ride and to shoot, but being Territorials they lacked battle experience. He trained the regiment hard in the surrounding country, with frequent night marches and, ever the soldier–scholar, took them to see the ruins of ancient Zimbabwe.

In due course the Yeomanry were inspected by a Visiting Officer, who congratulated them on their efficiency and their shooting. The Inspector, a colonel of the 16th Lancers, reported: 'These are the best squadrons I have inspected and much credit is due to Major Sykes for their training. If they are not to see active service from Bulawayo, I would suggest that they be sent to Mafeking and be replaced by less well trained units.' Within twenty-four hours, much to their delight, the regiment was ordered to join Lord Methuen's command at Mafeking.

Lord Methuen, who had heard of Sykes's eight years' experience in Persia, gave the Yeomanry some experience in a trek with his column and then sent them in charge of a large convoy of ox-wagons with an escort of one squadron of his own regiment, a company of infantry and two field guns. Since oxen could not

work in the heat and died quickly if overworked, they marched
from 4 a.m. to 8 a.m. and again from 4 p.m. to 8 p.m. They soon
saw action:

At the beginning of September we had a real scrap. I was in
charge of flanking patrols in the hills, while the column was
marching down a valley. But galloping hard I joined in and was
soon fighting Van Tonder's commando. After a fairly hot time the
Boers fled and we captured a dozen wagons, the baggage and the
Boer ladies. Among them were six girls, who had recently
returned from school at Cape Town and seemed quite pleased to
be captured. The wagons, owing to the flight of the Boers and
the natives, were left without drivers. Perforce I told the Boer
ladies that they must drive them. At first they laughed at me but,
upon our lighting fires near the axles, they called out, 'Mr
Officer, do not burn our wagons! We will drive them!'
Consequently, two hours after dark, the camp turned out to greet
the unusual sight of Boer women driving in the captured wagons.

On September 5th 1901, the captured wagons, which moved
at only two miles an hour, were sent off with a screen furnished
by the 5th Imperial Yeomanry. I was in command of the
advance guard of the column and we were moving through
thick scrub. When my screen was about to overtake the other I
was ordering the officer in charge of it to draw it in. Suddenly
heavy fire broke out and he was shot dead, as was another officer
who came up to report to him.

The position of the column was serious as it was marching
down a cutting with a shallow river. The front portion had
forded it and was marching uphill. I saw that the key to the position was a low ridge about a hundred yards ahead, so I ordered a
dozen men under Lieut. Jameson to dismount and started to run
ahead to the ridge. I was naturally the chief target. First of all my
field glasses were shot and then I was shot through the left leg. I
only had a dozen yards to run so, using my carbine as a staff, I
reached the ridge under a hail of bullets and threw myself down,
being partly covered by a tree. Firing was incessant and at close
quarters. The Boer fired at me with an elephant gun, but since
he used black powder I was able to locate him and bagged him.

Many of my men, who were extremely plucky, were killed and wounded and a Maxim gun crew had to withdraw their weapon. I had fired some fifty rounds and only Lieut. Jameson, who behaved extremely well, and one of the yeomen were left unwounded or dead. Suddenly a shell burst some thirty yards ahead of me. Lord Methuen had dragged a gun up the river and was firing across me from my right. The Boers all retreated. The wounded were put into ambulance wagons and late at night we reached Zeerust, where a mug of Bovril and a piece of bread ended a fight in which my regiment earned high praise.

For this action Lord Methuen mentioned Sykes and many of his men in despatches. Many years later, in 1930, the two were talking and Sykes told Methuen how concerned he had been to hear of his capture by the Boers. Lord Methuen replied that he would never have been taken prisoner by the Boers had Sykes been with him in command of his regiment. Sykes said that this was the greatest compliment that had ever been paid to him.

Sykes's view of his own involvement in this action comes across in a letter to his mother, written from hospital, one of the only two of his letters home to have survived. It reads much like a letter home from boarding-school reporting a victory in a cricket match:

My dearest mother,

As usual, I have been very lucky. We were marching through a thick forest much broken up with ravines, when 800 Boers attacked and killed or wounded most of the men on ahead. This gave me my chance and I rushed up with some of my men under a hail of bullets. There was a ridge which I saw was the key of the position, so with three or four others I ran for it across the open followed by one or two men.

When half way across my glasses were hit and I got a bullet through my leg from left to right, but I ran on and kept the Boers at bay with two men and one officer who were 20 yards behind.

It was quite exciting as some 20 or more Boers were firing only 30 yards away, but I kept up heavy fire and so we saved the situation. It was nearly an hour before aid came when I found that we had suffered terribly, two of my men being killed and seven

wounded. In fact only three were untouched. However, Lord
Methuen said that I had saved the situation, which I think was
true and as he has done me well in his despatches, I am content. I
was in a hail of bullets, even my moustache being shot off.

Since then I have been on my back. The bullet passed
between the two bones of my leg and had done no harm. I am
on crutches but a month will see me all right, I expect. In any
case I am glad to have earned my medal with honour.

Lord Methuen wrote that my command bore the brunt of the
fight and says we are the best fighters in the division, which is all
very pleasant. The reaction was trying as, what with dead and
wounded men and horses, the sight was terrible.

One officer was shot as I gave him orders and a second who
was coming up with reinforcements. It is by far the hottest fire I
have been under . . . Don't feel anxious about me as I have got
much credit and enjoyed myself at the same time.

By way of contrast to Sykes's somewhat self-satisfied account of
the action, *The Times'* history of the war[1] gives a drier version:

Four days later – and this was an ominous sign of revival –
Kemp, reinforced by De la Rey, was turning the tables on Lord
Methuen by attacking him on his way to Zeerust in the bush-
clothed valley of the Marico River. The bush, too thick for
proper deployment, was infested with Boer riflemen; the ox-
transport was a dangerous burden and, to make matters worse, a
gun stuck in a spruit for four hours. Forty men, chiefly of the
Welsh companies, were killed or wounded in a fight which,
after Vlakfontein, was the severest as yet experienced by any of
the new yeomanry.

The official history of the war[2] gave British casualties of sixteen
killed and twenty-five wounded, with slightly more on the Boer
side, plus some prisoners.

[1] *The Times History of the War in South Africa*, vol. 5, p. 327, action of Marico River
(Rhenosterfontein), 5th September.
[2] *History of the War in South Africa*, vol. 4, p. 292.

Sykes, who had been bored by the inactivity of his early army days with the Bays in India, had at last seen some action. His description of his part in it, however, is illustrative of his temperament. The Yeomanry lost many men in the action, largely because, being a local regiment of volunteers, they had a strong team spirit and charged in to help each other, regardless of the Boer firing which their senior officers had got them into. For all his energy and courage, Sykes's egocentrism and self-congratulation were dangerous characteristics, as became clear later, when he was given command of the South Persia Rifles during the First World War.

Sykes returned to Britain on leave, a wounded hero, in the autumn of 1901. During his leave the Foreign Office conferred on him the CMG for his consular work at Kerman, and the Royal Geographical Society awarded him its Gold Medal for his exploration work in Persia. The paper that he wrote for them about his travels in Baluchistan ran to forty-nine closely printed pages, of which he presumably delivered only a part as his lecture. The discussion afterwards was filled with tributes to him, particularly from Sir Thomas Holdich, who had been his chief on the Boundary Commission:

> I can personally testify, as no-one else can, to the extraordinary influence which Major Sykes exercised over the people with whom he had to deal in that quarter. It was an influence gained by just those same qualities of ready adaptability to the country and the people with whom he had to do, of keen insight and participation in their sports and pastimes – the same qualities which afterwards fitted him so well to become a distinguished leader of yeomanry in South Africa under one of the best of our fighting generals.

He also gave much praise to Sykes's geographical work and to Asghar Ali, his Indian plane-tabler, who accompanied Sykes on all his map-making travels, 'a patient, painstaking, hard working topographer who, under Major Sykes's direction, has succeeded in securing a very fine acquisition of fresh geography in that country'.

Hercules Read of the British Museum then spoke at length on the importance of the Persian tiles, bronze artefacts and pottery that Sykes had brought back and shown at the lecture. In his vote of thanks to Sykes, the President of the Royal Geographical Society, said:

> What I think must strike most of us . . . is the exhaustive and complete manner in which he acquaints himself with the country and the people among whom he has to live and serve. I do not think, as a Persian traveller, that there has been one since Sir Henry Rawlinson[3] who has combined so great a knowledge of Persian history with such valuable geographical investigations.

Sykes – now thirty-four – was feeling the urgent need of a wife. His home leave was short and, like many another colonial in the same position, he needed to do something about it rapidly, for if he failed he would not get another home leave for at least three years. He he turned to his family for help.

His wife-to-be, Evelyn Seton, had been born in 1881, the daughter of Colonel Bruce Outram Seton. The Setons came from Normandy with Henry II and in the early thirteenth century were invited to Scotland to support the king against the unruly clans of the north and west. They were quickly absorbed into Scotland and indeed fought against Edward I. Sir Christopher Seton, who was Robert the Bruce's brother-in-law, saved the latter's life in one battle but was captured not long afterwards and suffered a grisly death for treason. The family came out for the Old Pretender in 1715 and lost everything, but two junior branches of the family kept their baronetcies, bestowed by Charles II. Evelyn was always aware of the distinction of her lineage.

She had been brought up in the gatehouse of the Norman castle of Usk in Monmouthshire, after her mother died at the age of twenty-three. Her father was a keen sportsman, a notable rider and steeplechaser; he was fond of salmon fishing and tied his own flies. He was good at drawing and caricatures (he had been taught in

---

[3] Rawlinson travelled in Persia 1833–8, was Consul-General in Baghdad 1843–55 and Minister at Tehran 1859–60.

India by Kipling's father), and was well read and broad-minded. When Evelyn was about twelve he took her and her sisters to Brussels for seven years to learn languages, music and dancing. They went to concerts and the opera, but *Tosca* was taboo. In the summer holidays they went to the coast and rather daringly rode bicycles with specially divided skirts, or went to southern Germany and Switzerland, walking and fishing, or touring battle-fields. Her father then died young, leaving her in the care of her cousins, but she was already an adventurous and self-reliant young woman. Sykes's daughter Elinor Sinclair later described the legacy left by the colonel to Evelyn and her sisters: 'My grandfather died before his daughters grew up, leaving them unprovided for, but certain that they came of aristocratic lineage. They were equally certain that Jews, coloured people and business people must be ignored socially. The working class, like domestic animals, provided they behaved properly, must be treated kindly.'

In a memoir written in her old age and remarkable for its clarity and wit Evelyn described her first meeting with Percy Sykes at Lydham, the family home in Shropshire:

Major Sykes of the Queen's Bays had just returned from the Boer War wounded in the leg and in need of rest and recuperation. He came to Lydham with his charming sister Ella. He was then over thirty and his family were anxious that he should marry; it was suggested to his cousin Mabel that she should ask a selection of her friends to meet this promising young soldier. He had already written a successful book, *Ten Thousand Miles in Persia* and made himself *persona grata* to influential Governors in Persia, which had pleased Curzon, who was Viceroy at the time.

Percy had turned down some of Mabel's friends like Lavender Bryant of matches fame and one of the Playfairs who, with their smart London manners and money, were all determined to marry peers or their sons. His courtship was short and I might say almost violent. I was very attracted by this young man. He had explored a great deal of the then almost unknown country of Persia. I listened enthralled to these adventures. He and I were soon talking and to his pleasure I had read a good deal and took a real interest and let him know that I would like to travel.

My father had given me a taste for that by taking us to so many foreign parts as children. At any rate matters travelled fast and I did not need much persuasion when he proposed.

We went to stay at Lyndhurst in the New Forest [with his widowed mother and his two sisters] where we rode and walked for miles and finally were engaged. Percy had promised to return home to Kerman so that his replacement could be in time to travel to Delhi in time for the arrival of King George and Queen Mary for the Great Durbar, so the wedding was hurried forward to 1st October [1902] and we spent our honeymoon mostly in London and Brighton.

Thus, with due dispatch, Sykes had bagged a wife. His engagement present to her was a copy of his *Ten Thousand Miles in Persia*, beautifully bound in tooled jade-green leather – hardly the conventional object of personal adornment that she might have expected. According to their daughter Elinor, the honeymoon was 'spent by my father rowing my mother up and down the Thames in the chill of late autumn'. But he had found a woman of unusual character and 'portability', while she had found a man who was not terrified by her originality and independence.

Sykes's haste in the matter, quite apart from being thoroughly in character, was also due to the fact that while he had been on leave from Kerman, discussions had been taking place between Curzon, the Foreign Office and the India Office about future policy in Persia, and his career was about to take a new turn. In January 1901, while Sykes was in South Africa, Curzon had been reproaching Salisbury, who had been preoccupied with the Boer War, for ignoring his warnings about the impending collapse of Persia and the need to take action. Curzon had also written from India to Lord George Hamilton, the Secretary of State for India in Whitehall, to say that he was waiting for confirmation of Sykes's appointment to succeed Colonel Picot as military attaché at the Tehran Legation. The confirmation never came. Charles Hardinge at the Foreign Office, who remembered Sykes from his days at the Legation in Tehran and could not stand him, had made sure that it never would. But Curzon still wanted his man and got in touch with Sir Arthur Godley, Lord Hamilton's deputy.

Godley reported back to Curzon in February 1902: 'I have been seeing Sykes, who has distinguished himself in South Africa. He is anxious to settle his career and intends, if not transferred to Indian Service, to take some military office.' Curzon replied to Hamilton: 'I have a high opinion of that officer in spite of his somewhat truculent manner and appearance. We are about to address you offering to take over the Kerman consulate from the Foreign Office with the idea of bringing Major Sykes on the list of our Political Department and employing him in this and other Persian posts that may hereafter be vacant.' Hamilton pushed hard at the India Office and replied: 'I will do all I can to bring Sykes on the list of our Political Department. Over zeal is a good fault, though the eastern side of Persia is not a good place to exhibit it, especially when you have a nation so prompt through its representatives to outdo on their side any slip or incautious transaction which any of our officials commit.'

Sykes had sent a copy of *Ten Thousand Miles in Persia* to Curzon, who not only wrote to thank him for it and to compliment him on it but added a table that he had carefully drawn up, showing nine direct quotations, with chapter and verse, which Sykes had lifted from his own two-volume book *Persia and the Persian Question*, with the comment: 'I observe you have made a clean sweep of all my most cherished quotations . . . Either our reading must run on curiously parallel lines or you must have absorbed what I wrote with a completeness which is in any case a compliment.'

In July Sykes wrote to Curzon from Lydham to thank him for his kind comments and added: 'I was asked by the War Office whether I was prepared to leave the Foreign Office and join the Indian Political Department. Since the FO has dismissed me with a blessing in the shape of a CMG, I replied that I was quite ready.'

Curzon had got his man. Not only that, but he had removed the Kerman consulate from the control of the Foreign Office to report directly to the Government of India, putting it on the same footing as the Meshed consulate. Sykes had to bustle Evelyn off to Persia promptly to answer Curzon's call.

I I

Return to Kerman

EVELYN AND PERCY, accompanied by his cousin Herbert Sykes, took the usual route to India, going by train to Marseilles and from there by ship to Bombay.[1] Evelyn took with her a nursemaid from England, who had had three months' training in midwifery and who at first thought she was bound for service not in Persia but in Perthshire. She died within two years of smallpox.

On board they met the Aga Khan, who promised to visit Kerman to see his relatives and Ismaili followers in the region. At Bombay they were entertained by various notabilities, and got about in a carriage drawn by a pair of beautiful Arab horses which the Aga Khan had insisted on lending them. Bombay was the base of the Parsees in India and a delegation of fifteen of them came to deliver an address of eulogy for the help which Percy had given to the Parsees of Kerman. In reply he urged the influential Indian Parsees to visit their kinsmen in Persia and to imbue them with more modern and progressive ideas. They then placed a massive garland of tuberoses and tinsel over his shoulders and put a huge bouquet of flowers into his right hand, while in his left hand he held the address, contained in a handsomely engraved silver cylinder.[2] And so, with profound professions of respect, the deputation withdrew. Herbert found the sight of his cousin comical, but he

---

[1] Herbert's account comes from a series of articles that he later wrote for the *Stockport Advertiser*.

[2] Now with the Sykes papers in Oxford.

failed to realize how much Sykes had done for this honest, hard-working and much harassed minority of what were the original inhabitants of Kerman.

From Bombay they went up to Karachi to pick up their consular escort of six Sikhs of the Central Indian Horse and embark for the ride to Kerman. The Sikhs rode small grey active horses and each carried a sword, a lance and a .303 rifle. They also took on board an Indian medical orderly, who disgraced himself by not only omitting to bring any medicines or equipment but also by not mentioning his forgetfulness until Karachi and telegraphic communication had been left far behind.

They travelled up the Persian Gulf on a returning date boat. Evelyn later remembered that it was infested with cockroaches which, after the dates had been unloaded in India, set about feasting on the passengers. Although a cabin was supposed to have been specially cleaned for her, hordes of them were crawling about below her bunk, but she did not make a fuss. Her memoir continues:

> In Muscat we stopped for lunch, tennis and dinner with Major and Mrs Cox. He was the Consul and afterwards became the 'King of the Persian Gulf'. She never cared about travel in the wilds, which I always enjoyed. That night there was a storm in the Gulf and Percy lifted me out of my bunk and carried me up on deck where, if the boat capsized we would have had a better chance of surviving.

The next day they arrived at Bandar Abbas, where the water was shallow and there was no quay for the vessel to dock at. Under the blazing sun passengers and luggage were piled into a small dhow, which tacked about for two hours before it could get ashore. It finally deposited them on a sandbank in shallow water where a chair was brought for Evelyn and she was carried ashore. Already pregnant, and the wife of the prestige-conscious Sykes, her first welcome to Persia was not what she expected:

> We had hoped to stay with our Consul, but not at all. Plague had broken out in Gwadur and, in case we spread it, the Persian

Government made us spend six days in quarantine outside the
town in a tent, which Percy's head man had made all ready for
us, with a couple of cooks. Colonel Gray the Consul came
often to see us and put us wise as to the ways and means of life in
Bandar Abbas, one of which was that the water was quite
undrinkable and had to be diluted with any strong drink which
could be spared from the date boats passing up the Gulf.

Bandar Abbas was then a small town with a population of about
6,000 Persians, Arabs and Baluchis, who lived in white houses or
palm huts which straggled along the shore. Behind these was a
wide expanse of sand leading up to the foot of a mountain range
eight thousand feet high. In winter the air was so clear that the
mountain seemed to be on top of the town, but it was in fact
fifteen miles away. Herbert took a walk through the bazaars and
was pleased to find Edgeley bleached cottons on sale.

Before they could set off for Kerman, consular duties intervened. A young Hindu merchant from Kerman, hearing that
Sykes was at Bandar Abbas, had come down with a letter from his
father asking Sykes to persuade the young man to marry his
betrothed forthwith, since he was over twenty-five and the old
man did not see why the young lady should be kept waiting.
When the young merchant protested that his business was pressing
and his time was precious, Sykes suggested that he propose to his
father that he should be allowed to wait just two years more in
order to provide a better establishment for his wife than if the marriage were contracted at once. This was agreed and, *Pax Britannica*
thus established, the Sykeses were ready to move off. Evelyn
described their departure:

Our camp was soon organized and, our escort of Lancers in
readiness, on 15th December we set forth on the three hundred
mile trek to Kerman. We left Bandar Abbas with their pennons
flying but, since they were tiring for the men to carry on long
stages, they were put away on the journey except when we were
passing through villages. I had a nice grey Arab to ride, with
smooth paces well suited to a long journey. Progress was slow
since the double camp of camels and mules had to keep to the

pace of the camels, which could not cover more than a hundred miles in a week, with a rest at the end. The camels were fed on dates, spitting the stones out neatly, one out of each side of the mouth.

Herbert Sykes had his own camp, with a staff of five. His head servant waited at table and supervised the two *farrashes*, the cook and the groom. The *farrashes* pitched the tents, carried water and did all the odd jobs. The camp consisted of two sets of tents, the *pish-khaneh* (advance camp) and the *pas-khaneh* (rear camp). The former set off at midnight with the day tents and the non-personal baggage, which would all be set up and ready by about ten or eleven the next morning, while the travellers spent the night in the *pas-khaneh* with just the essentials. The march routine was to rise at six and have breakfast in the open air on tinned bacon with eggs, if any were to be had, and then set off to reach the day's stage before the midday heat. Lunch, ready cooked, was carried on the *abdari* mule and served on arrival. In the afternoon they bathed and changed to pursue partridge or francolin, or sat in the shade reading and writing. In the cool of the evening they took a stroll or played a round of impromptu golf.

The camp was made up of twelve tents. The largest, the dining- and living-room, was twelve feet square. There were two sleeping tents of Swiss cottage type, eight feet square with a bath alcove, and four tents for the cooks and *farrashes*. The Sikh escort had three tents and the rest were for the medical orderly, muleteers and grooms. After breakfast the tents were struck and loaded on mules while the party mounted their horses and rode the stage to the next camp, about fifteen or twenty miles on, where they would find the *pish-khaneh* already set up: the *pas-khaneh* arrived about two hours later. Camels carried the advance camp and the mules, which travelled faster, brought up the rear camp. The whole caravan, carrying Percy and Evelyn's complete outfit and Herbert's travelling kit, amounted to twenty horses, thirty-five camels and twenty-four mules, with one man leading seven camels or four mules. It was no simple matter to organize all the packing for such an expedition, and the first stage of a march was traditionally only three miles, to allow things to shake down and sort themselves out.

It also made it possible to go back to collect any items that had been forgotten or left behind in the confusion of the *bandobast*.

The main roads were mere tracks worn down over the years, and no effort was made to remove boulders, make marked routes or build bridges. Rivers had to be waded through, and rocks stumbled over. There was no question of using wheeled vehicles. At the end of each day's march the horses were given chopped straw and barley and tethered for the night under a couple of felt rugs.

One afternoon they hit a cloud of locusts and, by way of a special delicacy, the cook planned a locust curry, but the wind blew them away before enough could be collected for a meal. They made slow progress, covering fifty-five miles in twelve days, and many of the party fell ill from being in Bandar Abbas. There was no medicine and the worst sufferer was the medical orderly himself, who declared noisily and repeatedly that he was dying of a dozen diseases. When Sykes firmly limited him to half a dozen he began to feel better.

For Christmas Day the caravan halted in the Jiroft valley. Lunch was tinned plum pudding and brandy, but holly was not to be had. They read the service and strolled in a date grove watching dragonflies. Dinner was tinned soup, tinned salmon, lamb cutlets, francolin pie, mince pies and tinned cheese. They drank the health of King and Queen in burgundy, with hyenas shrieking just outside their tent, while Evelyn kept a good hold on their two terriers in case they should rush out at them.

The Governor of Jiroft gave the party a very cordial welcome by sending out twenty mounted men to meet them and conduct them to his camp, where a guard of honour drew up and saluted them with a long bugle call. They sat on cushions in the governor's tent while they took tea and Sykes expatiated on the Boer War. After tea they rode back to their own camp and the governor, according to the rules of Persian politeness, returned the call, bringing with him his pointer, which he lent them. The next day it put up an unrecorded species of wild cat which Sykes shot; he sent its skin to the Natural History Museum.

Up in the Jebel Bariz (Cold Mountain) they pitched camp at the entrance to a narrow gorge through which the wind whistled, blowing the tents down as soon as the *farrashes* had put them up.

All hands had to set to to lash them down with boulders and camel-ropes before they would stay up. Evelyn recalled:

> As we travelled inland, climbing all the time, the weather became uncomfortably cold and the thermometer went down to 8°F. I remember putting on all the clothes I had to keep the icy cold out and the food cooled very quickly between the cooks' tent and ours . . . I was glad that I was escorted by a very solid husband.

After crossing a blisteringly cold pass at 8,400 feet they descended into the Kerman plain and made for Mahan, where they stayed in Farman Farma's garden, the Bagh-i Shahzdeh. The Prince himself was now in disgrace, following some court intrigues at Tehran, and had been banished to Baghdad, leaving the house very dilapidated. On 4th January 1902 they were met outside Kerman by Major Phillott of the 1st Punjab Cavalry, who had been acting as Consul during Sykes's two-year absence, and by two of Sykes's Persian friends who had braved the bitter cold to ride out of town to greet him with proper Persian ceremony. They entered Kerman in English-built landaus with the coach springs lashed down with cords to stop the passengers being bounced right out of them; there was no road and they flew in to the Consulate at a terrifying gallop over ditches, streams and irrigation channels, ridges, furrows and pot-holes that would have astounded any English coachman.

Sykes later gave a lecture to the Royal Geographical Society about this journey of three hundred miles. There had been much sickness and one death in the party on the way and it was a 'matter of congratulation' that they had not been caught in a blizzard. Astonishingly he made no reference to the fact that for the first time in Persia he was travelling with a wife, a young bride barely two months married and already pregnant. In his address of thanks the President, clearly startled by this unchivalrous omission, gave her due credit. Perhaps Sykes felt that his wife was none of the business of the Royal Geographical Society, or that the spotlight should shine only on himself, or perhaps he had been influenced by years of living among the Persians, who considered it the height of ill manners even to mention one's wife to a stranger. This very public omission spoke volumes about his relationship with Evelyn, whom he undoubtedly sidelined throughout their married life.

Evelyn settled efficiently and without fuss into the Consulate, transforming the bachelor quarters into a home with the collapsible furniture which had been sent up by camel from the coast, together with a supply of stores for three years. They were short of horses when they arrived and had to buy some, which they made into polo ponies for their entertainment. Herbert bought one from a Persian prince who had recently been appointed district governor without salary. The prince had accepted the post a poor man but soon rode into Kerman with about twenty horses and a large retinue of servants. He had robbed right and left and was in no way discomfited when Percy suggested he might have been going rather too far when he took to stealing the post horses.

Herbert entertained himself with some amateur archaeology, digging for remains in some caves in the hills behind the Consulate. He discovered a skeleton covered in a shroud but, although he ordered his men to cover it up again, there was a day's delay, and rumours began to spread round the bazaar that the foreigners were defiling graves. More than that, they said that the *farangis* had taken the body to the Consulate and were using alchemy to extract gold from the brain. Sykes was bombarded with letters of protest, the mullas threatened to complain to Tehran and one of the workmen was jailed.

Percy got Herbert out of the way by sending him down to Bandar Abbas to collect his sister Ethel. Not greatly loved by the family, she had decided to come out and have some adventures in Persia along with a doughty Miss Tanner, who had been travelling for the past sixteen years, and had already been there twice. Percy wanted Herbert to go back to the coast by a different route to explore and report on what he found. Evelyn set him up with stores for a month, with everything from soap to tinned butter, flour, candles and bloater paste. No interpreter could be found to accompany him, so he bravely set off without one, hiring twenty mules to cover the journey. After the cold winter barrenness of Kerman he reached the fertile town of Bam, with its oranges and date groves, where word had gone ahead that the cousin of Consul

Sykes was on his way. The Governor sent six of his servants to escort him through the bazaars to his lodgings in town, and every-where he went Herbert was treated with the greatest of respect, which he attributed to the high level that British prestige had reached through Sykes's efforts. The possibility of its being also due to natural Persian courtesy did not seem to occur to him.

After some tough travelling – at one point he was nearly swept away in a flash flood – Herbert reached Bandar Abbas just in time to catch the mailboat bringing the ladies. They disembarked in the usual way but then the coolies in the luggage buggalow all jumped off the same side of the boat as it was about to beach, tipping it over and depositing ten of their trunks in three feet of sea water, ruining their clothes. The stalwart women laughed this off and rode up to Kerman with Herbert by the shorter summer route. After staying a month in Kerman, much of which he spent stalking mouflon in the mountains with Farman Farma's head stalker, he took the two women off on a long expedition across the desert via Yazd on the pilgrim route to Meshed.

Back in Kerman life had not been dull. The harvest had been disappointing and there was a shortage of wheat, which was com-pounded when some of the landowners immediately took to hoarding grain to raise the price of flour to famine levels. The townspeople rioted in protest and Farman Farma feared for his life. However, the mob was well disposed to the British Consulate and, after two hundred of them had taken *bast* in the garden, Farman Farma removed the corrupt official who had been principally responsible for organizing the shortage and put an end to the inci-dent by cutting off a judicious number of hands and noses. Throughout all this the unflappable Evelyn patiently awaited the arrival of her first child.

Just before it was due, Sykes abandoned her and went off on a trip to the high summer pastures of the Buchaqchi tribe – the principal tribe of robbers in the district – as a guest of their chief, who had invited him to go shooting. The chief's eldest son, as a sign of respect, rode out sixty miles to meet Sykes and conduct him to the camp. The Buchaqchis complained of the exactions made on them by the Persian government and its officials and said that they would be happy to come under British protection. Sykes had the inspired idea of turning poachers into gamekeepers and employing them as telegraph line guards.

On his way back to Kerman, Sykes visited Hasan Khan, the chief of the 18,000-strong Afshar tribe of nomads, who came to meet him riding on a donkey. Hasan Khan had never seen a European and was very suspicious of Sykes until Sykes told him that he was a friend of his favourite son, after which his attitude changed. In his long report to Lord Lansdowne he wrote, showing his characteristic modesty:

I enjoy the immense advantage of either knowing or being known to every khan or chief and wherever I travel I am considered to be the representative of a power which desires that Persia should remain independent and should progress. The people are weary of an effete and corrupt Persian administration which is constantly compared with the upright and just character of British rule.

Shortly after his return Evelyn had her baby. She later told the story in her cool and matter-of-fact way:

In early July Frank was born. A young English doctor working on the new telegraph line being laid from Tehran to India was sent for and he hurried down. He had never seen a baby since his student days. When my nurse went to find him he had disappeared. It turned out that he had drunk the bottle of ether which Percy had brought down specially from Tehran and had passed out. Percy threw him out of the house . . . How the baby survived the journey from Bandar Abbas to Kerman still surprises me. Had anything gone wrong I might have left a little grave in the desert, myself perhaps with him. In those days childbirth was a very haphazard affair. In all I had six children and three miscarriages.

Like the nurse, Frank caught smallpox but, unlike her, he survived.

Now with a family, Sykes was travelling much less and spent most of his time near Kerman cultivating the officials, landlords and village headmen, while Evelyn cultivated her garden, bringing in English insecticide for the fruit trees, Sutton's seeds and, for the house, English soap. Prince Farman Farma gave Sykes an open invitation to make free use of his country pleasure-house, the Bagh-i Shahzdeh, his magnificent archetypal Persian garden a short way outside Mahan, which was (and still is) venerated for its shrine to Shah Nematullah Vali, the fourteenth-century founder of the Nematullahi order of Sufi mystics.

Farman Farma's garden is about twelve acres in area and stands on the barren mountain skirt, protected from the wind and summer dust by a high wall of ornamental brickwork. Approaching it across the desert, one enters through an archway of patterned brickwork inlaid with tiles, to be faced by a Persian vision of paradise. The eye is led up to the house by a line of twelve pools, one above the other, with clear ice-cold water cascading from one to the next in a stream fed by a *qanat*, which brings the water underground from the mountain behind. Running parallel to the staircase of water are rows of tall cypress, pine, poplar and plane trees, all bending and rustling in the breeze coming down from the hill. This was all laid out with a vision in mind, for in Persian poetry the picture of a cypress bending in the breeze is a symbol of divine but invisible love touching its creation. The tall thin cypress is like the Arabic character *Alif*, the first letter of *Allah* and also the figure 1, which gives the idea of the unity of creation. The bending cypress, which is never burdened or bowed down with the weight of fruit, is also likened to a willowy young damsel.

Below the trees, safely shaded from the desert sun and lining the running water, are beds of roses. At the top of the avenue stands the airy two-storey whitewashed house with its arched *iwans*[3] to catch the breeze and give shade from the sun. Here the Prince's guests could sit in peace, far away from the cramped and narrow streets of the city.

In his idle moments Sykes wrote about some of the characters that he had come across. Following the manner of James Morier's *Haji Baba of Isfahan*, a classic caricature of Persian life, he worked on *The Glory of the Shia World: The Tale of a Pilgrimage* (published in

---

[3] Porticoes or verandas.

1920), which was fancifully supposed to have been translated from a work written by one 'Nurullah Khan', the grandson of the original Haji Baba. Nurullah Khan was a thin disguise for Sykes's Kermani friend Haji Muhammad Khan, the mildly eccentric old man who claimed to have refused the Order of the Garter from Queen Victoria. Sykes used his book to put together many local stories of consular life that he could not include in his official reports. Some of them, although written in leaden prose, give a good flavour of the precarious and lawless nature of life in the provinces. At one point he criticizes some of the Young Persians who had been sent to Europe for a progressive education but had learned very little:

The Vakil ul-Molk[4] sent one of his sons to Europe with plenty of money to study history, law, geography, all sciences and languages and above all Parliament. Fazlullah Khan spent several years and much money in London and wrote to his father such accounts of his learning and of the attentions paid to him by its Viziers who, according to him, vied with one another in honouring him, that the Governor-General was transported with delight and frequently exclaimed in durbar that without the slightest doubt Fazlullah Khan would one day be Grand Vizier of Persia, or if not that, he would certainly become Vizier for Foreign Affairs.

At length Fazlullah Khan wrote to his father that he was returning to his service and His Excellency, who was camping in the hills during the Forty Days of Heat, gave orders for him to be met with the highest honours by all his servants, of whom I [Nurullah Khan] was one of the chief.

The reception party consisted of three hundred sowars under a general. There were also twenty mounted servants leading superb horses with collars of gold round their necks and gorgeous Rasht saddle cloths; and the Governor's favourite horse was sent for Fazlullah to ride upon. In truth, had he been a prince more honour could not have been shown him.

---

[4] A Governor of Kerman famous for his probity and public works, many of whose buildings survive today.

Near the camp, ten servants with silver maces and sixty *farrashes* led the future Vizier to where His Excellency awaited him alone. Fazlullah Khan flung himself off his horse and wished to do obeisance to his father; but the latter, kissing him on the mouth, led him by the hand to a tent which they entered alone.

After a short silence His Excellency said, 'My son, during the course of your many years of travel, tell me what is the most extraordinary thing which you have observed.' 'Lord of my life,' was the reply, 'may I be thy ransom; but in London, even the little boys spoke the English tongue.'

The Governor made no reply, but rose and left the tent. He was immediately surrounded by the nobles of the province, who expressed hope that he was satisfied with his son. The only reply I heard was, 'My money has been burnt.'

Needless to say, none of us Kermanis have, since that date, thought of educating our sons in Europe.

Provincial Governors-General bought their appointments from the Shah and recouped their outlay by selling local sub-governorships to the highest bidders. The local governors, in turn, extorted whatever they could from the populace before they were outbid by a rival and replaced. Sykes gives a good illustration of the high value placed by Persians on the sort of ready wit which, if it pleased the Shah, could turn a sentence of death into a reward of having one's mouth filled with gold.

There is a story which runs that [a Governor-General] once appointed a man to a governorship and this individual, knowing what to expect, bethought him of a plan by which he might be secured in his post. So one day, when the Governor-General was sitting at the window of the Hall of Audience, he saw such a one riding on a horse with his face to its tail and holding a paper in his hand. On seeing this, His Excellency remarked, 'What animal is this?' and immediately ordered the individual to be brought to his presence and asked him what was the meaning of such behaviour. Such a one replied, 'May I be your sacrifice! This slave [polite Persian for 'I'] was appointed Governor of

Bam, but knowing that a second Governor would soon be appointed, he sat on his horse looking back towards Kerman and holding the appointment all ready for his successor.'

The Governor-General, upon hearing this, rolled over with inextinguishable laughter and, when he was able to speak, he shouted, 'Go, mount thy horse with thy head towards its head. I grant thee Bam for five years.'

In criminal investigation honeyed words and subtlety were more effective than crude threats of violence:

It happened that one of the Hindus [who were British subjects], of whom there are several at Kerman, was robbed and murdered in the Rafsenjan district and the English Consul *Sahib* sent repeated telegrams to the English Legation, with the result that every day fresh orders came from the Minister of the Interior for the murderers of this Hindu to be caught and punished; there was also a threat of dismissal unless this was done quickly.

Now all the while the Governor knew who the robbers were, but he did not wish to show great severity as, after all, the killing of a Hindu was not a great crime. However, he was obliged to seize the men and informed the Consul *Sahib* of the fact and that he was ready to have them executed. But that official, who had been hard throughout, to his surprise refused to have the men executed without proofs of their guilt.

The Governor pondered for a while and then asked the interpreter of the Consulate to go into an adjoining room and expect the proof desired by the *Sahib*. The prisoners were brought in and all the *farrashes* were dismissed.

The Governor then spoke most affectionately to them and said, 'Oh my brethren, we are all Muslims and I, like you, rejoice at the death of this infidel, may his soul remain in hell! I have dismissed all my servants that I may secretly congratulate you; and I wish to know to whom is due the most credit in this meritorious deed.' Hearing this, Iskandar Khan replied, 'Praise be to Allah, we were all partners in this pious deed. Ibrahim Khan seized the Hindu, Abdullah Khan held his donkey and I shot the infidel and Allah knows he bled like a pig.'

No sooner had he finished than the Governor asked the interpreter if he was at last satisfied of the guilt of the prisoners and, upon his replying in the affirmative, he ordered the executioner to take them to the Great Square and execute them. That dread official afterwards mentioned that the men were as if in a dream and never seemed to realize what was happening, so simple were they that they could not understand the astuteness of a high Persian official.

To illustrate the sheer tyranny and bloodthirstiness of some of the provincial governors, Sykes tells a tale of one of the local Afshar khans:

One of the leading landowners had some months before complained of the Khan's tyrannical behaviour, and the Governor-General had rebuked him for oppressing the people he ruled. Upon receiving this message from Kerman, the Khan summoned the landowner and addressed him as follows: 'Thou art the first man who has been brave enough to complain of me to the Governor-General and thy heart must be different from other men's hearts.' He then roared out to the Chief Executioner, 'Take out his heart and let me see it.'

In Nurullah Khan, Sykes showed a side of himself that he had referred to only fleetingly in his travel memoirs. After describing the various religious sects of Kerman he concluded:

Yet it is the Sufi creed which really attracted me. Many are the hours I spent listening to the *Murshid,* or spiritual head of the Mahan shrine, and my heart approved when he repeated again and again that all religious fanaticism was the result of ignorance, and that it must be swept away to make place for universal Love.

In the spring of 1904 Sykes made another short journey northwest and west of Kerman in country new to him, returning at the end of April in bitter weather. He crossed the plain of Rafsenjan, which at that time produced annually five hundred tons of the best pistachios in the world. His narrative of this journey included a discussion of whether the manna that came down from heaven to Moses was, as is still commonly believed in Persia, the sweet and sticky nougat-like substance which comes from the tamarisk that the Persians call *gaz*, or a similar exudation of camel-thorn called *toranjebin*, as maintained by Sykes's Qoran teacher, for the story also features in the Qoran. Sykes, curious about everything that he came across, was inclined to accept his Qoranic teacher's view on the matter. This is practically the only mention that Sykes made of his reading of the Qoran. It had nothing to do with his official duties. This military man wished to absorb Persian culture.

In October 1904 a commercial mission from India arrived, led by Mr Gleadowe-Newcomen of the Calcutta Chamber of Commerce. Sykes met them on their way up from Bandar Abbas at Sirjan, south-west of Kerman, and led them back, not by the direct route but by some wide detours to the west via Pariz – at an altitude of 7,500 feet – and Bahramabad. When the expedition finally reached Kerman, they rested for nearly two months, making extensive preparations before setting out on a long tour in January 1905. The declared purpose of the mission, as reported to the Persian authorities at the time and to the Royal Geographical Society later, was to explore the possibilities for developing commerce between south-east Persia and India. The expedition, with its escort of Indian cavalry and, this time, a Persian military escort, duly marched north-east to Khabis (now called Shahdad), an oasis on the edge of the Lut desert, where dates and oranges were grown for export to Khorasan and even Afghanistan. They then travelled south to Gowk, well known for its grapes, and on to the fortress city of Bam, which even today is famous for its delicious fresh dates. Here they hit winter in all its severity and battled south-east to the henna-growing region of Narmashir. From there they proceeded south and then in a wide westerly circle back towards Kerman, through gales and torrential rain. They lost a horse through oleander poisoning and a mule through drowning, but at one point they were rewarded for all their tribulations by a spectacular day's francolin shooting, with forty brace falling to three guns in two and a half hours. They had visited every district to the east and south-east of Kerman, not only noting local products that might conceivably be of interest to the Indian market but also making detailed maps of the topography, marking the availability of forage and transport animals.

The Persian authorities refused to believe that the purpose of the expedition had been simply to ascertain whether there might be a market for Persian dates or henna in India, or for Indian tea and indigo in Persia, and their concern was shared even by the French. *Le Courrier Européen* reported that, after a hundred Persian soldiers had been killed in a bloody incident with some Russian frontier guards in the north, Sykes had rapidly organized this expedition, which paid generously for every sort of local information and spent far more time drawing detailed maps than pursuing commercial matters. There could be no doubt, it said, that the British were looking for suitable advance bases to halt a Russian invasion of India. *Reynolds' Newspaper* also wrote of this 'secret Anglo-Indian mission to Persia', whose real object was to bring pressure to bear upon the Shah to prevent the Russians establishing themselves on the Persian Gulf. The Shah, who had hitherto been pro-Russian, had had a change of heart after the border incident, it reported, and the Persians were now suspicious that Russia was planning at last to conquer Persia. *The Times* was much more coy and devoted two disingenuous columns to the commercial benefits of the expedition: 'The one object of the mission is trade, and no attempt will be made to survey possible routes for roads . . . It will be known as the prototype not of peaceful penetration but of honest shopkeeping adventure.' *The Times* did, however, note that the Calcutta Chamber of Commerce had sent no representative of the tea trade on the expedition, which was perhaps a nod to the wise reader between the lines as to its true purpose. *The Times of India* reported at length on the mission, noting that the Government of India had paid all the costs and that the Calcutta Chamber expected very little commercial return. The *Morning Post* reported a speech given by Herbert Sykes to the Royal Central Asia Society, with Sir Thomas Holdich in the chair, which mentioned the mission and stressed the importance of following trade with the flag. To demonstrate the urgent necessity of taking pre-emptive action against Russian intentions he produced a map, recently published in St Petersburg, which showed a projected railway line from Baku to Tehran, with two branches down to the Persian Gulf – one ending at Bushire and the other at Chahbahar, next to the Indian frontier. Curzon's forward policy was very much alive.

Meshed: mullas, spies and pilgrims

BY 1905 NORTHERN Persia had effectively become a Russian province, ruled by Russian officials. Persian officials were not allowed to collect taxes, which were levied by Russian consuls and paid into the state-subsidized Russian Banque d'Escompte de Perse, no accounts ever being rendered. The Russian Bank functioned not as a commercial bank but as a branch of the Russian Ministry of Finance and was lending large sums to landlords against their property, using its whole so-called banking machinery to substitute itself for the Persian government. Under every kind of open illegality vast acreages of the best agricultural land were transferred to Russian immigrants. The Russian officers of the Cossack Brigade of the Persian army, although paid by the Persian government, acted under the orders of the Russian Minister of War. In 1901 Major Chenevix-Trench, the British Consul at Meshed, had reported that the Persian government intended to let Russia farm the revenues of the strategically sensitive frontier province of Sistan, or even sell the province outright to them. Similar intelligence later came in concerning Khorasan. At the same time the Russians were making military advances eastward across Transcaspia into Central Asia, constituting an ever more serious threat to India. Their railway now ran right up to the border of Afghanistan. By 1890 Britain had established a small consulate at Meshed and was using it as a base to keep watch on Russian movements in Central Asia. Previously they had been able to report on troop movements only from the consulate at Batumi on the Black Sea, which was much too far away. Terence Keyes, the Consul at Sistan on the Afghan border, on his way home on leave through Russia in 1904, reported a conversation with some hospitable Russian officers at Ashgabad, the garrison town of Transcaspia the other side of the mountains from Meshed, who told him that they expected an imminent invasion of India.

When Curzon passed through Khorasan and its capital city, Meshed, in the late summer of 1889, he was unimpressed by what he saw of the British consular presence there and wrote to the Foreign Office calling on the government to provide a bigger establishment. He also recommended naval visits to the Persian Gulf ports and an upgrading of the telegraph service. When they did not respond, he cabled them demanding a reply, noting that not only had the Russians granted Persia a monopolistic loan, but they had then appointed consuls to new areas and even invaded the quiet waters of the Persian Gulf. A Foreign Office memo recorded that 'our influence has gone' and advocated inaction. Frustrated, Curzon wrote to *The Times*, saying that the government should provide the Meshed consulate with 'quarters of sufficient splendour to impress the native mind with the prestige of a great and wealthy power'. Agreement was finally obtained for the building of a new and imposing consulate. This splendid edifice stood in a walled eight-acre compound, with residences, offices and stabling for a twenty-four-strong Indian cavalry escort and for twenty-two Turkoman mounted *sowars*, who provided the courier service between Meshed and Herat, where the mail to India was handed over to the Amir of Afghanistan's officials.[1]

The building had been designed by Ney Elias and had been under construction when Sykes passed through Meshed on his first journey through Persia in 1893. It was a two-storey structure, with

---

[1] Colonel C.E. Yate, Consul at Meshed 1893–8, in his memoir *Khorasan and Sistan* (London, 1900), told of a *sowar* he sent to deliver a telegram for Lieutenant Napier, who had left for home via Ashgabad several hours earlier. Riding a good Turkoman horse, the *sowar* caught him up sixty miles out, delivered the telegram and returned to Meshed the next day, all on the same horse, which was as fresh as if it had been ridden for one stage. Ella Sykes recalled one of these Turkoman *sowars*, who in fact was a Persian who had been kidnapped as a boy by the Turkoman and lived with them until he met a long-lost uncle working as a muleteer with the British boundary commission, who persuaded him to enter the British service.

a veranda all the way round it. Corinthian columns supported a balcony and on the roof was a pointed cupola, while the principal reception rooms boasted two excellent sprung dancing floors. The Russian consulate on the edge of the bazaar quarter looked distinctly dowdy by comparison. Following Curzon's recommendations, this lavish establishment was paid for out of funds provided by the Government of India, including liberal secret service funds for the intelligence operations, whereas the Legation at Tehran and the other consulates were paid out of the much more meagre Foreign Office funds. This quirk led to some jealousy between the generously paid 'Indian' officials and the underpaid home government staff who reported to Whitehall. The Meshed consuls were appointed by India, not London, and acted independently of the Tehran Legation, although they did the Legation the courtesy of sending them copies of their reports to India.

Khorasan is very different from the province of Kerman; where Kerman is an isolated and untroubled land of deserts and barren mountains dotted with oasis villages and date groves, Khorasan is a fertile province at one of the great crossroads of Asia, known for its turquoise mines and saffron. Historical Khorasan extended well into present-day Afghanistan, Turkmenistan and Uzbekistan and considered itself more part of Central Asia than of the Persia to the west and south.

The holy city of Meshed lies in a river valley 3,200 feet above sea level. To the west, north and east are mountains which shut it off from the great plain of Turkistan. A hundred miles to the south-east is the point where the borders of Persia, Afghanistan and the old Russia meet. Long before the Russians made their move into Central Asia the Persian empire stretched well up into Turkistan, to Bokhara and beyond, and down this route came successive waves of Turkic invaders, culminating in the devastating appearance of Tamerlane.

Meshed is a European corruption of *Mashhad*, 'the place of martyrdom'. The martyr referred to was the Imam Reza, the eighth of the Shia imams in line of descent from the prophet Muhammad, renowned for his piety and spiritual and miraculous powers. Around AD 800 the Caliph Mamun in Baghdad, who was a Sunni Muslim, decided in order to win the favour of his many Shia sub-

1. Sykes, disguised as a Russian, in Baku, before embarking on his spying trip to Samarqand, 1892

2. Prince Farman Farma (in terai hat) and hunting party, 1893. The friendship between Sykes and the Prince was a crucial element in Anglo-Persian relation until the end of the First World War

3. Sykes with his escort of Sikh Central India Horse, on tour in Kerman province

4. The British Consulate, Kerman, 1894

5. A typical house in Kerman. The wind tower draws a cooling draught into the basement, where the family retreats for the hot summer

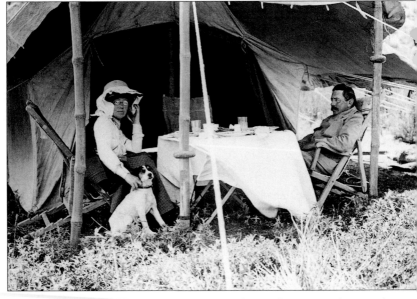

6. Sykes and his sister Ella in camp on their ride to open the British Consulate in Kerman. Sykes was unmarried at the time and Ella came out to keep house for him

7. Travelling light

8. The first British Consulate, Sistan. Sykes had raced across the desert to raise the flag before the Russians came. The subsequent fortified Consulate had a staff of 137

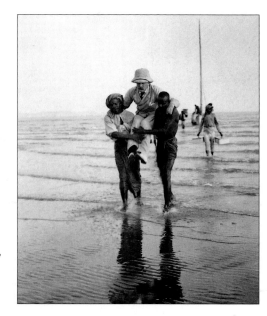

9. Sykes being carried ashore, Bandar Abbas. There was no jetty. A chair was found for Evelyn when she came

10. Evelyn in the Consulate carriage, Kerman. Just married and pregnant, she had ridden up with Sykes from Bandar Abbas to her new home at Kerman in the middle of winter

11. Frank, born shortly after Sykes and Evelyn arrived in Kerman. The doctor drank all Evelyn's chloroform at the birth and passed out

12. Bagh-i Shahzdeh: Farman Farma's pleasure garden at Mahan, where the Sykeses spent much of the heat of the Kerman summer

13. Pilgrims in front of the Shrine, Meshed. Spies of all sides passed unnoticed in this mix of Persian, Afghan, Turkoman, Arab and Uzbek pilgrims

14. Courtyard of the Shrine of Imam Reza, Meshed, the holiest site in Persia and the burial place of Imam Reza, the eighth descendant of the Prophet Muhammad in the Shia line

15. The British Consulate, Meshed, built on Curzon's orders to impress the Persians with the might of imperial Britain in this sensitive post close to the Russian border

16. Evelyn in her garden, Meshed. During the eight years that she spent in Meshed Evelyn hardly ever left the confines of the Consulate, even to go shopping

jects to appoint their most holy man as his successor. While he was at Merv, in the outer reaches of the Caliphate, he summoned the Imam to his presence, where he proclaimed him as the next Caliph and gave him his daughter in marriage. This move proved popular with the Shia but not among the Sunnis, who caused many uprisings in protest at the appointment. A year later Mamun and the Imam Reza left Merv for Baghdad. At Nowqan, where Mamun's father, the famous Haroun al-Rashid, was buried, they stopped and there, after eating an immoderate quantity of grapes, the Imam died. The Caliph, showing great signs of distress, had him buried next to his father. The Shia, however, believed that the Imam had been poisoned with a pomegranate at the orders of the Caliph, who, alarmed at the disturbances, had decided to be rid of him. The tomb of the Imam rapidly became a holy spot and place of pilgrimage for the Shia, who remembered a saying of the prophet Muhammad: 'A part of my body is to be buried in Khorasan, and whoever goes there on pilgrimage will surely be destined for Paradise.' The fervour of the Shia was increased by their belief that the Imam Musa al-Kazem, the father of Imam Reza, had prophesied that his son would be poisoned and that he would be buried next to Haroun al-Rashid and had declared that anyone making a pilgrimage to his tomb would be credited with seventy thousand pilgrimages to Mecca.

Over the years the shrine was built up and then destroyed by various Uzbek or Afghan invaders, and Meshed grew into a town. In about 1415 Gowhar Shad, the remarkable wife of Shahrukh, the son of Tamerlane, made many improvements to the shrine and built the mosque, with its vast courtyard and stunning tilework, that still stands beside it. After Persia had become officially Shia under the Safavids in the sixteenth century, Shah Tahmasp and Shah Abbas added domes and minarets, in the style of their mosques at Isfahan. Further additions were made in the nineteenth century by the Qajar Shahs. Around the shrine there grew a magnificent library and a number of theological colleges or *madrasehs*, which attracted students from all over the Muslim world.

In his book *The Glory of the Shia World* Sykes told the Arabian Nights-like story of how one of these theological colleges had been endowed.

One of the *madrasehs* was endowed by a Persian who gained his wealth in a remarkable manner. One day a rich merchant asked him whether he was willing to work at a place to which he would be conducted blindfolded. Being a fearless Kermani and very poor, he agreed and was led through many streets to a courtyard, where the blindfold was removed and he was ordered to dig a hole and bury gold coins and jewellery. This he did for several days and, being searched before he left, he saw no chance of bettering his condition.

However, one day he saw a cat, which he killed and ripped open. He then sewed up some of the money and jewels inside it and threw it over the wall. When his work was done, he wandered about until he found the cat, and not only secured the money hidden inside it, but also learned the position of the house.

Its owner shortly afterwards died, and the astute Kermani bought his house with the gold sewn up inside the cat and, as the merchant had never revealed his secret to anyone, he became his heir and in turn, when dying, bequeathed his money for the pious task of founding and maintaining a religious college.

When Sykes was at Meshed the town was a sprawl of bazaars and houses in narrow twisting streets, surrounded by a wall with a number of outer gates which were shut and barred at night. There was only one straight street, which ran east–west either side of the shrine, with a stream nine feet wide and five feet deep running down the middle of it. Although spring-fed, the stream was filthy, as it was used for washing and other purposes. The road was rough and unpaved, full of snow in the winter, muddy in the spring and dusty in summer and was lined with shops, with their wares spilling out into it.

The population at this time, as far as anyone knew, was about fifty thousand, but this number was doubled by the constant stream of pilgrims to the shrine, who came from all over Persia, Mesopotamia, India, Afghanistan, the Caucasus and Turkistan to pay their respects and to pray for miracles. There is an overwhelming sense of power to the shrine. Many pilgrims were, and indeed still are, cured of afflictions there when all hope of cure by the doctors has been abandoned. Others came just to die or, if it was too late, to be buried near the Imam, grisly caravans bore partly embalmed and stinking bodies, wrapped in shrouds, six to a camel, to be buried in the hallowed ground. The shrine was endowed with vast wealth and surrounded by a great bazaar, where pilgrims and travelling merchants mingled over the money tables.

The wealth and power of the clergy at Meshed came from the system of covenants known as *vaqf*, whereby individuals could keep their estates and property safe from the constant threat of government confiscation by making them over to the supposedly charitable institution of the Shrine, which allowed them to enjoy a proportion of the income during their lifetime. The Shrine thus acquired vast landholdings and became an independent power in its own right. It was administered by the chief custodian or Mutawalli-Bashi, who, although appointed by the Shah, ran it as an autonomous empire and was regarded as the mouthpiece of the Imam himself. He was allowed to retain a tenth of the *vaqf* income for himself and could quickly accumulate a large personal fortune. He was also the source of all important legal documents, which provided further income. Acting as a check on the Mutawalli-Bashi was the Qaim-Maqam, a hereditary office held by the chief of the Seyyids, or descendants of the Imam.

With its constantly shifting population so conveniently close to the Russian and Afghan borders, Meshed was considered by the British to be ideal for recruiting secret agents without attracting attention, and it became their most important and sensitive consulate in Persia. Consular life there was a heady cocktail of power politics mixed with religion, espionage and arms smuggling. After the departure of the formidable Ney Elias in 1896 British prestige in the province of Khorasan had diminished and the Russians had things all their own way.

In the early spring of 1905 the British Consul at Meshed had caused a scandal by taking a local woman to live with him and Sykes was ordered to proceed there immediately and take over as acting Consul-General on a temporary basis. He was to stay there until 1913. The journey from Kerman across the desert to Meshed is described by Evelyn Sykes in the memoir she wrote some sixty years later. Life at Kerman had been basic enough, but this move amounted to more than the usual upheavals suffered by army wives following the drum. 'My first fear and thought was how a baby under two years old would withstand such a journey. After both whooping cough and small-pox it seemed a terrible risk. No doctors – my heart sank. There was no alternative; it had to be.'

The direct road was the eastern one, shorter by two hundred miles, but it was considered too rough and impassable for a carriage and would have entailed the baby Frank and his nurse travelling in *kajavehs*. (A *kajaveh* was a pair of covered cradles, used by lower-class women and children, slung over the back of a camel or mule.) They rolled and shook at every step and were very tiring, so Sykes decided to take the longer but carriageable route via Yazd and the Lut desert, which had the attraction of the missionary doctor at Yazd. They got a little Russian *droshky* carriage drawn by four horses for the boy and his nurse, while Percy and Evelyn rode their Arab horses so as to be always within sight and reach of it.

They left Kerman in a snowstorm in late March, with an escort of six Bengal Lancers, travelling with the usual double camps, the mules going by day and the camels by night. About ten days took them to Yazd, 240 miles from Kerman, in the middle of the sandy desert. Here they rested with the hospitable missionaries, who gave them some of their rooms. The doctor and his staff were very helpful but wearied Evelyn by repeating ad nauseam their single joke that all the local milk and butter tasted of castor oil, since the only available fodder for their house cows was the castor oil plant that grew in their gardens. She tells the story in her memoirs, in her inimitably unflappable way:

After this week of rest and making plans for the longer part of the journey, the long march to Meshed of four to five hundred miles, we set out to cross the real desert on which nothing will grow – in contrast to the rest, which only needs a little water to make anything grow. There were many miles of this salt-encrusted soil, once, it is thought, the bottom of an inland sea. There were a number of hazards to be faced. The first was a dry river bed with high banks. So far we had had no trouble with the carriage. The horses were unharnessed and the carriage was manhandled over the steep bank. Another obstacle was forty

miles of waterless country, a long and tiring stage for man and beast. The animals had to be watered, however sparsely. The camels were the easiest probably. We had to start about 3 a.m. and were glad to see the last animals in late that night. I think our worst stretch was eight miles of sands. All our belongings and baggage had to be removed from the carriage and arranged on the pack animals. Although only the nurse and child were in the carriage it still sank to its axles in the sand. The poor horses dragging it along with great difficulty had to be beaten through it. One of the three horses abreast died at the end of the fortunately few miles. After that the going improved.

On the way they met a caravan of pilgrims:

Men of position rode horses, their wives being packed into *kajavehs*. The poor rode donkeys or walked, and every now and then a prayer would be started and repeated with genuine fervour by all present. A few sleek *mullas* were particularly assiduous in reading prayers, mainly to ladies, as the caravan moved on in picturesque confusion. Percy had been told that some brigands were holding up and robbing travellers and advised the leader of the pilgrims to come with us; we had our escort of Lancers, all well armed. The man refused, saying that his people and animals were too tired to keep up with us. Poor things, they came in to the next stop on foot, having been robbed of all their possessions and animals. We saw the ruffians sitting on the rocks watching us with their rifles on their knees.

After halting at the British Consulate at Torbat-i Haidari on the far side of the desert, which also had an English doctor, they reached Meshed.

Arriving in the Consulate at Meshed we found everyone in a state of nerves and jitters. The Consul, Minchin, had contributed to this by ordering a supply of arms and ammunition from India, making a little armoury in the centre of the Consulate and sand-bagging the roof. This was caused by memories of the massacre of the English after they retreated from their legation at

Kabul and were attacked by wild Afghanis about the year 1840. Opinion afterwards was that they should not have left their own buildings. We listened to all these fears, then waited for the departure of the Consul-General going on leave. We were glad when this alarmist took himself off.

Percy immediately made an appointment to call on the Governor-General, very soon had him friendly and calmed the fears of the naturally alarmed staff. All the same we learned to handle a rifle and the parapets of the house were sand-bagged. We settled down, glad of the comforts and good arrangements after our seven weeks of camp life. I can only say that we lived there happily until 1913, barring six months' leave every three years, with Persian staff and other English and some Indians for office staff, without any threats to us or our people. No hand was ever lifted against us . . .

I only felt sorry that it was impossible to have any contacts with Persian ladies. Owing to the restrictions of their faith, we had only men servants in the house, who would not have been allowed into the harems or allowed to conduct me there. I went into the town and bazaar once only and never into a mosque. I remember a cousin saying when she heard my stories, 'Oh, I should have gone in disguise'. 'Yes,' I replied, 'you might have done so, been discovered and brought the whole place down on our heads.' Sixty thousand fanatics were not to be despised. Percy's rule resulted in a friendly atmosphere and a knowledge that their religion and customs would be observed. We had no missionaries, which was just as well.

Evelyn's calm and matter-of-fact account is impressive. Totally loyal to her husband, she unquestioningly put up with not only the travelling conditions but also the social isolation. Except when on her travels, she was almost entirely confined to her house for years, with only the tiny European community for company. The English wives were not very exciting but the Russian ladies all sang and played the piano and Evelyn, with her musical upbringing, spent many convivial evenings with them. Sykes delegated the family side of life to her and expected her to keep house and children in good order ready for his occasional inspection when he was at home. As her youngest daughter, Elinor Sinclair, said, 'Mother was certainly long-suffering, but not always in silence.' According to Elinor, Evelyn's attitude to her children was loving but distant: 'She loved her children but did not understand them or consider it her duty to do more than make sure they were being properly fed and clothed.'

Sykes himself, in his official diary, recorded that on their arrival outside Meshed the Governor-General of Khorasan, the Asaf ud-Dowleh ('Wise Man of the State') and the Karguzar (the official responsible for liaison between foreign representatives and the local governor) sent their representatives to greet him officially and lead him in with a full *istiqbal*. A typical programme of an *istiqbal* offered by a governor-general to a British consul arriving at Meshed would consist of:

A *sartip* (brigadier) in full uniform, as head of the reception party
A *yuzbashi* (senior NCO) with ten Persian cossacks
A led horse with gold trappings
A riding horse with gold trappings and English saddle (for the consul–general)
One *mustaufi* (financial secretary)
Two *munshis* (secretaries)
One *naib mir-akhor* (assistant master of the horse)
One *jelodar* (outrider)
Two majors
Eight orderlies, four mounted and four on foot

There would be smaller deputations from the Karguzar and from the Begler-Begi, the chief of police. Tents were set up outside the town and tea, sweetmeats, coffee and *qalyans* were offered before the whole procession moved off to make a ceremonial entry into the city, ending up at the Consulate.

With the arrival at the Consulate of Sykes, whose reputation had preceded him, Britain's standing showed signs of immediate improvement. The Asaf sent him a friendly message of welcome, recalling their joint expedition to capture the murderers of

Graves seven years earlier. Within the week his 'very old friend' the Khabir ud-Dowleh ('Omniscient of the State'), the local Director of Persian Telegraphs, called on him. 'He was extremely glad to see me and said that the Russian Consul-General had that very day shown him a message from the Russian Minister at Tehran to the effect that the Persian Government had agreed to allow the Russian military signallers to make use of the Persian telegraph offices on the Sistan line. The Khabir ud-Dowleh had asked for instructions from the Mukhbir ud-Dowleh (Reporter of the State), the Director-General of Telegraphs at Tehran, and promised to keep me informed of what happened.' Four days later Sykes returned the call on the Khabir, whose latest information was that the Russian *knyaz* at Khaf had an instrument that enabled him to tap all the telegraph messages on the Sistan telegraph line.

Minchin, the outgoing Consul, was visibly put out by this volte-face on the part of the Khabir ud-Dowleh, who had not paid him a visit him until some months after his own arrival at Meshed and had hitherto been notably pro-Russian.

Sykes made official calls on Ivan Ivanovitch Reschetoff, the drunken Russian Consul-General, and on other leading Russians, followed by a call on Victor Castaigne, the Belgian director of customs, whom he disparagingly described as 'a rather typical Belgian bourgeois'. On 14th May Minchin officially handed the Consulate over to Sykes and prepared to leave.

Things went well for Sykes from the beginning. Almost immediately after his arrival there 'came into his hands' a copy of a letter from Mir Asadullah Khan, Shaukat ud-Dowleh ('Glory of the State'), chief of the Timuri tribe, which he had addressed to the Russian Consul-General concerning a band of thieves on the Afghan border. The chief of this important tribe, which straddled the frontier, had not visited the British Consulate-General for years and was known to be very close to the Russians. The very next day he came to visit Sykes: 'He was extremely cordial and pointedly remarked that he hoped to be a close friend of mine and that he had come to call as he had heard all about me.' Other grandees called in quick succession: the Begler-Begi (chief of police), Mirza Abdul Hossein Khan Muzaffar ul-Nizam

('Victorious in Public Order') – 'he knows me well, having been with Farman Farma at Shiraz in 1898 when I was on special duty there' – followed by Mirza Farajullah Khan, the Mutawalli-Bashi ('Custodian of the Shrine'), who had kept away from the British Consulate for a very long time. A feather in his cap was a visit from one of the divines, Seyyid Shah Sowar, the Mansur ut-Tawlieh ('Triumphant of Trusteeship'), the seventeenth descendant of the Sufi mystic Shah Nematullah Vali. 'He is considered extremely saintly and dresses entirely in green. Hitherto, although he has been a Shrine official for many years, he has not visited a European official. He was immensely pleased and flattered at the intimate knowledge of his family which I displayed.'

More visitors followed, among them the Qaim-Maqam of the Shrine, who complained that 'everyone is in debt to the Russian Bank', and Ibrahim Khan Shaukat ul-Mulk ('Glory of the Kingdom'), the new Amir of Birjand, on his first visit to the British Consulate-General, which he had hitherto ignored. This was the beginning of the long association with the British of this family of progressive landlords, culminating in Asadollah Alam, the late Shah's Minister of Court.

The Persians were pleased to see Sykes in Meshed. So many previous consuls had regarded Persia as a tiresome posting in their Indian careers, but Sykes understood them and was a trusted friend. His cultivation over the years of all manner of people was bearing fruit, as was the effort he had made to learn not only the language but, more importantly, what to say in it, together with the visibly genuine respect and admiration that he felt for the Persians and their civilization.

Although Sykes made much in his despatches of the high esteem in which the Persians held him, the real key to the sudden friendliness being shown to him was the annihilation of the Russian navy at Tsushima by the Japanese in the spring of 1905. This one event had given heart to patriotic Persians who, seeing that Russia was no longer invincible, felt that they could turn to Britain for ·support without fear of Russian retribution. The Russian grip on northern Persia could at last be loosened and Sykes was the person to help them.

Although the Persians were now emboldened, the Russians

were still capable of exerting pressure on the government. When the Russians discovered that the Khabir ud-Dowleh had a habit of passing copies of their telegrams to Sykes, he was, at their insistence, sacked – despite Sykes's efforts to intervene on his behalf. His replacement, before setting off from Tehran to take up his post, was warned by his superiors, who resented this heavy-handed Russian interference, that he should not be too friendly to the British by reporting *all* the Russian telegram traffic to them.

The Consul's first and foremost job in Meshed was the gathering of intelligence about Russian activity in Central Asia and monitoring the Russians' moves towards India. Much of the Russian military activity was based on Tashkent, but a consulate there would have been useless for intelligence gathering, by being too conspicuous and under constant observation. The British had established in Central Asia a network of semi-official 'newswriters',[2] who were often Indian traders well known to the Russian authorities, as well as unofficial native spies, who came and went unnoticed among the great numbers of pilgrims coming to the shrine from Samarqand and Bokhara, from Baku and Baghdad and from Afghanistan and beyond.

In the Public Record Office there is a volume entitled 'The Great Game – Meshed' with monthly accounts of the money paid to these men, who were spread all over Turkistan. Some of these newswriters carried their own despatches while others sent trusted couriers. They were brave men. Occasionally there is a note that one has disappeared, while others record their narrow escapes. It was noted that the Persian newswriters were prone to exaggeration in their reports, while the Uzbeks were more reliable. Their existence was known to all sides, which aroused much suspicion. In 1906 a harmless trader from Torbat-i Haidari travelling to Turkistan was flogged and imprisoned by the Russians in case he was an Afghan spy and, on the way back, suffered the same fate at Herat on suspicion of being a Russian spy.

---

[2] In 1892 there were newswriters reporting to Meshed from Sarakhs, Panjdeh, Yolatan, Merv, Charjui, Bokhara, Samarqand, Ashurada, Bojnurd, Quchan, Kerki, Kalat, Uzunada, Herat and Tashkent.

Apart from gathering intelligence from Turkistan, the Consul's other function was to maintain as good a working relationship as possible with the Persian authorities. The civil authorities were almost totally under Russian control, whether they wanted to be or not, but the religious authorities were more independently minded and were prepared to resist Russian pressure, in return for some help. While visibly pious and known not to be open to bribery by any Persian, the chief priest, or Mulla-Bashi,[3] had hinted that he had 'many dependants to support' and could be helpful to the British if he received a discreet monthly allowance from them, provided that the Persians never got to hear about it. His code name in the British records, appositely, was 'Archbishop'.

By 1904 intelligence work had become too much for the Consul to handle alone and a full-time military attaché was appointed. This was Captain Henry Smyth, a young officer from Indian Army Intelligence, who went on to lead a very colourful career. He went home on leave to get married shortly after Sykes arrived and was temporarily replaced by Captain Redl, who arrived from Tehran at the end of September, having ridden hard all the way in six and a half days on a succession of post horses, at the rate of about a hundred miles a day. His baggage followed at a more leisurely pace.

The Consul's official duty was to maintain good relations with both the Governor-General and the Shrine authorities. Unofficially, he was meant to support them in any efforts they might make towards exercising independence from the Russians. The Governor-General's job was to collect revenue from his province and to keep order within it. To be appointed in the first place he had to make a substantial payment to the Shah. Once in office he could recoup this outlay by purloining as much of the provincial revenue as he could get away with. However, when he was seen to be doing particularly well out of the job he could expect a rival to make a move to unseat him. Occupants seldom lasted more than three years in the post.

Sykes was an acute observer of the Byzantine machinations in Persian government circles. In his September diary he recorded:

---

[3] Sheikh Mohammed Zakki is shown in the file as a man who 'has always been most friendly'.

It is whispered that the Asaf ud-Dowleh is about to be got rid of by the Crown Prince. If however, the Asaf can bring about a *sholouq* [disturbance] here just at the psychological moment, on the return of the Shah to Tehran, the Shah will be compelled to rescind the order [of his dismissal] so that the Asaf may hold the necessary authority to quell the disturbances.

The Governor-General was being threatened not only by per-ennial personal rivals but also by the new phenomenon of the Constitutional movement, which was beginning to stir in Persia. Sykes heard through his agents that the local *mujahideen* ('Volunteers') of the movement had decided to raise a militia. Suspecting that the Asaf might have these potentially dangerous revolutionaries arrested, which would have been disastrous, Sykes suggested to him that he invite them to his residence, where, after a long discussion, he persuaded the young idealists that, instead of raising a force of soldiery, they would do much better to start a co-operative for the purchase of spinning wheels. For a time there was no further trouble from them.

The Consul also had to be on good terms with the Russian authorities, on whom he was, of course, energetically spying, as they were on him. Shortly after his arrival in Meshed Sykes began to hear from 'friends in the postal service' that arms and explosives were being delivered to the Russian consulate. One day, when he was due to have dinner with the Russian military attaché, he heard that a donkey driver had brought in two boxes of gunpowder and bombs, hidden in a load of fodder. That evening, although his retainers knew the story, he politely forbore to inquire of his host whether the boxes had arrived safely. Such stories, spread around the bazaar by the servants, added to Britain's reputation for all-knowingness about Persian affairs.

Even while he had to be on good social terms with the Russians, Sykes was nevertheless competing with them on several levels. When the Shah's birthday came round at the end of July he had the consu-late illuminated with lanterns for the first time. This, he reported, was a great success and was much commented on, as was the fact that the Russians, not to be outdone, had managed to respond with a show of only six lamps, a cause of much public merriment.

Another official and 'above board' consular duty was to represent the interests of British-protected persons in Khorasan and to intervene in their disputes with the Persian authorities. This arrangement had resulted from the Russo-Persian treaty of Turkmanchai in 1828, under which Russian citizens were entitled to be tried in special courts and to enlist consular support in case of need. These capitulatory rights were later extended to British citizens and British-protected persons, mostly Indian traders and, since Afghanistan was a British-protected territory, some Afghans. By a diplomatic quirk, the Meshed consulate was also nominally responsible for looking after Ottoman Turkish subjects, since Constantinople, although it had an embassy at Tehran, had no representation in the province of Khorasan.

Dealing with minor disputes between Indians or Afghans and the Persian authorities was very time-consuming but on occasion Sykes could be robust with them. A deputation of aggrieved Afghan nailmakers from Herat came to complain that the local nailmakers had 'given a present' to the Begler-Begi, who had then revoked their trading licence. They asked him, as the representative of Great Britain and their protector, to intervene on their behalf and do something about it. Taking a direct approach, Sykes roundly advised them to give the Begler-Begi a present as well, 'since, like other people, he must live and he gets no salary'.

The Consulate was in the middle of a walled garden full of fruit trees near the *Arg*, or government citadel, on the west side of the city. The main building was in the centre, with smaller buildings for the staff round about, and under the walls was a row of old houses for the servants, which were overcrowded, damp and insanitary, with overflowing latrines and stinking ponds of standing water. One hundred and twenty-nine souls inhabited the compound, with forty-five horses and cows. In 1907 the servants' quarters were knocked down and new land on an adjacent plot was bought to rehouse them. Fresh water was carted in daily from a *qanat* which came to the surface outside the city walls. The townspeople, however, preferred to draw water from their own wells, which were sunk next to their cesspits. Such was the general contamination that even bread was unsafe to eat if the bakery ovens were not hot enough. Evelyn remembered the Consulate thus:

[It] was a pleasant two-storey building with running water round three sides. Our house stood in the centre and small houses were built for the other inhabitants in the corners, with their own gardens and offices. There were a doctor's house, one for a military attaché, a small hospital, stables and quarters for the escort of Bengal Lancers, also a little street for servants and their families. There was a large office with a mostly Indian staff of clerks and reception rooms for the various callers who looked in on business. These were a weird collection of the bordering peoples: Afghans, nomad tribesmen, Russians of all kinds, travellers. Sometimes English would look in having come up from India via Sistan. All brought a retinue of servants and other hangers-on who were housed and fed and interviewed, if only temporarily.

The Consulate supported an English doctor supplied by the Indian Medical Service (IMS), with a dispensary and a small hospital, which also catered for the people of Meshed. (The Shrine, although supposedly a charitable institution, supplied nothing comparable.) The British motivation was not entirely altruistic, however; quite apart from being good for public relations, the doctors had private access to a great number of people and were privy to many confidences.

Sykes held the title at Meshed of 'Consul-General of His Majesty the King of England and Emperor of India, resident in Khorasan'. This was a simplification to avoid confusing the Persians, who might have held him in less regard if they knew that he was the servant of two masters; his real title was His Britannic Majesty's Consul-General and Agent of the Government of India in Khorasan. His salary and budget came from India, which expended reams of paper arguing how much of his expenses could be allocated to the Home Government in London, whose precise share was always a matter for dispute. An idea of the expenses is given by the Meshed consular accounts in the Oriental and India Office Collections files:

Sykes's salary	27,000 rupees	(£1,800)
Native attaché	4,320	(£288)

Newswriters	5,160	(£344)
Secret Service fund	9,000–12,200	(£600–£813)[4]

In each of the large towns of Khorasan where there was no sub-consulate there were accredited British agents, usually Indian traders, who reported on any news and looked after the interests of British subjects. To remind the imperial Consul-General at Meshed of their existence and importance they submitted tedious, long-winded reports and, to maintain their local prestige they cultivated petty grievances which they could then contrive to have resolved with a flourish of the British flag. Composing correspondence over the affairs of these gentlemen took up much consular time; a typical example is this letter to the Governor-General of Meshed:

Gracious, Worthy, Kind, Respectable and Friendly Excellency,

It is respectfully brought to your notice that according to the letters of Excellency Mirza Hassan, the representative of the High Government of England at Kariz, one of Your Excellency's servants by name of Hussein Ali who is at Saadabad has created obstacles in the way of the collection of the share of agricultural products belonging to the horsemen of the great government of England.

The representative of the Consul-General has asked him why he was prevented in the crop collection of the horsemen and in reply he has been told some very naughty and rude words.

It is requested that Your Excellency will send me a letter addressed to your servant Hussein Ali ordering him to cease such behaviour and to pay the crop share of the horsemen, as the outcome of such behaviour will not be good.

With kind regards and wishing you happiness
P.M. Sykes/Major

Sealed with the Seal of the Consul General of His Majesty the King of England and Emperor of India resident in Khorasan

Dated 21 Jamad al-Sani 1327

---

[4] To obtain an approximate current value, these figures should be multiplied by 50.

The real hero and 'fixer' of the British Consulate-General at the time was the Native Attaché, Mubarik Ali, who knew well how to deal with the Persians and rendered invaluable service. As a Muslim, he could make private approaches to people who would not wish to be seen with the British. He also acted as intermediary with the authorities and passed on suggestions as to suitable rewards for their services, which would have been seen as indelicate if made directly.

One of Mubarik Ali's first calls after Sykes's arrival in Meshed was on the three leading clerics at the Shrine. Gangs of Karabaghi Turkish religious students from the Caucasus had begun to attack the Christian Armenian colony in revenge for Armenian attacks on the Turks back at home in the Caucasus. They were being encouraged to do this by the Russians, whose subjects they were. There had been similar trouble in the previous month of Muharram – the month of fanatical religious mourning – and Sykes did not want to let the Russians use the pretext of danger to Christians to justify bringing more troops into Meshed. Mubarik Ali was able to induce the mujtahids (the authorities on Shia Islamic law and theology) to promise to preach against this use of violence.

Sykes's next move was to present the Shrine with a hideous and gaudy clock, for which he had paid £7 (about £350 today). Consul Reschetoff was furious and tried to get the Shrine to remove it but, as Sykes reported, 'our attaché Mubarik Ali leads the Mutawalli-Bashi by the nose', and the clock was placed close to the head of the sacred tomb of Imam Reza, where all the pilgrims would have this sign of British respect for Islam imprinted on their minds.

With his profound knowledge of, and sympathy for, the people and the country Sykes undeniably played a crucial role in thwarting Russian designs at this period, but his self-importance gained him no friends among the junior members of the Legation at Tehran, most of whom thought of Persia as no more than a disagreeable step on their career ladder. They regarded him as something of a cad for associating with the Persians, whom they held in low regard, and the fact that he knew a lot more about Persia than they did, and had no hesitation in saying so, also irritated them.

They may also have envied his independence and his freebooting way of life, and they would certainly have been irritated by the fact that, being in the employ of the Government of India, he was much better paid than the officials of the Foreign Office.

One person who did hold Sykes in high regard, however, was Sir Arthur Hardinge, the Minister at Tehran,[5] who paid him a visit in September 1905 and wrote in his memoirs:

> A short ride brought us from Nishapur to Meshed: there we were welcomed at the Residency by our Consul-General Colonel Sykes[6] and his charming wife who had recently crossed, with a newly-born infant, the great waterless desert which extends nearly the whole way from their former home in Kerman to Khorasan.
>
> Colonel Sykes made a powerful impression on me as a man of the most multiform abilities, a soldier, a geographer and a historian, who had produced the most up-to-date and interesting History of Persia. He was, indeed, on all Persian matters, an almost encyclopaedic authority, and he had become, owing to his familiarity with the Persians and their customs and habits, a unique representative in many varied fields of British Imperial Power in the East.

Sir Arthur shared Sykes's friendly attitude towards the Persians. He had earlier written to Lord Lansdowne: 'Persians are like the Irish. It is very little use to argue in the light of pure reason; you have to enter into their peculiar sympathies, to make large allowances for the shams and vanities on which they live, and you will do more than a little good by a little cordiality, a little gush and, I would add, a little blarney, than by the most serious and sustained reasoning.' It is not surprising that he and Sykes got on well.

Sykes took Hardinge on an expedition to visit the forbidden ancient fortress of Kelat-i Naderi, near the Russian border. This was of particular satisfaction to both men, not least because Curzon

---

[5] Not to be confused with Charles Hardinge, his cousin, who had been at the Legation earlier and later went on to become Viceroy.

[6] In fact Sykes was still only a Major.

had tried to get there on his celebrated Persian travels, but had been refused permission to see more than a part of it by the local Persian officials, who were fearful of Russian retribution. From its highest point at six thousand feet they could see far below them a Russian train on the Transcaspian military railway. It was after Hardinge had reported on his visit that Sykes was confirmed in his position as Consul-General and at last began to be paid a salary.

Sykes was evidently pleased by the passage from Hardinge's book; he copied it out on Athenaeum writing paper and stored it among his own papers. However, he omitted to copy the rest of the passage, which shows that Hardinge had been sent by the Viceroy to Meshed to investigate a 'highly placed Indian official, reported to be in improper relations with a married lady, the wife of the Director of Khorasan Customs'. As Sykes's son-in-law Sir Patrick Reilly said, the 'official' in question was clearly Sykes. The tolerant Hardinge reported that Sykes was 'not entirely free from blame, but did not deserve serious punishment or even censure; the lady in question was only a Belgian'. The puritan Curzon was not pleased with the leniency of this report but Hardinge reminded him of the carryings-on of a previous Viceroy, Lord Lytton, which were on a much grander scale and went unadmonished.

Apart from the visit to Kelat-i Naderi, Sykes had managed to make a 'flying visit' with Evelyn in the late summer to the district of Kuhpayeh ['foothills'] to the west of Meshed. In this pleasant hill country there was a little side valley above the village of Jagharq, where the European community occasionally went to camp. It was about eighteen miles south-west of Meshed, approached up the river valley by a track shaded by trees for the last eight miles. The sides of the gorge were steep and irrigated by water channels taken from the stream, which allowed many kinds of trees to flourish. Everything was cool and green 'and so impressed was I with its charm and remoteness that I decided to convert it into a hill station for Meshed; and indeed no more ideal spot is conceivable, as a cottage perched on this spur overlooks a bend of the valley which forms a sea of greenery, and yet it is raised above the unwholesome damp of the valley, far from the still more baneful mosquito'. He acquired a large two-storey stone house on the side of a hill, with a wide upper balcony all round it to catch the breeze. This summer retreat allowed him to escape from the hothouse of political intrigue that Meshed later became. The only winter recreation was to ride out before dawn and wade through the icy swamps and reed beds outside the city in pursuit of snipe and duck, followed by an open-air lunch and a canter back to town for a hot bath.

At the end of October 1905 Sykes set off, again with Evelyn, on a month's tour surveying in the direction of the Afghan frontier, leaving Captain Battye in charge of the consulate. Battye was the army doctor and his wife was a distant cousin to Sykes. Captain Watson came up from the Torbat-i Haidari Consulate to join the party at Fariman, south-east of Meshed, where a large irrigation dam was being built. They continued southward to the district of Khaf, famous for its grapes and pomegranates, where the sound of the pines soughing in the wind 'gave one a touch of home'. There they visited the fourteenth-century *madraseh* of Khargird, built by Tamerlane, which had lost most of its splendid tiles. Sykes was, however, able to buy some of these in Meshed and later donated a superb collection of them to the British Museum. They then turned east and north-east to Kariz at the frontier on the main Meshed–Herat road and thence north to the Jam river at Dowlatabad, where there was excellent shooting, with a great variety of duck. They continued on to Torbat-i Sheikh-i Jam, Khitai and the squalid Afghan frontier village of Zulfikar, from close to which they spied through field glasses the two white pillars marking the Afghan–Russian frontier.

Sykes wrote a long and florid report on this trip, larded with historical, architectural and literary references, for the Legation and the Government of India to study at length in what he imagined was their excessive leisure. The Legation copy bears a red pencilled note in the margin by George Churchill, by now the Oriental Secretary, 'This is wearisome stuff': the useful part of his report was in the very detailed maps that he made of the region, which were of great value to Army Intelligence at Simla.

In Sykes's absence from Meshed the Russians had knocked a hole in the city wall and built an imposing new gateway to give them direct access to the Russian bank, which was just outside the wall. In front of it they planted a large stone with a Persian inscription announcing that the gate was for Russian use only. A Persian government official, unaware of this restriction, was turned back by the Russian gate guards. He was incensed but, although it was his own country there was nothing he could do about it. A more minor irritation caused by the Russians to Persian sensibilities was a series of theatrical performances in which actresses appeared. The mullas protested but Sykes considered that 'since the mullas indulged in the free use of dancing girls, their attitude was a trifle pharisaical'.

The new year of 1906, after the rumblings of the 1905 revolution in Russia had begun to be felt, was celebrated in style with a durbar in the British consulate. All the notables of Meshed were invited, but not the Russians. The previous practice at entertainments on such occasions had been to seat the Persians and Europeans at opposite sides of the table. Sykes created something of a pleasant stir by seating them together and this new precedent was later copied by the Russians. After dinner and the recital by the official poet of a long, turgid poem in praise of Persia and Britain commissioned for the occasion, Sykes made a speech in which he declared that Britain wished for stability in Russia since a weak Russia was against her interests. The following day he learned that Reschetoff had heard of this speech, which had been repeated to him by the Mehman-Bashi, the Governor-General's guest-master, who had been one of the principal guests at the durbar. The diary records: 'I was of course aware that Our Special Correspondent was present and framed my address accordingly. The present arrangement by which what we wish is accurately reported to our rivals and the effect on them accurately reported back to us is quite ideal.'

The irascible Reschetoff was still irritated by the presence of the clock in the shrine and sent a long telegram of complaint about it to his legation in Tehran. A copy of it was duly delivered to Sykes by the new director of telegraphs, the Khabir us-Saltaneh, who was beginning to supplement his income in the customary way. However, when he became a little too free with his favours and started delivering copies of British consular telegrams to the Russians, Sykes decided to deal with him. He went to the Governor-General and, knowing that a direct complaint would bring no result, informed him that he had heard that the Khabir was giving copies of his telegrams to the Russians. The Asaf was not pleased to hear this and said that he would try to get the Khabir us-Saltaneh dismissed and have the old Khabir ud-Dowleh reinstated.

The principal concern in Persia at this time was the rise of the Constitutional movement and the attacks on the monarchy. The economy was in a more than usually disastrous condition and there was a great deal of resentment at the high-handed behaviour of the Shah and his ministers. For nearly a century the Legation had been reporting that the country was about to collapse, but it had somehow survived. Now it was felt that the end really was near. In January rumours were circulating that the Shah had been deposed or even assassinated, but as the telegraph link to Tehran had been cut, there was no reliable news. Sykes sent a galloper to Tehran to find out from the Legation what the situation was. He returned with the news that the Shah was still in place, which indicated that the rumours were premature and nothing but wishful thinking.

The threat of Persia's collapse, and with it the collapse of the buffer against Russia's advance towards India, was a cause of constant anxiety to the Government of India. Not only were there conspicuous Russian troop movements across the border in Transcaspia, but there were also rumours that the Russians were about to build a military road through to Meshed from just across the border at Ashgabad. In January Sir Louis Dane, Secretary to the Government of India at Calcutta, asked Sykes for his views on the matter. He replied:

It appears that the end of Persia is approaching . . . Five sevenths of the debt that Persia can contract without insolvency is already contracted . . . The money is not used to develop Persia but is squandered abroad . . . There is a growing disgust of the Persians at the present state of affairs – thirteen years ago the late Shah was occasionally abused but more generally lauded. Today all classes unite in condemning not only the monarch, but also the vicious system he represents.

Should Persia break up, the occupation of Persian Baluchistan and Sistan would be of vital importance to the Government of

India. It is obviously urgent to exclude rival influences from the Helmand delta . . . This has been the motive underlying the opening of the Nushki trade route, the McMahon Mission and indeed the founding of the British Consulate at Sistan.

He went on to propose that as a first measure, a movable column of cavalry should be stationed at Kuh-i Malik Siah, the mountain in the middle of nowhere, where the frontiers of Persia, Afghanistan and India met.

13

Constitution and carve-up

The parlous state of the Persian economy not only meant that the government was unable to pay its servants, but also led to other bodies taking advantage of the situation and withholding payment of their debts. At the end of January the Shrine servants came to the British consulate to complain that the new Mutawalli-Bashi had cut their pay (and presumably pocketed it) and they asked to take *bast* in the consulate in protest. Sykes could not rightly refuse them sanctuary, but at the same time he did not wish to jeopardize his relations with the Shrine authorities; it required all of Mubarik Ali's powers of persuasion to get them to go away. Sykes went to see the Mutawalli-Bashi the next day and found him 'most polite but remarkably ignorant. He asked if I had ever visited London . . . He expressed a strong contempt for the Russians and remarked that one Persian is equal to thirty of them.' It was difficult to know how to deal with a person in such a position with so little knowledge of the outside world.

Another example of such insular ignorance came in April 1906, when the mujtahids of the Shia holy city of Kerbela in Meso-potamia sent a telegram to the Shrine in Meshed announcing the unlikely news from Japan that the Mikado, following the Japanese victory over the Russian navy, had converted to Islam. In celebra-tion of this religious success the Shrine authorities had the build-ings illuminated, causing great joy among the gullible faithful.

The Russians were continually engaged in making pinpricks

against the British. In April their telegraph signallers moved the end of the line to Sistan away from the Persian telegraph office into their own building, which enabled them to cut off the connection to the outlying British consulate at any time. Sykes duly protested to Tehran and the line was restored. When there was a report of an outbreak of plague in Sistan, the British Indian doctors tried to inoculate the people but the head mulla, who was a Russian agent, persuaded the people not to accept it. This gave the Russians the excuse to throw up a cordon sanitaire and disrupt Indian trade coming across the border. When there was a genuine plague, however, they handed the matter over to the Persian authorities.

As a relaxation from all the politics Sykes spent much of his free time shooting. A keen amateur naturalist, he sent a specimen of a native pheasant (*phasianus principalis*) that he had shot on the banks of the Hari Rud to the Natural History Museum in London. As a more complicated exercise, he sent to the London Zoo an onager that had been brought in from the Lut desert. These rare and legendary wild asses were hunted by the Sassanian kings of Persia on horseback with bow and arrow. Captain Keyes, the acting military attaché, succeeded in partly taming it before it was sent off. The diary reported: 'It is used for riding but it kicks freely.'

At the end of April 1906 the Sykes family left Meshed to take three months' home leave in England. Since 'every hour was precious' Sykes travelled fast and reached Kahka on the Transcaspian railway in two days and London on the tenth day. Evelyn had preceded him with the baby Frank and the nurse. Her memoir records that they were a party of eight, escorted by Major Redl, who was also going on leave. They drove for five days in carriages to Ashgabad, a hundred and fifty miles away on the other side of the Kopet Dagh mountains, in a procession of three-horse troikas; from there it was one and a half days by train to Krasnovodsk on the Caspian, then across to Baku and home by train via Rostov and Vienna.

While in London, Sykes gave a number of lectures to the Royal Geographical Society and other bodies and had meetings in the Foreign Office to advise senior officials and Sir Arthur Nicolson, who was about to depart for the St Petersburg Embassy, on the situation in Persia. After a lecture that he gave on the Parsees of Persia, Lord Curzon made several complimentary remarks about him and said that there was no living Englishman with a greater knowledge of Persia. Quite apart from the lectures on geography and politics, Sykes also wrote articles on his theories about the routes taken by Alexander the Great and Marco Polo, parts of which he had attempted to follow. He also wrote on Persian gypsies and their music and even produced a short glossary of their secret language, as well as a short article on Persian tattooing. Sykes's interests were wide-ranging and, although he was only an amateur, his opinions were taken seriously by the professional academics, even if they did not always agree with them.

While the Sykeses were away they missed the culmination of the Constitutional Revolution, which arose from a struggle between the Prime Minister and the clerical community. Under Muslim law the clergy ran the legal system, which enabled them to enrich themselves by taking 'fees' from the litigants on each side. The Prime Minister, Ain ud-Dowleh – who later robbed a caravan carrying £17,000 to the Imperial Bank of Persia's branch in Tabriz – was not only interfering with the old legal system but had also had publicly flogged some of the bazaar merchants who had been hoarding sugar to create a shortage. The mullas, the traditional allies of the merchants, brought the crowds out on to the streets to demand his dismissal and the restitution of the old courts, together with their ancient clerical privileges. Their policy was one of protest, pure and simple, and there was as yet no mention of a constitution.

Large public gatherings were organized by the clerics and when a seyyid was shot at one of these, the mullas asked the British chargé d'affaires, Grant Duff, for the assistance of the Legation. He replied that it was impossible for the Legation to support a movement directed against the government of the Shah. They next inquired whether if they took *bast* they would be ejected. To this Grant Duff responded that, in view of the acknowledged custom in Persia, it was not within his power to expel people who took *bast*.[1] The subsequent events were described by David Fraser,

---

[1] The grand mujtahid Behbehani, who was the principal British contact among the clergy and had stirred up action against Russian trade concessions in 1902, had approached Grant-Duff to arrange the *bast*. Persians subsequently believed, wrongly, that the British had organized it from the beginning. He went on to lead the Moderate party in the Majlis, in opposition to the Democrats. He was assassinated in 1910.

who was at that time the Tehran correspondent of *The Times* newspaper:

On the evening of 19th July [1906] fifty mullas and merchants entered the Legation grounds and took up their quarters for the night. They were followed by others in driblets, until on 2nd August fourteen thousand persons were assembled in the Legation garden. Of that number it is safe to say that not one per cent knew the meaning of the word Constitution, or indeed had ever heard of it. As they streamed up the Boulevard des Ambassadeurs they were asked why they were going to the British Legation, and who had told them to go. They answered that they did not know who wanted them to go or why. They were going just because everyone else was going, and because a *tamasha* [spectacle] in the summer time, when business was slack, in the leafy aisles of the finest garden in Tehran appealed irresistibly to the pleasure-loving Persian mind. Nevertheless, a full-blown democratic Constitution was the outcome of this curious situation.

Mr Grant Duff's only hope of getting rid of the people who were ruining his garden – it was done in the most orderly and considerate manner possible – was to help them to settle their differences with the government. No great difficulty was experienced. A short time before, the grossly obese Muzaffar ud-Din Shah had been struck down by paralysis, and was even then on his deathbed. He was not fit for business and only wanted peace. By agreeing to the people's demand for a Majlis, or parliament, he sought to please the people and escape from a dilemma, without realising the extent to which he was divesting himself of his most important prerogatives. The *bastis* desired British guarantees that the Shah's promises would be fulfilled but these, naturally, were not forthcoming. A deadlock ensued. Eventually a meeting took place between the Government and the popular leaders, at which a British representative was present, whereat a decree, granting a national Assembly and Courts of Justice, was drawn up by mutual agreement. This being duly issued, the *bastis* were satisfied and left the Legation. Since the final bargain between the Shah and his people had been made in the presence of a British representative, no matter that he took no part in the discussion, the implication was that the British Government was sponsor to the arrangement and morally responsible for its observance. The Persians henceforward assumed that they were protected by Great Britain from the consequences of anything which they might do or say against their own government . . .

The part played by the British in Tehran as mediator between the Shah and his people created a profound impression upon certain sections of Russian public opinion. British and Russian rivalry in Central Asia was usually focused in Tehran and had at times given rise to bitter feelings between the officials of either country . . . The weakness of the British position in Persia was perfectly apparent both to the Persians and the Russians; in their disregard for us the Persians for years had treated us with scant respect, ignoring our interest and flouting our blandishments. The Russian, in fact, was top dog.

And then suddenly it seemed as if the power in Persia was to slip from the hands of the autocracy which Russia had spent so much money in suborning, into those of a democratic regime hating Russia and leaning on England. Local Russian opinion immediately attributed the situation to a Machiavellian British plot to recover long lost ascendancy. We were supposed to have engineered the Constitutional movement from start to finish with the sole object of destroying Russian influence and uplifting our own.

Exactly how the situation arose is difficult to ascertain. In the beginning we . . . discouraged the *bastis* who proposed to honour us with their presence. The staff of the Legation being away in the country, however, a few took refuge without leave, and when they increased in number we began to take an interest. And then, as the number kept growing, we could not very well stop the influx, and we began to realise that our sudden popularity constituted a pretty dig at Russian supremacy in the hearts of the populace.

That our people in Tehran saw the far reaching consequence of what was being done, or that our Foreign Office ever realised the full significance of what was happening in Tehran, cannot be supposed. But the Russians were clear on the point. They saw that the success of our protégé meant the loss of Russian influence in Persia and the establishment of British instead. For that reason every Russian in Persia, as well as the reactionary party in Russia which professed the forward policy, became the bitter enemies of the reform movement, and therefore fought tooth and nail for its defeat.[2]

There were many, both Persian and Russian, who assumed that it was British money that had kept the Constitutionalists going, but this was not the case. In January 1907 Cecil Spring Rice, the new Minister at Tehran, wrote to Sir Edward Grey, the Foreign Secretary: 'It was supposed that the Constitutionalist Movement would collapse as soon as "English money" failed. Since we have withdrawn our patronage the popular movement has grown in strength.' A mixture of muddled foreign ideas and raw commercial self-interest with an overlay of Islam, the movement was a truly Persian affair which, after the end of the *bast*, owed nothing to the British.

It was not only in Persia that there had been disturbances. Henry Smyth's spies in Transcaspia reported railway robberies and an atmosphere of revolution, led by the railway workers, across the border at Ashgabad, with extensive military movements. His spies also reported that three Russian prostitutes, ordered by the Russian consul-general for the Cossacks, had arrived in Meshed. Officially they were registered as maidservants for the consulate.

In Meshed the feeling against Russia was strong. Captain Battye reported on 13th August that 'British prestige has greatly increased in Meshed as a result of the successful ending of the demonstration in Tehran. The Attaché is everywhere being congratulated. One mulla is reported to have said in a public meeting that he is now prepared to fall down and kiss the feet of the English as the champions of Persian freedom.' By early December, when the Sykeses were due back in Meshed, Battye was reporting that 'British prestige has much increased since the events of last August in Tehran and on all sides there is shown an anxiety to be friendly with us. The Governor-General, the Karguzar and many other Persians,

---

[2] *Persia and Turkey in Revolt* (Edinburgh, 1910).

official and otherwise, who know Major Sykes are vying with one another to do him honour on his return to Meshed tomorrow and the *istiqbal* bids fair to completely eclipse the one given to him on his first entry to Meshed last year.'

On 8th December he reported: 'Mrs Sykes arrived about 4.30 p.m., followed about half an hour later by Major Sykes, accompanied by a large procession. Although the reception accorded to him was strictly unofficial and entirely spontaneous, yet it proved to be, I believe, the largest *istiqbal* on record given to any British Consul-General in Meshed, consisting of an imposing procession of twenty-nine led horses with trappings and thirteen carriages, in addition to the four Russian and twenty Persian Cossacks and our own escort of twenty-four Native cavalry.' The *istiqbal* was unofficial because Sykes had already been accorded an official one upon his first entry to Meshed and was therefore not entitled to receive another – which makes the scale of his reception all the more impressive.

Notwithstanding all this good will, the year ended with the feeling that the Constitutional issue was far from settled and that the Russians would be making trouble. Smyth drew up extensive plans for the defence of the consulate, with a cellar, concealed loopholes and a crow's nest. With the Persian government unable to guarantee the security of diplomatic premises, the armoury was increased substantially; within two months it held sixty-three rifles and nearly ten thousand rounds of ammunition.

On the surface, however, relations with the Russians were good and Vassily Oskarovitch de Klemme, who had replaced the alcoholic Reschetoff as Russian consul-general, arranged for Sykes to take Russian lessons with one of the Russian bank clerks. He did not know that Sykes knew that at the same time Russian officers in Meshed were being given lessons in Hindustani by an Indian teacher brought down from Tashkent.

On 9th January 1907 the Tehran Legation sent Sykes a cipher telegram saying that Muzaffar ud-Din Shah had died at ten o'clock the previous night. Sykes at once informed the Governor-General and the Karguzar. His diary records, 'Neither of them had heard it and they were extremely grateful for this news.' When the news broke the next day, it was soon widely believed that the Shah had in fact already been dead for a month. As so often happens in Persia, rumour became indistinguishable from fact. The Meshed authorities expected trouble. The mullas in Tehran cabled their colleagues in Meshed telling them to preserve calm and wait to assess the new Shah's actions before making any moves. In fact, practically the first act of the new Shah Muhammad Ali, encouraged by the Russians, was to tear up the Constitution. Thus began a long period of rivalry between, on the one side, the reforming nationalist Constitutionalists and, on the other, the royalist and reactionary party. For the next year Muhammad Ali did his utmost to suppress the Majlis and in June 1908 he ordered the artillery to bombard it out of existence. The Constitutionalists, through wishful thinking, believed that they had British backing, while the reactionary royalists were actively backed by the Russians, who had no wish to see any change to the decaying order of things, which they had been controlling to their advantage.

The Meshed mullas soon fell out with the Constitutionalists, who were trying to introduce secular legislation to replace some of the Islamic *sharia* law and thereby reduce the stranglehold of the mullas over the affairs of the nation. The Constitutionalists also set up a number of Majlises in the provinces as an alternative to the central government. In March Sykes reported:

> All the officials of the Shrine, except Agha Seyyid Asadollah, the leading Meshed reformer, have sent a memorial to the Shah stating that the mujtahids, mullas and seyyids of the Shrine, as the rightful descendants and successors of the great Imam, are not disposed to submit to any national Assembly, or any authority other than the Shah himself. They are therefore entirely at his service in any movement he desires to undertake against the Constitutional Party. The religious rulers of Meshed have hitherto taken a part in the formation of the local assembly, not out of any sympathy for reform, but merely in order to control a popular movement which they feared would otherwise develop independently of them and perhaps end in the destruction of their power.

Constitution and carve-up

The reformers did not take this lying down and in early April five *fedayeen* (volunteers prepared to sacrifice their lives) from one of the *anjumans* or secret nationalist societies invaded a mosque and, tearing open their shirts to reveal the red cords of their order, surrounded the preacher, who had been speaking against the newly formed local Majlis, threatened him with their revolvers and made him recant in front of his congregation.

The new Russian consul at Meshed, de Klemme – who, although personally on good terms with Sykes, was none the less his professional rival – was still smarting enviously over the scale of the *istiqbal* given to Sykes on his return from leave, which had compared most unfavourably with his own reception. He announced to the Asaf ud-Dowleh, who took great pleasure in afterwards repeating the story to Sykes, that he was going to leave Meshed for a week and that he expected to receive a similar *istiqbal* on his return. The Governor-General, ever courteous, replied that Sykes's *istiqbal* had been entirely private and that all those present were Sykes's personal friends but he would be delighted to put his own horse at de Klemme's disposal for him to ride into town if he wished. The Asaf was a man of wit: he knew that de Klemme was a bad rider and terrified of horses.

The Asaf got on well with Sykes and had many informal conversations with him. On one occasion he asked Sykes whether he was not dismayed by the rise of the British Labour Party. Persia, the Asaf reflected, was cursed by the fact that its ministers were almost all men of lowly origin who, as soon as they reached high positions, immediately made it their object to ruin anyone of high birth. To do this they surrounded themselves with a team of low-class understudies, one of whom would later, in turn, oust them from power. The Farman Farma, he said, had made Moshir ud-Dowleh prime minister, but would soon have to bow before him. A week after this conversation the Asaf was himself unseated, having being unable to account for 80,000 missing tomans of Treasury funds. Sykes reports all these stories of official and clerical corruption with an amused and unshockable tolerance.

The British were regarded as being better informed about events in Persia than even the most senior Persians themselves. In February Sykes sent a cable to the Legation to say that the

Governor-General had asked whether he could confirm rumours of a serious riot in Tehran. This shows a remarkable degree of confidence between Sykes and the Asaf. In normal circumstances no Persian in the Asaf's position would have opened himself to the humiliation of admitting to a foreigner that he did not know what was happening in his own country.

The Asaf ud-Dowleh was replaced by the Rukn ud-Dowleh ('Pillar of the State'), who took a very long time to appear from Tehran because he first needed to raise the necessary money to pay for the usual 'presents' offered for the privilege of becoming Governor. His was not a popular appointment and a local Majlis was formed to resist Rukn ud-Dowleh and to introduce reforms. One of the first acts of the new Majlis was to close down all the opium dens and coffee houses. Sykes noted that 'many of these are owned by Russian subjects, so difficulties may be anticipated'.

Rumours came through that there had been riots in Tabriz and that the rioters had flogged the Governor in public, but Meshed remained relatively tranquil. Smyth, in his private memoirs, written after his retirement, gave much credit to Sykes for keeping the peace in Meshed during these disturbed times:

> Meshed revolted . . . and fighting ensued between the Royalists and Revolutionaries. Things did not go very far in Khorasan however, largely owing to the influence of our Consul-General, Major Sykes, as he then was, and in the end both sides agreed to a sort of truce to await the result of the fighting at Tehran and Tabriz to see who would come out on top. The Persians were sensible enough over all this but they were continually being stirred up by wild revolutionaries from outside: Russians, Caucasians, Armenians, Georgians and even Indians.

Smyth admired Sykes and made him godfather to his son, who was born in Meshed and baptized by the Russian priest.

In early March Meshed was settled enough for Sykes to leave on a tour to Torbat-i Sheikh-i Jam and Kariz, filling in the gaps in the military maps of the border regions. One of the villages that he visited was peopled by the Karai tribe, descendants of the Karaits of Mongolia, who had been Nestorian Christians before their conversion to Islam. The Karaits were behind the myth of Prester John, who was supposed by the Christian powers in Europe to be coming to save them from the invasions of the sons of Gengis Khan. The extremely lengthy report that Sykes submitted to the Legation was in his usual style, full of purple passages and overlaid with historical and literary references in the grand Victorian style, punctuated with descriptions of the bird life and the game that he had shot as he travelled. Sykes's inability to distinguish between composing an official report and writing a long-winded essay was unfortunate, because his maps and detailed information about the country through which he passed were of great value.

After his return from this journey Sykes aroused suspicion in Meshed when he imported a mysterious cargo of instruments to the Consulate. 'Public opinion is divided as to whether we are setting up a wireless telegraphy installation or are importing bombs', he wrote in his diary. In fact the instruments were meteorological, but the suspicious nationalist members of the Majlis were not satisfied until they were invited to inspect them. When the suspicions of the young men were allayed, they immediately warmed to Sykes and decided to open direct relations with the British Consulate-General, bypassing the Karguzar, who was the official channel of communication between the representatives of the foreign powers and the local government. The Young Persian nationalists soon became frequent visitors to the British Consulate.

In May Sykes decided to make a big impression by putting on a Grand Gymkhana, to which all the leading elements of Meshed were invited. Great consternation was caused by the simultaneous invitations given to the European officials, the Persian government officials, the Shrine officials and the members of the Majlis. This was an unprecedented mixing of groups who almost never got together socially, especially in public. No Persian could have brought all these rival parties together but they could accept an invitation from Sykes, who was respected for his impartial honesty, without giving cause for mutual suspicion or jealousy. Two tents were put together to entertain the seventy-odd guests, who were treated to a display of polo and cavalry manoeuvres, including tent-pegging, given by the Indian cavalry escort. Sykes reported that the event was very popular and that the British star was well in the ascendant.

The star was soon, however, to fall with a crash, as a result of the Anglo-Russian Convention of 31st August 1907. By this the two Powers agreed to split Persia into two zones of influence. A line was drawn in the west from Qasr-i Shirin, a small frontier town on the road from Baghdad to Kermanshah, through to Isfahan and Yazd and from there eastward to the point where the Persian, Russian and Afghan frontiers met. Everywhere north of this line, which was the fertile and populated part of the country, fell within the Russian zone. The British zone was to be the south-eastern part of the country, starting from the Afghan frontier east of Birjand, down to Kerman and Bandar Abbas: nothing but a strip of desert and some date groves. The rest of the country, including all of south-west Persia, was to be neutral. The neutral zone also included the area where exploratory oil drilling had just begun, the importance of which nobody had foreseen. It was agreed that each Power should have a free hand in its respective zone and would not compete or interfere with the other.

This agreement had everything to do with European politics and nothing to do with British interests in Persia, or those of the Persians themselves, who were not even consulted. As a lecturer at the Royal Geographical Society said a few years later:

It is the misfortune of Persia that the course of her history is determined far more by events and personalities outside than by the happenings within . . . which have much less influence on her affairs than the after dinner conversation of two gentlemen in a remote Scottish glen. The most important event of last autumn was the conference between Sir Edward Grey and Mr Sazonov [the Russian Foreign Minister] at Balmoral.

The concern of Sir Edward Grey, the Liberal Foreign Secretary, was the increasing threat of German power in Europe. In London there was grave doubt as to whether the Anglo-French entente cordiale and the Franco-Russian alliance would be enough to deter Germany from embarking on menacing adventures. It was therefore decided that these alliances needed to be supplemented by a separate Anglo–Russian entente to remove any cause of friction between these two Powers outside Europe that might weaken the alliance against Germany. To allay the suspicions of the Persians, who would naturally see this agreement as an imperial carve-up, the British insisted that the Convention be opened with a preamble containing the solemn declaration to respect the 'strict independence and integrity of Persia'. Why the British government, in spite of all the advice from the Embassy in St Petersburg, should have imagined that the Russians would have any intention of honouring even the preamble to the agreement is a mystery. In the eyes of the horrified Persians the treaty did nothing but dismember their country and was the end of any goodwill that might have been held for the British, who were seen now to be truly perfidious.

Long before the Convention was signed, Sykes was asked for his views on the British draft. On 31st May he wrote at length to Sir Louis Dane, Secretary to the Government of India, with the following objections, from the viewpoint of British strategic and imperial interests:

1. The whole of Persia worth having would fall into the Russian zone.
2. Germany would consider that south-west Persia had been left free to her.
3. Yazd should be included in the neutral zone.
4. Qaen was vital to the defence of India and should be retained in the British zone.
5. The consulates would have to be rearranged. The Russians would want Britain to vacate the northern consulates at Tabriz, Rasht and Kermanshah. They, in turn, would have to vacate their southern consulates at Bushire, Bandar Abbas, Kerman and Sistan.
6. Britain should retain the Meshed consulate, since it covered Qaen and Sistan, points of strategic interest to India. It was also necessary to retain Meshed as a base for gathering intelligence in Transcaspia, Turkistan and Afghanistan.

The Government of India was, of course, far more concerned with questions of imperial defence than with the more general issues of European politics and made strong representations against the Convention. Putting the Persian point of view, Cecil Spring Rice wrote to Grey after the Convention had been signed:

> It is clear from the date and manner of your communication that my opinion on this proposed arrangement is neither invited nor desired. At the same time it appears to be my duty as laid down in the King's general instructions to advise you as to the probable effects of such an agreement upon British interests in the country in which I reside. With regard to the effect on popular opinion here . . . there cannot be any reasonable doubt. It will simply be regarded as a treaty for the partition of Persia.

Spring Rice, during his residence at the St Petersburg embassy from 1903 to 1906, had became convinced of the worthlessness of any agreement made with Russia, whatever its terms. In numerous letters to the Roosevelts he had expressed his views on the futility of attempting to bind Russia by written contract. He also wrote to Sir Edward Grey, who had been his friend since Oxford days:

> You will be judged by your friends and associates; and if Russia, as is the case, is notoriously hostile to the patriotic movement in Persia, and if you make an agreement with Russia, the simple people here will take for granted that in your heart you think as Russia does . . . you must be prepared to pay the cost and, as far as I can judge, part of the price is a great loss of popularity here.

The American Minister at Tehran wrote that 'it was commonly remarked that the Bear had gotten the Lion's share'.

Curzon also opposed the Convention and concluded the Persian part of his speech given to the House of Lords on 6th February 1908: 'I have been reluctantly driven to the conclusion that, whatever may be the ultimate effects produced, we have thrown away to a large extent the efforts of our diplomacy and of our trade for more than a century; and I do not feel at all sure that this treaty, in its Persian aspect, will conduce either to the security of India, to the independence of Persia, or to the peace of Asia.' 'And in so prophesying,' wrote Harold Nicolson many years later, when he was serving as Counsellor in the Tehran Legation, 'Curzon was correct.'

The rising Persian nationalists and liberals were horrified by the Convention. Hitherto they had seen Britain, with its reputation for fair play and honest dealing, as their supporter against the Russians; now they felt betrayed. Emboldened by British support, they had been persuaded to stick their necks out against the Russians, who had now been given a free hand by the British in the whole of the country that mattered and would no longer be deterred from dealing with them in their usual way. The extreme suspicion in which Persians have held the British to this day dates from this misconceived agreement.

It was not only the modernizing nationalists, however, who were affronted by the Convention. The agreement also troubled those in government who were untouched by the new idealism. Persian foreign policy had for years been based on maintaining some degree of independence by playing off the two Powers against each other, raising the stakes at each exchange, and from this auction of favours ministers could reap great personal advantage. If Britain and Russia were no longer rivals, where would be the scope for personal enrichment?

There was a powerful faction in the Central Asia department at St Petersburg who had never had any intention of honouring the Convention, which they viewed as Britain's handing over of Persia to them on a plate. Outwardly and at chancery level the Russians showed every sign of the new spirit of co-operation but on the ground and out of view the old game continued. From now on Sykes's time at Meshed was to be spent in countering the Russian effort and in persuading his masters, who were reluctant to believe it, that the Russians had by no means become Britain's allies in Central Asia.

Reporting to Sykes at Meshed was the outpost consulate at Torbat-i Haidari, on the edge of the great central desert. The consuls there had no European company other than their Russian rivals, and their reports mostly concerned tribal raids from across the Afghan border. Their duty, apart from giving assistance to British subjects, was to provide a counterweight to the Russian presence and to give advance warning of any Russian moves towards India. Life in these outpost consulates is well described by Frederick O'Connor, who was Consul at Sistan, where his Russian opposite number was Baron Cherkassov:

> We knew where we were, and that we were not expected to make mischief in each other's spheres. Frankness and *bonhomie* were the order of the day; and whenever one heard of one's *cher collègue* attempting to carry on any little underground plot of his own, one immediately proceeded to tackle him with the most effusive friendliness, and to drag his proceedings into the light of day. He, of course, welcomed this exhibition of cordial friendship and the little game generally came to a premature end . . . Many a jolly evening we had, beginning with the usual lordly *zakuska* and vodka and finishing up with Cossack dances and music round a bonfire in the courtyard.[3]

It sometimes seems these consuls were playing the 'Game' just to relieve their boredom. There was little of great import in their reports but occasionally there were gems. The following example was sent to Sykes by Captain Keyes in Torbat-i Haidari. It tells the story of one Benjamin, who peddled tracts for the British and Foreign Bible Society.

> He had sold a few Bibles to the Amir and some respectable merchants and had had some discussions with them until some seyyids threatened to kill him and burn his books. He came to the consulate for refuge. I went to the Governor and requested a guarantee for Benjamin's safety, but the Governor replied that, since the formation of the new Majlis, there was no longer any order in the country and he could offer little in the way of guarantee. I then referred him to the Amir-i Panj [military commander], who sent some Cossacks to keep order, and Benjamin

---

[3] F. O'Connor, *On the Frontiers and Beyond: A Record of Thirty Years Service* (London, 1931).

was sent back to the caravanserai where he was staying. Next day I received a letter concocted by the Governor and the Karguzar after their opium sleep, informing me that it was not on account of his missionary activities that the seyyids had been incensed with Benjamin, but because he had committed an unnatural offence with a seyyid boy. They had now restored order.

Sykes's official diaries are full of the details of Meshed life, with vignettes of the local scene which the diaries both of his predecessors and of his successors conspicuously lack. He took a great interest in people's lives, in what they had to say and what they and their relations were up to, and his diaries show a side of Persian life not touched on by the drier historians. Because of his genuine interest in them, the Persians unbent towards him in a way in which they never did to other British officials.

On 2nd September 1907, the day after the assassination of the Atabeg-i A'zam, a most unpopular prime minister appointed by the avaricious new Shah Muhammad Ali to persuade the Majlis to grant him a personal loan, Sykes reported:

> The leading astrologer of Persia resides at Meshed. He had been consulted by the late Atabeg, whom he had warned not to return to Persia. He has now issued a prediction that disorders will increase in Persia and that there will be much bloodshed for two years, after which the English will take the country and introduce order. This prediction will influence large numbers of people and increase the tendency towards disintegration.

Astrologers were held in high regard at the time and were consulted before the undertaking of any great enterprise. Contemporary Persian paintings show the Shahs on campaign always with an astrologer and a water-pipe carrier trotting along in attendance and it is not hard to imagine the effect of this utterance on the public, particularly after the accuracy of his warning to the Atabeg.

At the end of September Sykes fell ill with a bout of fever that kept him in bed for two months. Battye took over the running of the consulate and the writing of the diary. The reports revolve

around ever-increasing civil unrest and unbridled highway robberies. The main topic of Meshed conversation was the Anglo-
Russian Convention and the common belief that Britain had sold
Persia to Russia. The Native Attaché did his best to peddle the
British line that the Convention would unite the Persian people
with the government in an effort to regenerate Persia and save it
from the grip of the foreigner, but he had little success.

The state of Khorasan is well illustrated by the account of an
unusually large Turkoman raid near a copper mine north of
Sabzevar in the middle of November, in which some four hundred
horsemen made up the *alaman* raiding party. Forty men had been
killed and fifty prisoners, mostly girls, had been taken. The size of
the robbery was such that it could not be ignored in the usual way
and a punitive force of 200 Persian infantry, 60 cavalry and 22
gunners was somehow assembled. This bunch of unpaid tatterde-
malions aged from thirteen to over seventy, armed with motley
weapons and ammunition that did not fit, was paraded and eventually marched out of Meshed in pursuit of the long-gone
Turkoman. The men got as far as the biggest carpet workshop in
town which, being a more attractive proposition than searching for
the bandits, they set about looting. This fiasco came about because
the previous Governor-General had sold off the contents of the
arsenal and had also been taking commissions on the sale of girls to
the Turkoman. The local Majlis had demanded his head for this
but the government in Tehran – in the acid words of Captain
Keyes, the consul at Torbat – 'decided that it would be a pity to
waste such a fertile financial genius and made him Minister of the
Interior'.

The hapless Governor-General, Rukn ud-Dowleh, sent for the
native attaché Khan Sahib Ahmad Din and told him that he
believed the Russians were responsible for the Turkoman raid. He
was a troubled man and asked the attaché for his advice as to
whether he should throw in his lot with the Shah, who was the
enemy of the Constitution, or with the people. The attaché's
answer, regrettably, is not on record.

Battye reported that the Turkoman did not get away with their
pillaging but were attacked in the dark by a tribe of Kurds from
Bojnurd, who took advantage of the Turkoman aversion to night

fighting. This tribe of Kurds had been transplanted to the north-east frontier of Persia by Shah Abbas in the seventeenth century to guard the marches against Turkoman raiders, who had been a constant source of trouble, swooping over the hills on their horses to reive cattle and women from the villages for themselves and men to be sold as slaves in the markets of Bokhara. The Kurds had killed a number of the raiders and were sending their heads to Meshed.

When Sykes finally recovered from his fever, he rapidly discovered the real truth of the matter. Some heads were indeed on their way to Meshed, but they had belonged not to the raiders but to surplus prisoners, shepherds and passers-by. They were later gruesomely paraded in the city, to the usually imperturbable Evelyn's horror. The Turkoman, far from being punished, had in fact been incited to go on this raid by the Il-Khan of the Bojnurdi Kurds. He had sent a message to Muhammad Geldi Khan, the chief of the Göklan clan of Turkoman at Astarabad, who had entertained Sykes on his first journey in Persia, to let him know that there was no effective government in Khorasan and that, should they wish to indulge in an *alaman*, the pickings would be easy. At the time the Il-Khan had been under arrest in Tehran and wanted to show that his presence at home was indispensable for the maintenance of order. Sykes knew how to get to the Persian bottom of such things.

Just before Christmas 1907 drama befell Meshed. The local Majlis took over the government arsenal and post and telegraph offices, blocking communication with the outside world, although Sykes managed to persuade the revolutionaries to allow foreign nationals to continue to use the telegraph. On 22nd December the Majlis took over full control of Meshed. In a telegram to the Legation Sykes stated, 'In Khorasan all parties united against Shah – one party favours a republic, the other a regency under Zill-i Sultan [the Shah's elder half-brother] until Valiahd [the Crown Prince] grows up. Both sides are listening to my advice to maintain order and avoid bloodshed.'[4] Bloodshed, in Sykes's view, would have given the Russians the excuse to introduce more troops to take over Khorasan and move into direct contact with the Indian

---

[4] Zill us-Sultan was disqualified from becoming Shah by having a non-Qajar mother.

frontier. As he saw it, it was now up to him to keep the peace in Meshed and save the Empire.

The Government of India was becoming concerned by the over-dramatic nature of the reports that Sykes was sending back from Meshed. Captain Keyes was deputed to Meshed to go up and try to calm him down. In one of the letters that he wrote to his mother he said:

> Sykes is the most energetic person I've ever met and very good at his job in spite of all his *bakh* [bombast]. Mrs Sykes is a dear person and he's really kind, but I'm always afraid of having hysterics – his self-complacency is so magnificent. I think he likes to imagine that the Viceroy and Louis Dane wake up each morning with a sigh of thankfulness that he is still safe. He's trying to make them think that he's single-handedly keeping a revolution in check. All the other Europeans laugh at him.

But it was 'the other Europeans' who were the complacent ones.

A footnote to the official diary for 19th December 1907 gives the only reference in Sykes's writing to Freemasonry. Sykes mentioned that the native attaché had gone to call on the new Mutawalli-Bashi and remarked: 'He is a Freemason and was anxious to know if I was one.' He had indeed joined as a young officer and this would have been of immense advantage to him in Persia because at that time many members of the leading Qajar families and notables in the Constitutional movement were also masons. The Persian Freemasons had links with the Sufi orders, on which their organization was largely modelled. They met in lodges known as *faramush-khanehs* or 'houses of oblivion', where they could speak their minds openly and safely on the burning subjects of the day, knowing they would not be betrayed by their brethren.

The year 1908 began uneventfully; other than the usual run of highway robberies and border raiding, the diary had nothing of interest to report other than an item of Meshed gossip about Farman Farma. The sum of £30,000 had gone missing from the government funds under his control, but the general feeling was that this was 'merely a new way of making money' and not much surprise was expressed.

Keyes, however, wrote to his mother:

> Sykes has had a cellar dug under the consulate with a well
> in it so as to be able to withstand a siege and has become the
> laughing-stock of Meshed. I was told by a very sensible Persian
> that the Meshedis were asking how we conquered India if we
> were such cowards. The Persians are no fools and understand
> very well that an attack on Europeans would mean Russian
> occupation . . .
>
> I really don't dare go to Meshed as I couldn't help letting
> Sykes see what an inflated ass I think him. He is so obsessed
> with the idea that Persia is going to break up and that he's going
> to be King of Kerman that he twists everything to fit in with his
> hopes. His capacity for self-deception is enormous. One of his
> favourite expressions is that he has his finger on the pulse of the
> people but he's hopeless at the language and has to rely for all his
> information on two or three people, who tell him exactly what
> they think he'd like to know.

It is interesting to note that not everybody agreed with Sykes's
estimation of his own facility with Persian. He certainly worked
hard at it and kept notebooks of proverbs and unusual phrases in
his own very passable handwriting. Since he had picked it up
largely from servants and villagers, it is hardly surprising that his
Persian was looked down on by those who had learned from
teachers.

The heightened sense of unreality and the tendency for alarm-
ists to spread unchecked rumours in the tense situation at Meshed
at the time is shown in the same letter from Keyes:

> Last week it was reported to the local Assembly that eight
> wagon loads of arms and ammunition had been smuggled into
> the Russian consulate on three separate nights. They sent a man
> to count the wheel marks and got into a frightful state of excite-
> ment. In fact, it was us that had been to visit them in the local
> phaeton or they had been to us three times, and once the
> phaeton had bolted past empty, which accounted for the 'eight
> wagons'. That's the way history is being made in Persia.

Back at Torbat-i Haidari, with no European company apart from his rival the Russian Consul and with nothing more interesting to report on than the occasional incursions of Afghan sheep-stealers, Captain Keyes was moved to write a lengthier report than usual, explaining why he had had to sack and send home two of the Indian *sowars* from his escort. The escort, all Indian Sunni Muslims, were allowed by the Consulate to marry locally but, since they were mostly either already married or betrothed to girls at home, they preferred to make use of *sigheh*, the Shia arrangement for temporary marriage which obviated the Muslim prohibition on prostitution. *Sigheh* marriages were organized, to their considerable profit, by the mullas throughout the country, particularly in Meshed, where there were great numbers of travelling merchants and pilgrims suffering from the absence of their more permanent wives. Few of the Indian cavalrymen's *sigheh* marriages lasted more than two months and there had been many complaints from the discarded women. One eighteen-year-old woman had been married fourteen times, twelve of them to the Meshed and Torbat consular escorts. Keyes had therefore been obliged to order them to stop taking *sigheh* wives, bringing the complaints to an end but greatly reducing the incomes of the Torbat mujtahids. Besides collecting the marriage fees from the soldiers, the mujtahids had also been taking a percentage of the bride price from the women, whom they had often introduced to the Indians.

The two *sowars* in question, with their local wives, were running a brothel to cater to the needs of their colleagues, who had become much frustrated by Keyes's ruling, and had gradually expanded their business to service the local menfolk as well, thus undercutting the mujtahids and their *sighehs*. During the Muharram processions, when tempers, fanned by the flames of fanaticism, ran high, a woman was spotted leaving one of the escorts' houses by a back window. A mob gathered and the mujtahids, seeing their opportunity, quickly whipped it up into an anti-Sunni riot. When the local governor told the mujtahids to restore order, they persuaded him that the only way was for the Consul to deport the two Indians. Normal business for the mullas could then resume. It clearly pained the normally laconic Keyes to have to report at such length on this affair, which had caused some damage to Imperial prestige.

Keyes wrote home to say that Ella Sykes was coming to stay in Meshed, bringing with her the children of Franklin, the vice-consul, who had been with Younghusband on the Lhasa expedition. There is no record of this in the consular diary, nor did Evelyn mention it in her memoir but, judging by the account Ella wrote of Meshed life,[5] she rode out on shooting expeditions and even accompanied Sykes on some of his tours. A very faded photograph in Henry Smyth's album shows her riding side-saddle to Turkistan, with Mrs Smyth, who was not a rider, in a *kajaveh*. Evelyn, meanwhile, was pregnant with her second son, Charles, and was in no state to take part in her sister-in-law's adventures. The remarkable thing about these two women is that, although some have suggested that Evelyn might have been jealous of her sister-in-law, with her closeness to Percy and her independence, they were in fact very fond of each other. By this time Evelyn had begun to weary of Percy's cavalier treatment of her – one contemporary, Clarmont Skrine, said that he treated her like a brood mare – and she found that Ella was much kinder to her than he was. Through her books on travel and her work with the Royal Central Asian Society Ella has been rather unfairly seen as the stronger character of the two, but Evelyn had needed far greater strength to cope with all her children as well as run the household loyally and unquestioningly, as was required of women in those days.

The temporary calm in consular life at Meshed was broken in April 1908 by a second gymkhana, another splendid display of horsemanship given by the Indian escort. This was another 'Sykes success', attended by a crowd of five thousand, but it might have backfired because the Volunteer Majlis, whose nationalist pride, not unnaturally, had been wounded by this imperial display, were stung into considering organizing a rival sports day to put Sykes and his colonial Indian cavalry performers in the shade. Nothing came of it.

The signing of the Anglo-Russian Convention had led to a new spirit of official co-operation between the two consulates at Meshed. This had been helped along by a British loan to the

---

[5] *Persia and Its People* (London, 1910).

Persian government of £200,000 at five per cent interest. The loan had been almost forced on the Persians by the Legation, in an effort to wean them away from Russian loans. Nevertheless, the Russians were carrying on with the old game. At the end of May Keyes reported from Torbat-i Haidari that they had appointed a military attaché to their consulate, where there had been none before. A minute in the margin of Keyes's report – saying, 'This is quite contrary to the spirit of the Agreement' – shows that the British Legation in Tehran took a serious view of this development. Sykes meanwhile, was again fortifying his consulate in anticipation of trouble.

In June there were reports of arms being smuggled from Afghanistan to the sensitive frontier zone of the Qainat. This was a new development, in that arms were usually smuggled the other way, from the Persian Gulf into Afghanistan, from where they could be used against India. Sykes reported that he had persuaded the Governor-General, Rukn ud-Dowleh, to order the Shaukat ul-Molk at Birjand to send every available man to the frontier of his district but that the governor was short of funds and unable to act effectively. 'I have requested the Legation to press the Persian Government to allow the money asked for. I have also suggested that we advance the necessary funds, as after all the matter is of great importance to us.' A week later Rukn ud-Dowleh got his money and issued new rifles and ammunition to the garrison. Sykes commented mordantly: 'The officers and men were ordered to keep this a secret, with the result that it was known all over Meshed in a matter of hours.' The diary does not reveal how the Governor-General had got his money, but it is unlikely that the Persian government could have provided the funds within a week.

Sykes was also keeping an eye on the distant disturbances in Tabriz and Tehran and, in case they had missed anything, reported regularly to the Tehran Legation on news that he had heard from the other side of the country, to their growing irritation. On 23rd June he informed them, 'It is reported that a hundred men from Tabriz and fifty from Qazvin have left for the capital. For the popular cause it would have been better if they had remained at home and telegraphed that thousands were ready to start.' The last sentence was underlined in red by George Churchill, the Oriental

Secretary at the Legation, with the acid comment, 'Napoleon grasps the situation.' Churchill came from a family who had served at the Legation and at various consulates in Persia since 1848. His brother Sidney was described by Gertrude Bell as 'speaking Persian like a Persian, having lived in every part of this country, disguised and undisguised: knows the people and their habits and prejudices as no European does: rides anything and anywhere and is one of the most capable people withal that I have ever come across.' George Churchill was not dazzled by Percy Sykes.

The name Napoleon stuck. When Sykes reported at the end of June that Rukn ud-Dowleh intended to re-impose the *Sar-i Sang* octroi or tax on goods in transit and that, to improve his personal finances, the Governor-General had sold the right to farm this tax to his Master of the Horse for 5,000 tomans, Churchill's minuted comment was, 'Suppose Napoleon will protest if anything of the sort is attempted'.

On 4th July the Rukn ud-Dowleh was in trouble. The Shah wanted to replace him with the Nayir ud-Dowleh ('Illumination of the State'), who had outbid him for the office. The Russian and British consuls intervened jointly through their legations to keep him in office and three days later he was reappointed, on condition that he paid the same revenue to the Shah as his predecessor, who had contributed more than the Rukn. Sykes wrote, 'The Rukn ud-Dowleh is extremely grateful for our assistance. He is reaping a good harvest but is, however, squeezing with moderation.' The Rukn ud-Dowleh was widely regarded as a compliant tool of Russia, although he was also very close to Sykes, albeit more discreetly. Sykes's reason for maintaining him in office was that the Imperial Bank of Persia had made the Rukn a substantial loan, and there would be no chance of the British getting it back if he were to be removed.

The new Shah Muhammad Ali was not only avaricious but also vengeful. He was much troubled by spreading rumours of his illegitimacy and the fact that his mother was not a royal Qajar. She seems to have been not so much blue-blooded as red-blooded. At the end of July Sykes reported to the Legation, 'The Mutamid us-Saltaneh ['the Trusted of the Realm'], the ex-vizier, is ordered to leave for Tehran immediately. He is very unhappy as he has heard that the Shah has prepared a black list of all the individuals who married his mother the Umm-i Khaqan ['Mother of the Great Chief'] and is killing them off systematically. Sad to say, the Mutamid was the husband of the princess once upon a time! The number of her husbands is said to run into three figures.' The Legation's pencilled comment was 'The lady had a large heart!'

Although Meshed was far removed from Tehran and Tabriz, where the Constitutional battle was being fought, as a centre for pilgrimage it was very much in touch not only with the countries across the border but also with the Caucasus and with Ottoman Turkey. The British Consulate-General at Meshed was responsible for Turkish subjects in Khorasan. In August 1908 a potentially awkward situation presented itself when the Tabrizis of Meshed – Turkish-speaking Azerbaijanis – wrote to the Turkish ambassador in Tehran asking to become Turkish subjects. The Meshed Tabrizis were mostly prosperous and enterprising merchants who suffered as much from Russian depredations as from the exactions of the Persian authorities. By becoming Turkish subjects these hardheaded merchants would be entitled to Sykes's protection and could appeal through him for relief from official and unofficial taxes, for British merchants had to pay much less tax than Persians. They approached him and asked if, to support their request for Turkish protection, they could take *bast* in the British Consulate. The British clearly could not countenance being a party to this perverse manifestation of pan-Turkism and Sykes turned down their request.

Two years later, in an ominous foreshadowing of Enver Pasha's pan-Turkic movement,[6] the Turkish embassy in Tehran asked Sykes to compile a list of all the histories of Persia and to give them full details about all the Turkoman tribes with their fighting value and their degree of loyalty to the Persian government. Sykes did not record whether or not he complied with this request.

On 14th August the Consulate fortifications were again strengthened, but not without a little drama. Sykes's despatch records:

Thanks to Captain Daukes, the explosives, pickaxes, wires etc. have duly arrived. Most of the explosives were suitably packed

---

[6] See also Peter Hopkirk, *Setting the East Ablaze* and *On Secret Service East of Constantinople*, not to mention John Buchan's *Greenmantle*.

in champagne cases but one box, peculiar to the Arsenal, was employed. The pickaxes, wire etc. were packed in gunny sacking, which was worn through, showing the contents. However, there were no Arsenal marks on the consignment, which makes this Consulate quite safe, so far as can be seen.

The last sentence was underlined by Churchill with the minute, '*Inshallah!* What an ass Napoleon Attila Sykes is in some ways.' It appears that the feeling in the Legation was that Sykes was getting delusions of grandeur. On 12th September he sent them a telegram to say, 'A robbery of goods to the value of 90,000 tomans on the Yazd road is reported. Constant robberies are occurring at or near Rizab in the Yazd district. I am keeping the Khorasan section fairly safe but unless something is done on the Yazd section commerce will cease.' The underlining, in red, was done by Churchill, with an exclamation mark.

After his successful venture into carpet exports from Kerman to India, in May Sykes became involved with a carpet manufacturer in Meshed, one Haji Abdul Rahim. He planned to export them for the first time directly to London, bypassing the middlemen in Constantinople, who took most of the profit. Feeling that the traditional Meshed designs had become corrupted for the market by European influences, he had given the Haji some classical Persian designs taken from an old book that he had obtained from London. He later recorded: 'The trial consignment of Meshed carpets which I sent directly to Messrs Allen Bros. in London so as to divert the trade to London and America away from Constantinople has been most favourably reported on. The only drawback is that these carpets sell better when chemically washed to give the effect of ageing. Hitherto this faking has not been done in London, but has now started.'

Far from Meshed, at Masjid-i Soleiman in the Bakhtiari mountains of the south-west, after five years of unsuccessful exploration the first oil gusher had been struck in May by the Yorkshireman William D'Arcy.[7] Hitherto Europe had got its oil from Baku but

---

[7] D'Arcy had made a fortune in goldmining in Australia before financing oil exploration in Persia. He never went to Persia himself and Curzon had initially poured cold water over his schemes, declaring them to be impractical. See Denis Wright, *The English amongst the Persians.*

the cost of transporting it overland to the port of Batumi on the Black Sea was making it uneconomical to exploit. With this new discovery of oil in commercial quantities, the British began to take more interest in Persia and soon realized the mistake of having left the oilfields in the Neutral Zone. Today, a hundred years later, after a brief Western enthusiasm for Caspian oil, history is repeating itself.

14

Dealing with Dabizha

THE PERIOD OF relative quiet in Meshed came to an end in September 1908 with the posting of Prince Dabizha to the Russian Consulate-General at Meshed. He was described by Frederick O'Connor as 'an official of the old school, a courtly old gentleman with a long grey beard and a benign aspect, and steeped to the brows in every imaginable species of intrigue',[1] and by T.W. Haig as 'famous throughout Persia for his vast flowing beard, which he was said to encase in a blue silk bag when he travelled, to protect it from the dust'.[2] Before his arrival Sykes, ever the stickler for protocol, had written to Charles Marling at the Legation, requesting clarification as to whether he or Prince Dabizha would be regarded as the senior in Meshed and which of them should therefore take diplomatic precedence. As the first to have been posted to Meshed, Sykes could expect to take seniority, but since Dabizha had been Consul-General at Isfahan for longer than Sykes had been at Meshed, the Russian could also be regarded as the senior. Marling, irritated by this pettifogging, minuted that Dabizha would have to be counted as the senior unless the Persian government issued a new exequatur for his Meshed appointment, thus giving precedence to Sykes. This was quietly arranged, and Sykes was subsequently able to invoke his seniority over the

[1] F. O'Connor, *On the Frontiers and Beyond*.
[2] Lt.-Col. T. W. Haig, *Memoirs*.

Russian when dealing with the Meshed authorities and also to insist on his rights of protocol when confronting Dabizha, who was later to cause him considerable difficulty.

In the autumn Major R.L. Kennion, the new consul at Torbat-i Haidari, reported that the Shaukat ul-Mulk was to be replaced as governor by his cousin, the boorish Hishmat ul-Mulk ('Magnificence of the Kingdom'). In October Sykes sent in a further report that he had heard from Tehran that the Hishmat was to be given not only the province of Qainat but also the adjoining one of Tabas, and that there were several reasons for the Shah removing the Shaukat. For one thing, the Shah was alarmed that British influence in east Persia was becoming permanent in the person of the Shaukat. For another, the Hishmat had paid the Shah 50,000 tomans for the governorship and would have been appointed if the Majlis had not refused to ratify the appointment. The Shah therefore wanted to repay the debt of honour and at the same time show his power over the reform party in the Majlis. Finally, the Russians had been pressing the Persian government either to pay back the money advanced to them by the Russian Bank or to allow their man the Hishmat to 'make hay' in Torbat. Sir George Barclay, the new Minister at the Legation, giving Sykes his due, minuted in the margin of this despatch, 'A much more reasonable explanation of the case than Kennion's'.

Mir Akbar Khan Hishmat ul-Mulk had changed sides. In 1891, when the first agent of the Russians had arrived in Sistan and recruited the chief mulla to incite the people against the government, he had had him arrested. Since it was not a crime to be a Russian agent the Hishmat had him flogged for 'unnatural offences' and confiscated his property. However, the Russian Legation in Tehran, with characteristic Russian brazenness when caught *in flagrante,* openly intervened on their man's behalf and his property was restored to him.

The holy month of Ramadan came round in October and Sykes reported with relish on the venality and hypocrisy of the religious authorities of Meshed, who were turning to their own advantage the fact that gambling is forbidden under Islam:[3] 'Ramadan is a

---

[3] Gambling on chance is forbidden, but gambling on speed, skill or strength is permitted.

great time for gambling and the Mutawalli-Bashi is making much profit therefrom. Yesterday he found out where the Shrine officials were collected and sent a message to the seal-bearer of the Shrine that he must resign, as it was not right for a gambler to hold so holy an office. A collection of 1,500 tomans was made and this encouraged the austere chief to charge them 200 tomans daily for the right to gamble freely during Ramadan.'

At the end of the month, after arranging for the Consulate staff to practise filling and throwing bombs in anticipation of possible anti-European rioting, Sykes departed on tour, handing over to the vice-consul Franklin. The object of the tour was to gather much-needed intelligence about the Russian-controlled part of the frontier and to undertake survey work for Army Intelligence in Simla. He was accompanied by Captain Watson, who collected natural specimens and took some remarkable photographs, with the attaché Mubarik Ali and an escort of eighteen *sowars*.

They started off riding through the Ulang-i Shahi, the Royal Meadow, a famous grazing ground of Central Asia, and followed the Kashaf Rud river for fifteen miles. They rode over marshy ground along the river, full of duck and snipe, and visited the early thirteenth-century tower of Mil-i Radkan, with its fine fluted brickwork. This was a tomb tower, with a crypt underneath, where the prayers of the passing faithful would speed the soul of the departed on its journey to heaven. The Royal Meadow and Radkan were summer resorts of the Great Khans when Persia was ruled by the descendants of Tamerlane.

The party went on to visit a turquoise mine, which they entered by a tiny grille hundreds of feet up the hillside. After descending about a hundred feet and creeping along a lateral gallery they reached a more open part where, 'by the uncertain and evil-smelling light of primitive earthenware lamps', two parties were quarrying the rocks with chisels and hammers. The blocks were roughly broken up and carried to the surface by boys. Above ground, more boys were sifting and washing the blocks, encouraged by a foreman with a long stick, who beat them whenever he thought they were slacking.

They continued on to Bojnurd, to the Shahdillu Kurdish Il-Khan's 'pretentious palace with its huge reception rooms and tiled

porticos, which are quite out of place at Bojnurd', as Sykes wrote
in his report, and

> lunched in a room crowded with musical boxes and candelabra.
> The Sardar paid us the extraordinary compliment of riding for
> several miles with us when we left, and I can say that nowhere
> have I been received with greater kindness or more genuine
> hospitality than at Bojnurd. This was partly due to the fact that I
> had known my host's father when he was himself a mere lad: at
> the same time, nowhere in Persia does the name of England
> stand higher.

The margin of the report was here marked 'Important' by the
recipient at Simla Army Intelligence.

> During the many hours we spent together the Sardar spoke
> very freely about his position, which is that he has been
> 'squeezed' *à sec* by the Shah and Court . . . He complained bit-
> terly of the Russians . . . I explained how the Anglo-Russian
> Agreement affected his position and advised him to improve his
> relations with Russia. He finally agreed to do so, and remarked
> that as the Shah was 'a dead dog' in his dealings with Russia, it
> was obviously foolish to quarrel with the representatives of that
> Power. I explained to the Sardar that I would help him, but that
> it was invariably my rule to work through the Persian
> Governor-General, as direct intervention so frequently did
> more harm than good. Finally I begged the Sardar to keep on
> good terms with his brother-in-law [the Commander-in-Chief
> of the garrison at Meshed], but this is almost impossible for a
> Persian to do. The Kurdish Chief struck both Captain Watson
> and myself as more virile than most Persians and as possessing
> more energy, but it appears that he has as many wives as years –
> he is twenty-eight – and this must constitute a drain on his
> impoverished fortune, besides being undesirable from other
> points of view.

From Bojnurd they went up to the hills after big game while
surveying the Turkoman border near Samangan, 'where Rustam

wooed Tahmina, whose son was Sohrab', as he informed his masters, who would all have read Matthew Arnold's poem as schoolboys. There, up in the hills with the Kurds, he got more news from the locals about a big Turkoman raid of the previous year:

> The Bojnurd *sowars* attacked them, both sides losing thirty or forty men. A month later they had their revenge as the Turkoman were seen returning laden with booty. The Turkoman, who always fight on foot, were defeated with heavy loss, many prisoners were taken and captives released. Among the Turkoman prisoners was an old man of ninety who said that he had joined the *alaman* in order to secure a wife! The damsel in question came up during the interrogatory and brained her captor with a stone! The Turkoman much preferred Persian women to their own and this was a keen incentive, apart from money and goods, to engage in these forays.

They marched down the Dehaneh-i Gorgan gorge, guided by the Turkoman Oraz Muhammad, who had been Sykes's guide sixteen years earlier. They saw plenty of tracks of snow leopards and tigers, and the woods were full of very large stag, roebuck and wild boar; they also saw tracks of a bear in the snow. In this splendid shooting country, which is now a national game reserve, Sykes shot an enormous mouflon ram with horns 38 inches in length and 11½ inches in girth, followed by a huge stag with fourteen points; Watson bagged two snow leopard. Coming out of the gorge, with its very fine oaks, beeches and elms, they came to a clearing inhabited by Göklan Turkoman who, not unnaturally, mistook them for a raiding party and disappeared into the jungle.

With ominous prescience Sykes commented in his report: 'All this country is a paradise for sport; but it is deplorable that Persia should be so weak as to allow a handful of miserable Turkoman – the Göklan tribe of no more than 2,500 families – to occupy thousands of acres of the finest and best watered lands, which are yet under the suzerainty of the Shah.'

Down on the plain they reached Gonbad-i Kavus and sent a letter of introduction from Prince Dabizha to the Russian

Commissioner, who lived in a house next to the extraordinary eleventh-century ten-sided brick tower, 206 feet high, that houses the tomb of Kavus. The Russians had established this post to reduce cross-border raiding by the Turkoman. They rode on eastwards to Qaravol Tepeh (Watchman's Hill), originally a post on the Sadd-i Iskandar (Alexander's Wall), where Sykes's report includes a rambling and verbose diversion on Alexander the Great and the Parthians.

But then a messenger arrived. In Sykes's absence Meshed had erupted in revolution, and he decided to take the fast caravan route back, to the south of the mountain range. They crossed the mountains and descended through the village of Tash. 'Throughout the journey we had noticed that Russian spies were occasionally attached to our party; but during this section Commissioner Dolgopolov had, somewhat ineptly, sent one of his own *gholams*, whom we had seen at the Consulate. However, we used him as a guide and found him most serviceable and obliging.' After paying their respects to the shrine of the eleventh-century Sufi mystic Sheikh Bayazid Bastami at Bastam they continued down the hill to Shahrud, and from there eastwards along the fast route back to Meshed. Wherever they paused to rest their animals, Sykes made notes. 'At Abbasabad the inhabitants are descended from Georgians posted there by the Safavid Shah Abbas in the early seventeenth century. At night there was a wedding in the village and a procession with torches and lamps fetched the bridegroom, the whole party dancing with great vigour to the sound of horns and drums, as if possessed.' From there they pushed on to Nishapur (where they visited the tomb of Omar Khayyam) and Qadam-Gah, a shrine built by Shah Abbas to cover the footprint of Imam Reza. 'The custodian was doing well out of the passing trade.' They had covered a total of 880 miles in fifty-three days.

A week after Sykes had left on this tour, turmoil had broken out among the clerics in Meshed. Franklin, deputizing for him, reported that the mujtahids in Kerbela, the second holiest city of the Shia, which was in Mesopotamia and therefore under the Ottoman empire, had sent a letter to the Shrine accusing the Shah of handing over to the Russians the two most important northern provinces of Azerbaijan and Khorasan and calling on the people to uphold the Constitution and to wage a jihad against the Shah. Copies of the letter were circulating in the town. Rukn ud-Dowleh believed that it was genuine but he was being pressed by the government in Tehran to treat it as a forgery. The mujtahids did not know which way to turn; one day their leaders were against the Constitution, the next day they declared themselves in favour of it and then, under pressure from the Tehran mujtahids, who were themselves close to the reactionary Shah, they were once more in opposition to it.

On 30th November there was open revolt in Meshed. The mob rioted, the Governor-General brought out the artillery and distributed arms, and at the British Consulate the military attaché handed out rifles to the staff. On 1st December the pro-Constitution revolutionary leaders took sanctuary in the Shrine, where they were joined by the artisan guilds from the bazaar, which closed in protest. Posters were put up urging the people to follow the lead given by the mujtahids of Kerbela. The Shah declared their letter to be a forgery.

The following day the Governor-General informed Franklin that he believed that the only way to satisfy the people would be to restore the Constitution, but that he could not tell this to the Shah. The revolutionary leaders, not trusting the Persian authorities, asked Franklin to forward a telegram to the Shah via the British Legation in Tehran. Aware of the delicacy of the situation, Franklin refused to send an original telegram but did agree to send a précis, stating that the revolutionaries desired a constitution and would follow the mujtahids of Kerbela until one was granted. That day almost all the men of importance in Meshed joined the revolutionary party.

On 3rd December the situation had changed and Franklin reported that nearly all the leading reactionaries had now joined the revolutionaries. The next day the revolutionaries seized the telegraph office but were careful not to interfere with the British signallers. The Governor-General was trying to gather troops to restore order but there was no money to pay them.

On 13th December the revolt collapsed as quickly as it had begun. 'The mob, on the advice of their leaders, agreed to some trumpery concessions from the Governor-General and dispersed.

The astute Rukn ud-Dowleh, although unable to pay for any troops, had apparently found enough funds to secretly pay off a few of the leading revolutionaries and then seen to it that the others were informed, so that they all started to fall out with one another.' This was much cheaper and more effective than bribing the whole lot of them. Ten days later, with the drama over, Sykes returned to Meshed and sent a breezy telegram to the Legation: 'Reached Meshed yesterday after an enjoyable ride.'

The attempted revolution may have blown over, but battle was about to commence with Prince Dabizha, who was already making his presence felt. The opening shot came with a letter that the prince sent to the Rukn ud-Dowleh, who immediately passed a copy of it to Sykes, 'demanding that four bad characters who had attacked the son of the Russian Tajir-Bashi [Chief Merchant] should be sent to the Russian Consulate-General, with a set of sticks and ropes, there to be bastinadoed in public. He also demanded the reinstatement of the Russophile chief of police, who had been dismissed.' Sykes forwarded the letter to the Legation, explaining that the chief of police had been dismissed as part of the Governor-General's concessions to the revolutionaries and adding that the Rukn ud-Dowleh was incensed at Dabizha's high-handed manner. At the British Legation in Tehran George Churchill minuted, 'We had better trust Napoleon to handle his colleague as best he may. The FO won't want to hear of this and it's too ticklish to handle here.'

During the rest of the winter the Meshed revolutionaries licked their wounds and formed themselves into secret societies. Storms were brewing, both on the Constitutional and the Russian fronts, but Sykes was always civil and correct in his dealings with Dabizha. He even offered him the use of the British Consulate-General as a refuge in case of civil disturbance, pointing out that the Russian Consulate-General, being surrounded on all side by bazaars, was impossible to defend against attack by the mob. This may, of course, have been an oblique hint that Dabizha might be hoist with his own petard if he stirred up trouble.

Dabizha now began to show the apparent paranoia that charac-terized his subsequent maverick behaviour. Sykes's first entry in the consular diary for January 1909 recorded: 'My Russian colleague has been trying to discover who are the members of a secret society which exists among the Russian subjects and of which he is very much afraid. After much spying, two men were arrested and imprisoned. It turned out that they had been sent by the Russian Consul-General of Transcaspia to spy on Dabizha!'

The first manifestation of what was seen by the Persians in Meshed as the Anglo-Russian carve-up of their practically bankrupt country came at the end of January, when Dabizha informed the Governor-General and others that the Russian and British Consulates-General would assume control over affairs. Sykes wrote: 'I have since informed the Governor-General that some control of the finances is intended. This would be generally welcomed but at the same time there will be much opposition, in as much as the opportunity for perquisites will thereby be lessened.'

The plotters against Rukn ud-Dowleh finally succeeded and in March he was replaced as Governor-General by his rival the Nayir ud-Dowleh. The Rukn asked Sykes for help, but he said that nothing could be done because, as he had heard, the Nayir had paid the Shah 120,000 tomans for the post a year before, whereas the Rukn had paid only 90,000 tomans.

Sykes was convinced that Dabizha's plan was to cause disturbances in Meshed which would justify his bringing in Russian troops from across the border in Transcaspia to occupy the whole of Khorasan. Dabizha began in earnest on 8th March 1909 by trying to incite a mob of Constitutionalist supporters – thereby confusing the issue and hoping to cover his tracks – to attack the *Arg*, the Governor-General's residence. His idea was to place a number of mullas at the head of the mob, on the theory that the soldiers would not fire on them. 'The holy men objected to this programme, so nothing was done.' ('Very funny!', Churchill commented.)

Three weeks later Dabizha tried again by starting a feud between the Azerbaijani Turks, who were Russian subjects, and the Meshedis.

The Persian authorities have asked Dabizha to either restrain his subjects or, if he cannot do this, to state in writing that he will not hold the Persian Government responsible if any of them are killed. My wily colleague, however, will only verbally state to the Persian authorities that he will not claim compensation if the men are killed. At the same time he promises that as soon as a Russian subject is killed he will bring in Russian troops. There seems little doubt that, whatever the avowed policy of the Russian Government may be, its agents mean that Persia shall be broken up as quickly as possible.

The last sentence was underlined by Churchill at the Legation in Tehran, which was on totally civil terms with the Russian Legation, as were the two governments in London and St Petersburg; Sykes was beginning to be taken seriously.

More trouble broke out three weeks later, this time nothing to do with Dabizha, but of an almost surreal nature. 'The reactionary party subscribed the sum of 200 tomans, which was given to two hundred prostitutes to go and break up a meeting of the Majlis. That august body being forewarned, they on their part engaged two hundred and fifty gypsy women to do battle with the prostitutes and so the attempt failed.'

Outside the city there was trouble on the Russian border at Dareh Gaz (Vale of Tamarisk). 'The Persian Army was sent out to quell the disturbances and returned with a dozen heads. One of them turned out to have belonged to a peaceful Yazdi merchant, along with bloodstained women's clothing and, worst of all, a seyyid's turban covered in blood. The Majlis was outraged and nearly lynched the commander, but arrested him instead. The Army collected, blew trumpets to warm themselves up for battle, but contented themselves with a fierce demonstration. The Assembly was demanding that the *Arg* be handed over to them. Meanwhile the new Governor-General Nayir ud-Dowleh was 'cowering at Nishapur and refusing to make his entry to Meshed. The Shah was ordering the Governor-General to have the revolutionaries blown from guns, but this only made him report sick.'

Another hardy perennial around this time in the correspondence with the Legation concerned the robbery of a large sum of cash on its way from the Imperial Bank of Persia to Nishapur. This had been part of a plot to oust the Rukn ud-Dowleh, who, since he could be held personally responsible for robberies that occurred on the road, could be broken if forced to pay compensation to the bank. The robber was finally caught and arrested by the Governor-General, but his father bribed the Prime Minister to order his release. When the Rukn asked Sykes for his advice, he was told that the Legation would never allow the robber to be released. Much later it transpired that the money had not been robbed at all but embezzled by a high Persian official. Sykes finally arranged for the money to be repaid in instalments and two years later, after much time and effort, he was able to report: 'The whole of the first instalment of 3,044 tomans of the money due has now been paid in. The Bank will receive twelve per cent throughout and the Karguzar's fee will be paid by the man who embezzled the money.' (Barclay commented, 'The Bank ought to be grateful to Sykes. I am afraid that they are not and that they would have preferred that the case should have been treated as the embezzler wished, as a case of highway robbery. This is a sordid story and in my opinion does no credit to the Bank.')

The constant trouble in the city did not prevent Sykes from holding another gymkhana, but this time only the Europeans were invited to what was a comparatively muted affair. By contrast Dabizha brought in seventy-five Cossack officers, two Maxim guns and a few officers 'to keep security'. The bazaar shut for two days in protest, but soon resigned itself to the situation. The most vociferous protest came from 'a speaker in the local Majlis who said that it was an insult that the Russians should have sent such ugly and undersized men to Persia'.

Finally, on 5th May the new Shah Muhammad Ali agreed to grant a new constitution. The new liberal and supposedly enlightened leaders of Meshed were, however, no saints. 'A Volunteer (mujahid) Assembly has been started and money collected. Haji Ahmed, a respectable merchant from Tabriz, was asked to subscribe 500 tomans. He did not refuse to pay but merely asked how the money would be spent. To encourage the others, he was shot dead.'

It was the same story in Tehran. A despatch from the Legation to London of 2nd January 1908 said: 'Of the corruption of the Majlis a single instance will suffice. Large sums have been collected, mostly by indirect menace from those suspected of reactionary leanings, for the foundation of a National Bank, and lodged with one of the Vice-Presidents of the Assembly. Of this money, which may have amounted to £50,000 (about £2.5 million today), no account has been given and is said to have been quietly absorbed by members of the Assembly and the Anjumans.'

Sykes, throughout all this, was constantly receiving copies of Russian correspondence. The weary Karguzar sent him copies of many letters from Dabizha, full of high-handed demands for satisfaction against petty slights or small robberies from Russian subjects, accompanied by threats to send his Cossacks to arrest the suspects.

Following the Shah's capitulation to the Constitutionalists a state of anarchy broke out in Meshed. The new Governor-General was forced by Russian pressure to resign, to be replaced once more by the Rukn ud-Dowleh. Dabizha immediately bombarded him with crazed and outrageous demands, implying that he had the support of the British Consulate-General. He sent letters full of ludicrous demands to the Majlis, who tore them up and abused both him and the Rukn. The Volunteers fired on the *Arg* and the citadel artillery replied, but succeeded only in damaging some houses in the distance. The people, opposed to the return of the apparently pro-Russian Rukn ud-Dowleh, demonstrated in front of the Russian Consulate. Dabizha, still looking for a pretext to bring in more troops, five hundred of whom were said to be in readiness across the border, was hoping for some outrage to be committed, but Sykes somehow persuaded the demonstrators to accept the Rukn as Governor. Ten days later one of the senior Shrine officials was found murdered, with a note pinned to his corpse 'for his friendship with the Russian Consulate-General'. The Begler-Begi, who had been reinstated at Russian insistence, was also murdered. Dabizha was threatened. 'Everyone of position has either taken refuge in the *Arg* or fled to distant villages, or is being blackmailed.' The Majlis appealed to Sykes for help, but he replied that it was up to them to make terms with the Governor-General. For two nights there was firing round the British Consulate, and the defences prepared by Sykes and the military attaché, Major Redl, were finally manned.

In her recollection of this period Evelyn Sykes shows something of her mettle and unflappability:

During our eight years in Meshed a little Persian revolution broke out. Away from the capital it was a bit half hearted. They seemed to spend their time potting at each other from a safe distance. Thanks to the good relations which Percy had so carefully fostered they never attacked us, but odd shots would frequently drop down unexpectedly. We never knew when they might start shooting. Then we counted one shot, which we assumed was just a mistake, then two shots . . . When it came to five or more, it was time to go in to seek the protection of four walls. I remember running round the corner of the house as fast as possible.

A month later, still faced with popular rumblings, Rukn ud-Dowleh sent a message to Sykes saying that he had no hope of holding on as Governor and that he wished to resign and take *bast* with him. With the terms of the Convention in mind, Sykes replied that it would be more fitting if he appealed for *bast* to both consulates jointly. In the face of this display of diplomatic correctness Dabizha responded with duplicity. The diary records in detail the ensuing drama of Rukn ud-Dowleh's rescue and the double-dealing of Dabizha.

The Rukn duly wrote to both consulates announcing his resignation and requesting their protection. When there was no response from Dabizha, Sykes sent Major Redl, who spoke fluent Russian and Persian, to give him a carefully worded message to the effect that it was undesirable to send troops to protect Rukn ud-Dowleh in the *Arg* and that it would be better to take him to a safe house under the combined British and Russian flags. Dabizha agreed. Redl and Dabizha then agreed that an escort of ten Indian *sowars* with ten Cossacks should meet the Governor-General at the *Arg* and escort him to the safe house, which was to be chosen by Dabizha and would be close to the Russian Consulate. An hour later the two native attachés compared notes and discovered that the Russian escort would now consist of twenty Cossacks. Redl immediately protested to Dabizha, who said that there had been a misunderstanding, but that he would fall in with Sykes's views, provided that the Governor-General agreed; he now proposed, however, to guard him in the *Arg*.

Since he was bound by the terms of the Anglo-Russian

Convention, Sykes was unable to react unilaterally to this situation. He sent his native attaché, with the Russian attaché, to the *Arg* to speak to the Rukn ud-Dowleh, who said that he was ready to follow Sykes. Although the Russian replied by threatening the Rukn with Russian hostility and loss of the Shah's favour if he followed Sykes's advice to leave the *Arg*, the Rukn finally came out, escorted by ten *sowars* and twenty Cossacks. The Cossacks then tried to divert the carriage to the Russian Consulate-General, but were thwarted by the Indian *sowars*, who held firm and took the Rukn to a safe house. He later sent a message to Sykes, thanking him for saving his life. Even then, Dabizha refused to fly the Russian flag over the Governor-General's house as a sign of Russian recognition. It was not until a day later that the two flags were flown over the safe house.

Following several messages from the Majlis asking for his intervention to resolve the situation, Sykes called a meeting of all involved, to be held at the British Consulate-General: the Rukn ud-Dowleh, Dabizha, the two leading mujtahids of the Shrine, and the leader of the revolutionary mujahideen. Dabizha tried to obstruct this meeting by refusing to supply his share of a joint escort, which in the circumstances was essential if the parties were to reach the Consulate safely. Sykes, however, 'took careful military precautions' and they all arrived without incident.

When the Persian deputation arrived, he tactfully left them to have a private discussion with Rukn ud-Dowleh for half an hour and then brought in Dabizha. The agreement that they reached had four points:

1. The anti-Majlis party would disarm within ten days.
2. The Majlis should keep twenty armed and twenty unarmed guards.
3. A proclamation should be issued throughout Khorasan that reconciliation had been effected between the parties.
4. After the Majlis had ratified this agreement, the Governor-General should return to the *Arg*.

The Majlis duly ratified the agreement, Rukn ud-Dowleh was restored and successfully disarmed the reactionaries, the bazaar reopened and life returned to normal. Meshed, as Sykes said in his diary, was 'grateful for peace'. He went on to note, modestly for once, that this was the first ever meeting between the leading muj- tahids, the Governor-General and the Russian Consul-General to be held at the British Consulate-General, and it was also the first time that a leading mujtahid had set foot inside a European's house. The irony was that if Dabizha had provided the Russian escort as requested, the Persians would have refused to accept it and the meeting would never have taken place.

Sykes's reputation was now at its height and his reports for this month resounded with references to 'British prestige being at its zenith'. 'The local press is full of gratitude to this Consul-General and pays many compliments to British policy', he wrote. Barclay minuted to Major Stokes: 'I am sending a circular ordering all to do their best to combat the impression that the recent revolution is a victory of British policy over Russian.' In the view of the Foreign Office, the Russians were allies and must not be upset in any way that would prejudice overall Anglo-Russian relations in Europe. As a footnote, the Afghan agent, fearful for his own life in all this turmoil, had requested some British flags to keep his house safe. Sykes sent him ten and reported, 'Meshed is now quite gay with British and Russian bunting'.

It was at this point in his career that Sykes best showed his talent for reconciling apparently irreconcilable parties of Persians. And while he later had a whole regiment of British and Indian troops to back him up, in Meshed he was entirely on his own, with nothing but a tiny escort of *sowars*, totally outnumbered by the Russian Cossacks, not to mention the mob. It was here that his years of travelling in the country, learning its language and history, study- ing the Qoran and listening to the people in their own homes had finally paid off. He was also astute enough to make use of the experience of the new native attaché, Khan Ahmed Din Sahib, when discretion was required.

Throughout this episode Sykes had been sending a stream of cipher telegrams to Tehran denouncing Dabizha's total breach of the terms of the Convention. These caused the British to make a formal protest to the Russian Legation, who immediately tele- graphed back to Dabizha instructing him to be more co-operative with his counterpart. His attitude then improved, albeit briefly. Although the Russian Foreign Ministry was showing an outward spirit of co-operation with the British, there is no doubt that the Russian military were independently planning an invasion of Persia. In 1909 British Intelligence had acquired 'through a source in Persia' part of a Russian document that showed detailed plans for the occupation of whole of Persia outside the Russian zone, extending down to all the Persian Gulf ports.[4]

Sykes tried to relax through this very tense period by riding up to his country retreat at Jagharq once or twice a week with his colleagues. He was sometimes accompanied by Evelyn, who recalls that on one of these occasions she went out with the guns looking for big game.

An ibex was sighted on the far side of a gully, too far away to distinguish its sex. 'Can you see the ibex?' I was asked. 'And her little kid at foot, too!' Great excitement! None of our friends with their telescopic rifles had picked that out. After that I was always welcomed on the outings. At a practice shoot for our escort, I was given an army rifle, everyone watching eagerly to see what I could do with it. I was lucky and pulled off several 'bulls' but I found the kick a bit trying and refused to go on being trained.

The impression she gives is that Sykes had been keeping her kennelled up at home until this occasion. A Victorian wife in England would not have expected to go out shooting with the men and Evelyn had nothing to do but sit in the consulate compound all day. Given the unconventionally freewheeling upbringing that her liberal father had given her, it is not hard to imagine her quietly champing at the bit. The memoir written by her youngest daughter, Elinor, gives an idea of the limitations of Evelyn's life in Persia.

[She] never visited the bazaars or the mosques, nor did she learn to read or write Persian. She could not accompany my father on

---

[4] This document is now in the OIOC, ref. I/MIL/17/15/26.

his shooting expeditions nor ride or play tennis because of child bearing. The only company she had were occasional visits from my father's two unmarried sisters . . . They wrote books, spoke Persian, rode with my father and criticised my mother and her children freely. In her loneliness my mother turned to gardening and made the consulate garden a place of great beauty.

While this excitement had been taking place at Meshed, the serious work of the revolution had been going on elsewhere. In the spring the Nationalists took over Tabriz. Another force was formed at Rasht on the Caspian coast and began to advance on Tehran, with reinforcements pouring in from Baku. At the same time the Bakhtiari tribe, led by Sardar Asad at Isfahan, raised a force two thousand strong and raced northwards towards Tehran, which they had to reach before a Russian force of three thousand, which had landed at Enzeli in support of Muhammad Ali Shah, got there first. This they did, the combined force avoiding the lines of the defending Cossack Brigade, and took Tehran with little opposition. The Russian troops gradually withdrew; Muhammad Ali Shah agreed to abdicate and left the country for Odessa, with a pension of £16,600. He was succeeded on 24th June 1909 by his son Ahmad Shah, who was still a minor. A regent was appointed, who was succeeded in the following year by Sykes's old friend Nasir ul-Molk.[5]

There was a brief political honeymoon, which soon descended into intrigues among the various factions. On one side were the Democrats, who advocated complete separation of religious from political power and distribution of land to the peasantry. The most famous of these was Taqizadeh, a striking figure and a blazing nationalist, who later turned to the Germans for support. On the other side were the Moderate party, equally interested in reform but favouring a more gradualist approach, taking account of

---

[5] He had been educated at Balliol, where he made friends with Curzon, Grey and Spring Rice. In 1906 he was made Prime Minister and attempted reforms, but he was too honest and was arrested and sentenced to death by Muhammad Ali on 14th December 1907. He was rescued by the prompt intervention of George Churchill at the Legation (see E.G. Browne, *Persian Revolution*, pp. 162–3, and private letters from one of his descendants). Some writers have it that his friends Curzon and Grey arranged for his rescue, but this is incorrect.

Persian realities and untainted by superficial European ideas. For this they were branded as reactionary. Prominent among them were the leading mujtahid Behbehani and Nasir ul-Molk.

In Meshed the Russians had become extremely unpopular: the Cossacks had caused particular offence to Persian sensibilities by bathing naked in the river with their horses. The Aghazadeh, the new head of the Shrine (son of Agha Muhammad Kazim Khorasani, one of the leading Persian divines based at Najaf in Mesopotamia, the holiest city of Shia Islam), had declared a general boycott on Russian goods, which extended to his even refusing to take sugar with his tea – at least in public. There were also some minor disturbances. The diary records, 'Much shooting in the night. It turned out to be the police, who had been unpaid by the Governor-General. Their commander was trying to disarm them by getting them to fire volleys into the air and thus use up all their ammunition, removing the weapons before they could reload.'

In August Dabizha, in the hope of emulating Sykes's successes, decided to lay on a Russian gymkhana. It was not a success. Sykes scornfully reported, 'Poor circus tricks – the horses were so starved that they had to be beaten into a canter! The Persians were critical of the Cossacks playing the accordion on horseback and of their shabby uniforms.' But while the Russian horses were unfed and the Cossacks without decent uniforms, Prince Dabizha was prospering by extracting protection money of up to 5,000 tomans each from several landowners. Those who did not pay up were duly visited by his Cossacks. When Sykes reported this to the Legation, it caused something of a stir and reports of Dabizha's conduct were passed back to St Petersburg. According to M. Courtin, the French manager of the Russian Bank at Meshed, with whom Sykes had a later conversation, 'the Russian authorities at both Tehran and St Petersburg are dissatisfied with Dabizha's conduct and wish to remove him; they are also determined to investigate his bribe taking'. ('Very interesting' noted Barclay.) Sykes went on to say that trade and agriculture were in a bad way and that 'both the Governor-General and the Karguzar state that only the Majlis and the Russian consul are making any money'.

Sykes had a personal reason for doing battle with Dabizha,

which involved his wife. One afternoon in September Evelyn and the children went for a carriage drive, escorted by two of the *sowars*. They unhitched the horses from the carriage and sat down outside the gate of an orchard to take tea. The Persian lessee of the orchard, who was a Russian subject, arrived, insulted the *sowars* by calling them *pedar sukhte* ('son of a burned father') and played with their loaded guns. He then untied the horses and set them loose. The *sowars* were most restrained under this provocation and eventually recovered the horses and took the family home. The incensed Sykes lodged a complaint at the Russian court at Meshed and the man was eventually fined the paltry sum of fifteen roubles. Sykes, not content with this, then sent several pages of statements to the Legation demanding proper satisfaction from the Russian Legation. Sir George Barclay minuted: 'Sykes had better not press for the case to be brought before the Russian Legation . . . If he knows what we know, that Major Sykes' tenure of the post is trembling in the balance, in Sykes' interest I shall do nothing. I do not share Sykes' view of the enormity of Dabizha's fault.'

There had been some discussion about bringing Meshed under the control of the Foreign Office rather than the India Office, and putting in a Levant Consular Service staff member to replace Sykes, but Sykes argued cogently against this when he heard about it later. Barclay could not understand why, when Sykes was 'always bewailing the state of affairs and the impossibility of finding one honest Persian, he wanted to stay on in Meshed', but like many other Englishmen who have got to know Persia, Sykes had become firmly attached to the great charm, humour and humanity of its people.

Barclay had mixed views about Sykes. In another despatch from Sykes to the Legation in which he reported, 'the Karguzar informed me of the appointment of the Ala us–Saltaneh as Foreign Minister. I am much pleased, as I have known him and his son for many years', Barclay underlined the offending words and commented, 'Surely it ought to be "We are" for so exalted a personage!' Sykes had become puffed up, but this was hardly surprising. He was isolated from the Legation at Tehran, which was run by the Foreign Office and not by the Government of India, to which he reported, and he was up against the Russians, with all of their bottomless resources and backed up by their army, only 150 miles away across the border. He was under pressure from all sides, with nothing to support him but his own wits and his very limited resources. It is not surprising that he felt he was fighting single-handed.

In October Evelyn was expecting her third son, Edward, and Sykes requested fifteen days' casual leave to take his family to Krasnovodsk, the strategic Russian port at the head of the Transcaspian railway, to send them home. He found Krasnovodsk 'swarming with officials as usual, but espionage seemed rather slacker than usual. In other words, I was not followed about.'

On his way he made a courtesy call on the Russian Governor-General of Ashgabad, General Evremiov. Evremiov opened the conversation with an abrupt demand that the British should return the family of the chief of the Afghan Jamshidi clan, who were being held hostage. This tribe had been causing constant trouble across the frontier and Sykes was surprised to discover that the Russians should admit to supporting them. He explained that the Afghan authorities were very difficult to move and also inquired whether, if the family were handed over, the Jamshidis would cease to raid across the frontier.

General Evremiov next said that he wondered whether the British Government meant to work with Russia and added that he personally admired the English: but that he did not believe that we really meant to be their friends. He asked whether the British would obstruct Russian proposals to improve the roads around Meshed. I replied that of course we would not.

He then asked me to express a view on whether it was necessary to retain two squadrons of Cossacks at Meshed during the winter. I frankly replied that, with Russia's gigantic military resources, the locking up of two *sotnias* of Cossacks was a mere bagatelle. He appreciated the compliment and replied that the holding of India by seventy-five thousand British troops was the military marvel of the age.

Finally he escorted us arm in arm back to our hotel and in saying goodbye with the utmost cordiality, said that next time I passed through I must be his guest or he would never forgive me. In conclusion I venture to think that the hours we spent with His Excellency have tended to remove some misgivings and doubts and to improve our relations with so important a person as the Governor-General of Transcaspia.

Sykes, in spite of the pompous tone of his report to the Legation, had obviously got the measure of his Russian rival. He does not mention how much of Evremiov's eventual cordiality was owing to the shared consumption of vodka and how much to his own diplomacy. Sykes was a big, convivial bear of a man, which no doubt appealed to the Russian. And while he may have been pompous, it should be remembered that genuine modesty was no virtue in Persia and still less so among the officers of Imperial Russia.

At the end of December 1909 Sykes had a call from the Young Persians, the young, European-educated, would-be patriotic reformers.

They declared that they would resign from the Majlis unless the Rukn ud-Dowleh, the Karguzar and the Vizier were immediately dismissed. I advised them to be less hot-headed, and persuaded them that the Governor-General was as good as one could get and was certainly not in Russian hands, even though he had to work with them and put up with their treatment. If they worked at small reforms they would eventually win the day. They wanted Nasir ul-Mulk as Governor-General, being 'a nonentity', which I resisted.

Sykes took a dim view of the pretensions of the Young Persians, who were scorned by the traditionalists for their affected modern dress and stiff collars, which had earned them the nickname of *fokoli* (from the French *faux-col*). He nevertheless did them the Persian courtesy of paying a return call shortly afterwards, when 'to my surprise, I was told that they had accepted my advice'. A fortnight later he invited them back for lunch. To his further surprise these young men, whom he and most of the Europeans, along with the traditionalist Persians, had long regarded as ignorant, bombastic, conceited and arrogant youths with half-baked 'modern' ideas acquired abroad, 'who had arrived here with a flourish of trumpets', had the good grace to inform him 'how grateful they were to me for having induced them to work with the Governor-General'. Rukn ud-Dowleh also thanked Sykes for helping him to establish good relations with the Young Persians. To have brought two such disparate parties together was an achievement of which very few foreigners would have been capable. It required great understanding, patience and, above all, courtesy – qualities in Sykes that were not revealed to his compatriots.

In the countryside, outside the relative security of Meshed, banditry and murder were common. The gang leaders were allowed to operate freely, provided that they shared their business profits with the authorities. The first brigand to feature in the consular diary for 1910 was Salar Khan, who was being pursued towards Torbat-i Haidari by a force of two hundred government *sowars*. This was causing concern in high quarters: 'The Aghazadeh (the Custodian of the Shrine) is in a very evil frame of mind. He and others are daily praying that Salar Khan should either escape with his papers or be killed and his papers burned. He has kept an account of all the money which he has given to the Aghazadeh and others, which he will use in his defence if captured.' He was surrounded in his fort at Aliek for a while. One of his Baluchi spies was caught, had his ears cut off and was paraded in the Torbat bazaar, but when the Persian commander was slightly wounded the force withdrew. Salar Khan fled and disappeared into the Lut desert. 'The question now will be to find the money that he has buried.' A week later Salar Khan sent a message to the Torbat consulate requesting British protection, on the grounds that his grandfather had come from Baluchistan, to which the Legation telegraphed back pithily, 'Not sufficient reason'. Two months later Sykes reported that Salar Khan had brazenly turned up in Tehran, where he 'has squared the authorities and is returning to Khorasan loaded with honours!'

Another robber chief, Timur Khan, had been operating on the Yazd–Tabas road. Sykes had asked the Governor-General to have him captured. 'He has been caught and is being brought in to Meshed. As he was protected by both the Governor of Tabas and by the leading mujtahid, who took a percentage of the profits, it will be of interest to see what revelations this bandit may make. In any case, the action of the Rukn ud-Dowleh shows that he really does his best to please me.'

Nearly sixty miles west of Meshed lies the city of Nishapur, near which were a number of Ismaili villages. The Ismailis were followers of the Aga Khan – himself a British subject – and, as such, were entitled to British protection. They were regarded as heretical Muslims and consequently fair game for the orthodox. Many of them had been persecuted, robbed and even murdered and, although Nishapur lay outside Khorasan and therefore outside Sykes's jurisdiction, he did as much as he could to help them, not least because he had met the Aga Khan during their voyage out to India together and had been entertained by him at Karachi. After one particular outrage Sykes extracted a promise from the Persian government that the Governor of Nishapur would be dismissed, that the murderers would be jailed for life and that the stolen property would be restored. (There had been some difficulty in obtaining this promise since the Minister of the Interior had already received an advance on account from the revenues of Nishapur 'which affected his attitude'.) The Aga Khan's agent in Bombay expressed his gratitude for Sykes's intervention.

Sykes's own peace was also disturbed by robbers.

Last year a robber of Torkoba established a reign of terror in the Jagharq valley. I insisted on his being hunted down and he was finally caught, but although he had many murders proved against him he was not killed. The reason for this was that he was a seyyid. He was released after his tendons had been cut. He has recently raped a girl and for this he has been hanged. The Governor-General had offered the Chief of Police 100 tomans if his life were spared.

This chief of police was a newly appointed man of Turkish origin from the reforming party who was proving more zealous and effective than any of his predecessors. The merchants and general public all supported him, but the authorities, including the Young Persians, who ran the police, opium department, security department, municipality and courts of justice, opposed his honest efforts to establish order. He doggedly persevered for some time, but such was the lack of finance for his operations that by the end of the year he had become high-handed and corrupt, assaulting and arresting British and Russian subjects with demands for money to such an extent that both legations pressed for him to be dismissed. This was but a brief check to his career and soon afterwards he was appointed chief of police at Shiraz.

At the end of February the Asaf ud-Dowleh, who had been Governor-General when Sykes first arrived in Meshed, died. Sykes remembered him fondly: 'He had always settled all my cases on my own terms, in which connection when I first came to Meshed, he settled more than sixty cases in a few weeks. He was a very capable Governor of the old corrupt type and so far I have not met anyone with equal experience and capacity among the Young Persians.'

Discussions had been going on for a year about closing down the Torbat-i Haidari consulate, which had served its purpose. Sykes had written to Barclay: 'Until we had our finger on the pulse of Transcaspia, alarmist reports of Russian preparations were constant and caused numerous scares. Now that is all a thing of the past.' However, it had been decided to maintain the Consulate's existence for as long as the Russians were operating their cordon sanitaire along the borders of Khorasan. In February agreement was reached with the Russians, who also withdrew their consulate on the Persian Gulf at Bandar Abbas, and it was wound up, with an Indian native agent installed in its place.

Although this agreement had been reached between the British and Russian governments, Prince Dabizha, again making trouble, sought to diminish British prestige by putting about rumours that the British Consulate-General in Meshed was also to be closed. Indeed, for a time the effect of the closure of the Torbat consulate was that it was widely believed that the British were about to abandon Persia altogether.

In May the Sykes family went on home leave for eight months. Evelyn gives an account of it:

In 1910 our leave came round again. I went ahead to find a house. I had Frank and Charles and a nurse with me. At Baku in the night thieves broke into the hotel, shot the poor old porter – he had taken me off the boat that day – and made off with the cash. We then had to wait a couple of days for a new escort. We travelled through Tiflis and the Caucasus to Batoum, then by steamers to Constantinople and Naples and Marseilles, then across France by train to Calais.

We returned to Meshed in October. What a cortège: a governess for Frank, a nanny for Charles and the baby Edward. We travelled via the Hook of Holland to Berlin. We found we had some hours to wait for the train to Alexandrovsk at midnight, so took seats for *Götterdämmerung* and afterwards picked up the children and nurses. At the last moment it was found that Nannie had left a package behind. A man was hastily sent off for it. Percy stood on the platform anxiously looking out for the man and parcel. When the bell of departure rang out, a porter tried to keep Percy back, but a powerful thump on the chest sent him staggering and Percy was on the train. As he had all our passports, money etc. we might have had a tiresome time in Russia until he arrived.

Returning, the family took the usual train to Baku, ferry across the Caspian to Krasnovodsk and train to Ashgabad, where carriages for their party and wagons for the mountain of luggage met them.

We soon settled back into the comfortable Consulate. . . . The two Indian cooks were still with us, but the Chargé d'Affaires holding the post while we were on leave complained bitterly of having felt ill all the time. I was not surprised when in the kitchen a parade of utensils and cloths were produced for inspection, the latter absolutely black. I had a bonfire to see that they were destroyed, after which all went well.

Their fruit garden now began to bear. Evelyn had imported stone fruit trees from Tashkent when they first took over the Consulate. Gooseberries, currants and strawberries imported from England also grew well, but the cherries were disappointing. She moved the cherry trees to the foot of a wall and the next year they started bearing cherries as large as plums.

Water in Meshed was scarce. It was delivered once every eighteen hours and was paid for by the hour. It came sometimes by day and sometimes by night. 'We used to hear the gardeners shouting to each other as they opened or closed the *jubes*, as the irrigation channels were called. During the summer we had our camp beds put out on the top of the flat verandah. It was lovely sleeping out in that climate, to be woken only by the pigeons going off for a drink at dawn.'

15

Saving Persia single-handed

WHILE THE SYKESES had been away the situation at Meshed had changed considerably. Sykes's first report after his return, dated 9th December 1910, summed up his thoughts:

> When I went on leave in the spring the Young Persians had been at Meshed for four months and, having got the upper hand of the Old Persians, had begun to quarrel among themselves. The Chief of Police has been dismissed; the Chief Justice, who was corrupt from the first, has also been dismissed, but the other three Young Persians are still Deputy Governor, Chef de Cabinet and Commander-in-Chief, though there are rumours that the latter, too, is about to be dismissed.

The Young Persians were the first callers at the Consulate on Sykes's return, and the circus of unreality resumed:

> The Deputy Governor came to me with the following scheme and an urgent appeal for my support in carrying it through. He pointed out that the present revenue was inadequate to meet the expenses of government and he then went on to say that his scheme, which everyone approved of, was to augment the revenue by trebling the taxes. As however, a few people might give trouble, he wished, in the first place, to raise and equip an additional force of one thousand five hundred well

armed men and he was expecting sanction from Tehran to take this step. I ventured to enquire how he proposed to raise the money with which to equip this force, whereupon he naively replied that this question was quite easy as he had no doubt that either the English or the Russian Bank would lend him 250,000 tomans, or £50,000, on the excellent security of the revenues of Khorasan. He concluded that he had determined to suppress the newspapers until his scheme was in good working order.

The Ala us-Sultan also came to me with a rival scheme which was to select five honest and truthful men who would be appointed ministers, with absolute power of life and death. These incorruptible Persians should appoint fifty equally honest and truthful officials: Persia would be despotically ruled, the taxes would be increased, the press abolished and other similar measures taken until everything was in perfect working order. Such are the schemes of the two leading Young Persians of Khorasan!

Many well-to-do Persians are utterly weary of the present chronic state of unrest, tempered by anarchy, and are resigning themselves to the idea of ultimately accepting Russian rule. The Qaim Maqam, head of the descendants of the Imam at the Shrine and a very large landowner, said to me most frankly that he was thinking of leaving Persia and of not returning until Russian rule was established, as neither his life nor his property was safe. The fact appears to be that the new regime has been given a fair trial and has been found to be singularly wanting as, even though corruption has been lessened to some extent, expenditure has been increased and new taxes have been raised which hit every class and, above all, security has become less and less.

Only a day or two after his return the important frontier post of Bajgiran, on the road to Ashgabad, was seized by robbers and there were further disturbances along the frontier at Dareh Gaz. A previously respectable citizen of Nishapur, who had been unjustly stripped of his property by the previously incorruptible chief of police, had turned to banditry, seizing the district of Gonabad on the edge of the Lut and raiding right up to Torbat.

In January 1911 the mujtahids at Najaf sent a telegram to the Meshed Majlis ordering them to organize a boycott of Russian goods. One of the Meshed mujtahids theatrically tore off his turban, made of Russian cotton, and threw it into the stove. Other patriotic members of the Majlis followed suit and in a gesture of Persian mourning, ripped off their shirts and threw them into the fire as well. Cotton, tea and sugar were all to be banned: the people were to drink milk and honey instead. However, as so often in Persia, the public theatricals were but a mask. Sykes reported that a few days later an Indian merchant took delivery of forty camel loads of Russian sugar and sold them at an unusually large profit. The boycott, although it had been ordered by the most senior divines, was not popular. A meeting was held, in which a hostile crowd asked the mullas to suggest just where these banned staples might be obtained from, if they were not to be got from Russia. The nationalists sent threatening letters to merchants dealing in Russian goods but within a fortnight the boycott had fizzled out.

Banditry was rife throughout Khorasan, but some of the more notable culprits were being dealt with in spectacular fashion. Muhammad Geldi Khan, the chief of the Göklan tribe of the Turkoman, met a traditionally Persian end. He was invited to Nardin by the governor and treated as a distinguished guest. Once asleep, he was tied up and his men were all killed. His seal was taken off his finger and used to invite the rest of his followers, who duly received the same treatment. He himself was blown from a gun. If the Turkoman chief had read any Persian history he would have known better than to accept such an invitation.

A minor incident in the June diary was filed as the 'Case of the Dak Sowar'. 'The Kariz agent reports that a certain Sarvar and a certain Gholam Nabi of Ghurian told a friend of theirs that they had seized a man who had saddlebags and said he was carrying the English post, and that they had murdered him and found only papers. I am following up this clue.' The Legation's comment, in red ink, was 'Sherlock!' – a change from Napoleon.

Although the bandits had little fear of the Persian authorities, they were careful not to 'play with the tail of the English fox'. The local brigand of Nishapur was told by one of his spies that the

17. The fourteenth-century madraseh of Khargird near Khaf, eastern Khorasan. Sykes presented tiles from the madraseh to the British Museum

18. Kurdish horsemen parading the heads of the supposed Turkoman robbers, Meshed

19. Big game country: the Dehane-i Gorgan, north-east of the mountains from Shahrud

20. The Turkoman chief, Muhammad Geldi Khan, and his wives. He was later blown from a cannon for brigandry

21. Pamirski Post, the Russo-Chinese frontier in the Pamirs

22. Shuja ul-Nizam, the Deputy Governor of Bandar Abbas, who was instrumental in obtaining the first recruits for the South Persia Rifles

23. First recruits of the South Persia Rifles

24. The Yazd police of 1916 . . .

25. . . . and robbers, who are about to be released by the Governor of Yazd

26. Isfahan, the Meidan and the Masjid-i Shah

27. Triumphal joint parade of South Persia Rifles and Cossacks, in front of the Âli Qapu, Isfahan

28. Shiraz, seen through the Darvazeh-i Qoran

29. Entry of the South Persia Rifles into Shiraz, November 1916

30. Tribal fort in south Persia

31. Saulat ud–Dowleh and his Qashqai horsemen, gathered to sign a treaty with Sykes

32. Sykes with Farman Farma (*right*) and Qavam ul-Molk (*centre*), the two principal personages of Shiraz, on whose support he depended during the South Persia Rifles occupation of the city

Imperial Bank of Persia was sending a large sum of money that way under escort. Instead of congratulating the spy, the brigand beat him, pulled out his beard and sent him to the Governor-General for punishment, with a message that he knew better than to touch English money.

As an illustration of the total absence not only of order but of law as well, Sykes sent an anecdote, entitled 'A Case of Persian Justice', to Barclay at the Legation. One afternoon he had heard the roar of a mob and in a few minutes five hundred people were in the Consulate, all wildly excited because a certain Khan Agha had been hanged but the rope had broken. He had been reprieved and deposited unconscious in the Consulate garden, where he later came to. Sykes gave instructions for the man to be looked after but a few hours later was surprised to receive a request from the chief of police that he should be handed back. Still greater was his astonishment when he was informed that the Russian Consulate also wanted the man. By this time there were police pickets and Cossacks watching the Consulate. Sykes had meanwhile got in touch with the Karguzar, who asked him to keep the man until his case could be settled. He continued with his account:

> Khan Agha was a simple young village man, who had been to spend the night with his uncle at a neighbouring village. On his return home he was told by the village barber that he had found the body of his father-in-law, who had been murdered on his way back from a trip to buy bullocks. Khan Agha went to the spot and found the tracks of three men, who turned out to belong to a local gang of brigands. The twist in the story was that Khan Agha's wife had recently become the mistress of an *Akhond* [religious teacher], who persuaded the dead man's son to charge Khan Agha with the murder, the *Akhond* hoping thereby to be able to marry the woman and get possession of Khan Agha's property. Khan Agha was arrested and although several witnesses, including the two leading mujtahids of Nishapur, had declared that the case was a trumped-up one and ordered his release, the son of the local governor was bribed to send him to Meshed, where he was imprisoned again. Meanwhile, a minor

mujtahid of Nishapur was bribed to draw up a death sentence, which was sent to the leading mujtahid of Meshed who, for another bribe, confirmed it. A leading Shrine official then offered to save Khan Agha if he would make over to him all his property; but the young man replied that he preferred to die rather than live as a beggar. The official then went to the opposite party and arranged for them to bribe the acting Governor-General to carry out the sentence. A total of 1,980 tomans [£400 at the time] was paid in bribes to the six parties concerned.

After the execution had failed through the miraculous breaking of the rope the son went to the Chief Mujtahid and demanded that either Khan Agha should be hanged again or that his money should be returned, to which the reply was given that the condemned man, on his way to the gallows, had called on Hazrat-i Abbas[1] to save him and that, since the Saint had performed a miracle, it would be impious to hang Khan Agha again. Moreover, strictly speaking, the money had been paid to obtain the passing of the sentence, which had indeed been done, so that his side of the bargain had been fulfilled.

The Chief Mujtahid was much upset to realize that Sykes, who had always respected him, now knew that he had sentenced an innocent man to death for money. Sykes then approached the Karguzar, who told him that he knew that the case was made-up, and he had little difficulty in securing an order from the Chief Mujtahid that the death sentence should not be carried out. Meshed was indeed a Holy City.

During Sykes's absence on leave Prince Dabizha had been recalled, to be replaced by Grigoriev, an old acquaintance who, in a gratifying new spirit of co-operation, immediately suggested having weekly meetings to co-ordinate their consular reports to the respective legations in Tehran. However, in April Dabizha returned. Despite the Convention, the Russians were still setting their sights on the route to India. A small sign of this, which 'came into' Sykes's hands, was a copy of the instructions given by Dabizha

---

[1] The brother of Imam Hussein, martyred at Kerbela in AD 680.

to a Hazara[2] seyyid who had promised to go to Afghanistan as a spy but whose heart had failed him. He had been asked to find out everything, from bridges to arms and from river fords to details of the population. As Sykes commented, 'he has been asked to produce an Encyclopaedia'.

There was a rapid turnover of governors–general at this period. One who stayed only briefly was the Sahib-i Ikhtiyar ('Possessor of Authority'), who was replaced after a few months by Rukn ud-Dowleh, who, having 'paid highly for the post, considers that he <u>owes his appointment to the British Legation</u> [underlined in red by Barclay] and so may be expected to be most friendly'. On the Sahib's departure at the end of June Sykes wrote, 'He is the most agreeable Persian I have ever met and it is a great pity that he should be so hopelessly incompetent and corrupt. Of course one knows that an honest Persian is as rare as a black pearl, but there are limits which they usually observe.' ('They say this man may be Minister of Interior – He won't stay long I should think under the Shuster regime', Barclay noted.)

Morgan Shuster was a young, liberal and anti-imperialist American brought in by the Majlis to put the Persian finances in order. He was chosen because he came from a neutral country that was seen to be progressive. With Persia now practically bankrupt and no Persian individual or institution able to remedy the situation, Shuster was appointed Treasurer-General. To enforce the collection of state revenues he raised a regiment of well-paid and effective Treasury gendarmes. In command of this force he wished to appoint Major Stokes, the British military attaché, who was sympathetic to the Democrats and a friend of their leader Taqizadeh. The Russians, however, objected strongly to this infringement of their sphere of influence and forced Stokes out. He was replaced by the American Colonel Merrill. Shuster's lack of subtlety and oriental *savoir-faire* made him many enemies, not least the Russians. They had no wish to see Persia becoming prosperous and free of their clutches, and in the end they forced the Majlis to dismiss him.[3]

---

[2] The Hazara were Shia Afghans of Mongolian descent, living mainly in the centre of Afghanistan.
[3] See Morgan Shuster, *The Strangling of Persia* (London, 1912).

The Young Persians then began to impose new taxes on the landlords and merchants, most of which were in fact pocketed by the Young Persians themselves. This, combined with the almost total breakdown of order throughout the country, led to demands for the restoration of the exiled Muhammad Ali Shah and a return to the old way of doing things. The landowners went back to their old habit of hoarding grain and, despite the good harvest, engineered a scarcity of basic food supplies, thereby raising the prices to famine levels. This was a further cause of discontent which was easy for Dabizha to exploit.

In June 1911 Sykes reported that Dabizha was paying Yusef Herati, his principal agent, to instigate riots in support of Muhammad Ali Shah. Yusuf Herati was an agile *luti* gang leader, frequently wanted by the police. The Persian authorities, because of the Russian consular protection given to him, could not lay a hand on him. Barclay minuted: 'Poklevski [the Russian minister at Tehran] will telegraph reminding Dabizha of his injunctions to observe a neutral attitude.' Sykes also reported that there was much local support for the ex-Shah, who was about to return to Persia, and that the pro-Constitutionalist Agha Akhond Khorasani of Najaf had issued a fatwa to the effect that the Democrats were not Muslims and should be treated as infidels.

In July Muhammad Ali landed in Persia, prompting a stream of frantic telegrams from Sykes to the Legation. The political, religious and ethical confusion of the times is graphically related in this report from the diary. The police had tried to arrest a Shrine official accused of embezzlement, who had taken refuge in the house of a respected mujtahid, Agha Mirza Ibrahim. A crowd had gathered to protest against the violation of his sanctuary, and a tent to entertain them was pitched inside the courtyard of the Agha's house, at the expense of the notorious Muavin ut-Tujjar (deputy chief merchant). Various officials, in an attempt to calm the situation, called on the Agha and dismissed the police, but Dabizha then intervened to exploit the situation for his own ends and sent his men, with some money, to call on the holy man and persuade him to break off negotiations and proceed to the Shrine. This he agreed to, and a camp grew up round him. The diary continues:

The demands now formulated were: the abolition of the Court of Justice, prohibition of the sale of liquor and the recognition of the inviolability of the sanctuary. These conditions were agreed to by the local authorities but were not ratified by Tehran. The excitement increased and the roar from the Shrine became as loud as a football match and, as the Agha was always supported by the Russians, he was encouraged to make further demands as follows – (a) the abolition of the tax on pack animals and (b) the closing of all government offices and their reorganisation by local men of proven honesty.

During the night there was some firing, mainly indulged in to show that the warriors were alert, and in the morning the mob found the Shrine surrounded by a body of police and soldiers. To show how the Persians grade their own valour, the Persian police were disarmed and sent home and only the Turkish members of the force were armed!

Dabizha's agent Yusef Herati opened proceedings by firing at the police, who replied. There were a few casualties, especially among the spectators and, as honour was now satisfied, negotiations were opened. In the evening the Karguzar and other officers visited the Shrine and induced the Agha, who was by now very tired of the whole business, which was interfering with his hours for opium smoking, to return home.

I have made inquiries from every quarter and I hear that my colleague supported the rising until <u>he received a telegram from his Legation to the effect that he should stop</u> [underlined by Barclay]. As I had reported the matter to Tehran it looks as if this telegram has something to do with his instructions. I may add that the Manager of the Bank, who has been many years in Persia and is in close touch with the Persian community, absolutely confirmed what I had heard.

There is no doubt that if the rioters had gained the upper hand, <u>they would have declared for the Shah</u> [underlined by Barclay]. So far as I can learn, the large majority of the people are so tired of the tyranny of the Young Persians that they will welcome the ex-Shah, should he regain the throne.

Meanwhile on 25th July four hundred Turkoman horsemen had crossed the mountains and reached Shahrud, which they occupied on behalf of Muhammad Ali, who was advancing on Tehran via Mazanderan, on the coast, with a large force from Persia and Russia. He sent telegrams to the Governor-General at Meshed, the Director of Telegraphs, the Commander-in-Chief, the head of the Shrine and the Chief of Bojnurd to announce his arrival and demand their support. The chief of the telegraph office prudently referred these to Sykes, who duly informed the Karguzar, who in turn suggested that instructions should be requested fromTehran. The reply came that the telegrams should not be delivered and that the whole matter should be kept secret.

This was fortunately done, as, had the news leaked out, the rioters would have been encouraged to seize Meshed . . . Throughout, both parties appealed to me to intervene but, under the peculiar circumstances, I limited myself to giving advice in the direction of moderation. However, the attaché Mubarik Ali Shah is a persona grata with the mullas and it is to him that the chief credit is due for the riots ending without any serious results such as the looting of the bazaars and the introduction of a brigade of Russian troops. The Young Persians, with their utter lack of tact, wished to start the obnoxious new taxes immediately, but I persuaded them, at the urgent request of the Agha, to wait for four or five days until the excitement had died down.

The lesson to be drawn from these riots, which are likely to break out again, is that under the new order taxes are becoming higher and higher, interference of all sorts is greater and greater, security is less and all commodities are much dearer. Finally, each department is a law unto itself. The advantages to Khorasan, except to the officials themselves, have so far failed to appear. Indeed it is difficult to avoid the conclusion that the Persians are attempting to organize a scheme of government for which they are traditionally, mentally and morally unfitted.

No sooner was the rioting over than Sykes reported, 'Dabizha, to consolidate his influence, is offering Russian protection freely but Persians with liberal views are most unwilling to accept it. The presidents of both the Anjumans [revolutionary societies] and other most respectable Persians have asked me for British protection. I have referred the matter to Tehran.'

While Sykes may have been ridiculed for exaggerating the importance of his role in preventing the Russians from installing their puppet Muhammad Ali, he was regarded by all parties in Meshed as an honest broker, sympathetic to all sides and impartial.

Meshed itself was quiet for the time being but the ex-Shah was on the move again. 'Muhammad Ali left Astarabad for Mazanderan on 30th July with a force of a thousand Turkoman and a band of desperadoes, some of whom are possibly Europeans and the majority of whom are Russian subjects. He is now believed to be at Larijan. The four hundred Turkoman who reached Shahrud on 25th July were reinforced and started for Tehran. The Persian government has apparently offered a reward of 100,000 tomans for his murder.' A week later, after the mullas had once more changed sides, Sykes cabled: 'The mujtahids of Najaf have declared the ex-Shah an infidel and the faithful are exhorted to defend their country against him. Quite a number of young men have gone off to win the blood money on his head.'

Persians still believe that the mujtahids, particularly some of the senior ones at Najaf, were agents of the British. The late Shah himself held this view. The belief goes back to the Oudh Bequest of 1849, a fund set up in India for the welfare of British Indian pilgrims to the Shia holy sites in Ottoman Mesopotamia. In 1899, after complaints that the mujtahids were misappropriating these funds, the British Residency at Bushire appointed supervisors to control the mujtahids in charge of the distribution of the fund. In 1903 it occurred to Arthur Hardinge, the British Minister at Tehran, that use could be made of this contact with the mujtahids, whom he saw as a last resort to prevent the Shah from selling his country to Russia. A clumsy and indiscreet approach was made to them, which they had to decline since they could not be seen to be dealing directly with the British. Another attempt in this direction was made with a 'loan' of £2,000 (about £100,000 today) to the Shrine at Meshed through the Imperial Bank of Persia. It was all very irregular and Hardinge wrote that he was doing all that he could with the clerical party, 'but it is rather a delicate matter to work with them without . . . transgressing the bounds of diplomatic propriety'. Subsequent Russian propaganda successfully branded many of these anti-Russian patriots as agents of the British.

Muhammad Ali made good progress and on 12th August Sykes telegraphed, 'Government troops at Damghan have surrendered and joined the Turkoman. Ex-Shah apparently waiting result of his engagement at Sari. All important hereditary chiefs desire his success.' (Barclay minuted, 'All Mazanderan is for M-A.')

By the following week Muhammad Ali's forces had moved even further westwards towards Tehran: 'The Turkoman have passed through Semnan . . . A battle is expected in a day or two, but since Persians hate fighting, the unexpected may happen. Everyone in Khorasan is waiting to see which side will win. Revenue is not being sent in at all. The Vizier told me that the Chief of Bojnurd had actually despatched 20,000 tomans to the Treasury, but he sent after it to get it back!'

The unexpected did happen and the ex-Shah's forces were defeated in some small engagements in Mazanderan. In early September 1911 he fled back across the border to Ashgabad, waiting for an opportunity to return.

With Muhammad Ali out of the way for the time being, the Meshed government decided to reorganize the police force, so inadequate during the rioting. The split in the Young Persian movement made things no easier. The new chief of police confessed to Sykes that he was not acceptable to his officers, as they were Democrats and he was a member of the Party of Union and Progress. He also told him that the first night he went on his rounds, every single policeman was asleep. And so in September 'it was decided to dismiss all the Persians in the police on the grounds that they are cowards and corrupt. A hundred Hazaras and a hundred Turks are being engaged. It is interesting to note what the Persians think of themselves!'

The new recruits however, were a disappointment and less than a month later Sykes reported, 'Fourteen of our Indian ex-sepoys have been engaged as policemen. They will be employed at night, as they are believed to be less likely to commit burglaries than the Turks.'

A picture of the state of the army at Meshed appears in a letter from Sykes to the Government of India at Simla, describing a conversation with Mirza Muhammad Aslan Khan, the 'newswriter' at Herat, across the border in Afghanistan, who had come over to Meshed to report in person.

> The Afghan Army, about which he collects detailed information for the Military Attaché, is very like that of Persia so far as officers are concerned, although they are not the poltroons that command the troops of the Shah. They serve to any age; the Chief of the Artillery is over ninety and requires two men to aid him when he walks. Our Meshed Artillery general is of the same age and equally infirm. The Afghan soldiers receive their pay regularly every two months and believe that they owe it to the British subsidy . . .
>
> The Governor of Herat, Muhammad Sarwar Khan, is a man of 70 and most energetic. He tries as far as possible that he alone shall be permitted to rob, and punishes all other cases of extortion and robbery which, however, continue to be frequent.
>
> The general opinion in Herat is that Persia is doomed within a year or two, owing to its attempt at constitutional government and foolish love of new ideas. There is no newspaper and noone, not even an official, is allowed to subscribe to Persian or other newspapers. In this connection I send the Governor of Herat Persian newspapers and also the English illustrated papers with descriptions in Persian – and the newswriter is sure of the warmest welcome when he brings his budget of news to the Governor.

Throughout the turmoil Sykes had managed to promote British business. The Indian merchants at Meshed were disadvantaged by the length of time that it took them to get delivery of their goods, when the Russian railway brought competing goods all the way to Ashgabad, just 150 miles away across the border. One Meshed trader had brought some Manchester cotton as far as Kermanshah in the west, but the roads were so insecure that he had to send it back and bring it up through India, since the British had made the east the only safe part of Persia.

Sykes had worked hard to organize a new postal system and in August was able to write a despatch headed 'English Boots for Meshed'. 'My first attempt to open up trade through the parcel post has been most successful. The Indian trader can clear 40% profit on ammunition boots and a little less on walking boots. As he receives the goods in a month he can turn over his money four or five times a year and so will soon be rich.'

The carpet industry was stirred up by the German company I.G. Farben, which opened up an agency in Meshed for the sale of its aniline dyes, and distributed free samples to the dyers. These were much easier to use than the traditional cochineal, walnut shells, pomegranate skins and other vegetable dyes. However, within a month the dyers refused to use the artificial indigo, and went back to using the natural Indian product. The Indian indigo importers had been badgering Sykes for months. The new customs officers, ignorant of normal commercial practice, were levying the duty on the gross weight rather than the net weight. Since the indigo was packed in heavy wooden boxes, the duty payable had been effectively doubled. Sykes finally referred the case to the Legation, which eventually obtained an instruction from the customs administration in Tehran to the Meshed customs that duty should be charged only on the weight of the indigo and not on the weight of the timber. This simple matter took over five months to sort out.

The end of December 1911 coincided with the beginning of the Muslim month of Muharram, the month of commemoration of the deaths of the Shia martyrs in AD 680. During this month religious emotions run high, fuelled by processions of mourners beating their breasts with chains and slashing their heads with swords. Meshed was tense and trouble was expected. The Russians, fearing that they would be lynched, were sleeping with their jewels sewn into the lining of their clothes. There was a strong feeling in Meshed both against them and against the British for failing to protect Persia from Russian domination. Ostensibly to protect the European colony, Dabizha brought in a new squadron of Cossacks and a detachment of four machine-guns.

On 20th December the Tehran Majlis was surrounded by a

force of Bakhtiari tribesmen and police, supported by the Russians, who demanded the American Shuster's dismissal. There was also a large crowd of Constitutionalist women, with firearms hidden under their chadors, who came to demand that the men stand up to the ultimatum – the first occasion in modern history that women had been involved in a political demonstration.[4] The deputies were forced to comply, the Majlis was disbanded and Persia virtually ceased to exist as a state. On the same day in the north-west of Persia at Tabriz, there occurred a Russian outrage that has never been forgotten.

It began with a minor incident. Ten Russian soldiers had climbed on to the roof of a private house next to a police station to repair a telegraph line. The Persian police drove them off but two of them were killed by the Russians. The next day fighting broke out all over Tabriz and Russian troops started shelling houses, with much looting, destruction and killing of women and children. After ten days of this rapine, on 31st December, which was Ashura, the holiest day in Muharram, the Russians committed the ultimate sacrilege of hanging the chief mujtahid of Azerbaijan, the Saqat ul-Islam, along with fourteen other mullas and nationalists. The Russian puppet Shuja ud-Dowleh entered Tabriz in support of Muhammad Ali, causing further slaughter and looting. Russian gunboats were dispatched to Enzeli and their forces moved on Tehran to restore the ex-Shah.

At the same time the British agent at Ashgabad reported that 10,000 rifles had been sent westward by rail for Muhammad Ali's force. The importance of this report may have been exaggerated at home because a clerk in the Legation transcribed the figure on the incoming cable as 100,000 rifles. It is interesting to note from the Russian archives that when Lord Grey came under attack in London for his soft stance towards Russia over their atrocities in Tabriz and for the outrageous demands for 'reparations' from the Persians, the Russian ambassador to London informed St Petersburg that they should scale down their demands on Persia to save the Liberal Lord Grey from being removed.[5]

---

[4] See Shuster's memoirs, quoted by N. Keddie in *Qajar and the Rise of Reza Khan*.
[5] Jennifer Siegel, *Endgame*.

The hanging of the Saqat ul-Islam, if news of it had reached the holy city of Meshed during the Ashura processions, would have led to serious and uncontrollable anti-Russian rioting, which in turn would have led to a Russian military occupation. Sykes therefore used his influence with the Telegraph Office to prevent any news about the Tabriz outrage reaching Meshed until after the processions were over. Nevertheless, four hundred Russian infantry arrived in Meshed shortly afterwards and at the end of January Sykes reported that they began marching round the Shrine in force 'trailing their coats' in the hope of provoking a shot which would fire a conflagration. 'The Aghazadeh was terrified and, mindful of the fate of the Saqat ul-Islam at Tabriz, applied to me for British protection. This I refused and he has left Meshed. It is said that he has made £40,000 from his position at the Shrine.'

Sykes, however, was not intimidated by these alarms and held another Durbar for the King's birthday, which 'was celebrated in beautiful weather. Although there is certainly a strong feeling against British policy, many warm congratulations were received. In the evening the Consulate was illuminated and a dinner was given for forty leading Indians etc.' (Barclay's comment was 'Sykes is more demonstrably loyal than I, I fear!') There was further cause for celebration as Evelyn had been expecting another child. Her first daughter, Rachel, like Charles, was born in Meshed.

More Russian troops arrived, in breach of the Convention. Sykes protested to the Karguzar, who stated 'that the Russian Legation had informed the Persian Foreign Ministry that only eight hundred Russian troops were being sent to Khorasan, whereas more than two thousand have been sent. The explanation appears to be that the Russian Legation recommended a smaller force, but the Governor-General of Turkistan insisted it was far too small, and has not informed the Russian Legation of the change.' (Barclay minuted, 'This is a good example of its kind.')

The Russians, through their principal agents Yusef Herati, who was then sheltering in *bast* at the Russian Consulate-General, and Akbar Boland Tehrani, who was in the employ of the consulate, then organized a demonstration against the local police, demanding that Russians troops patrol the streets in their stead. Dabizha muddied the waters by telling the Karguzar that the return of the ex-Shah had been agreed to by both Powers and that Sykes's denial of this was due to instructions from the Government of India. 'The Persian authorities are in much perplexity and have appealed to me', wrote Sykes.

The British government was incensed by what it saw as Dabizha's independent actions in breach of the Convention. Telegrams flew between Tehran, London and St Petersburg. The Russian government accepted the British protests and on 3rd February 1912 Barclay sent a telegram to Sykes:

> RG [Russian Government] sent instructions to RC [Russian Consulates] at Rasht etc. to effect that they are to do their best to quell any agitation on behalf of Muhammad Ali. Please report whether your Russian colleague seems to be acting in the spirit of these instructions. I am endeavouring to get sharp instructions from St Petersburg for your Russian colleague, who appears to be acting in diametrical opposition to spirit of Russian Minister's instructions.

Sykes cabled back two days later: 'My Russian colleague has stated in writing that he will do what he can to calm the mob and that he has ceased to protect Yusef Herati.'

Dabizha was playing a deep game, keeping both his masters and the British in the dark. Barclay, returning from a meeting with the Russian Minister at Tehran, with whom he was on good terms, cabled to Sykes: 'Your Russian colleague reports that ninety percent of your province, as of all other provinces, are in favour of the ex-Shah and that the change of the two Governments from neutrality to opposition to him is likely to cause very serious disorders. What do you think of this view?' In a long letter to Barclay of 14th February 1912 Sykes summed up the situation. Through his encouragement, he said, the Persian authorities were doing their best to ignore all Russian provocations; even drunken Russian officers and men were being treated with deference.

While Dabizha was trumpeting abroad an astrologer's prediction that Muhammad Ali would reach Meshed and then march on Tehran, Grigoriev, the Russian First Secretary and a refreshing contrast to his superior, was horrified by all the proceedings, as were some of the Russian officers. General Redko, the military attaché, in a comradely gesture asked Sykes to teach some of the Russian officers to play polo. Finally Dabizha withdrew his *agents provocateurs* and the disturbances went briefly quiet – until the mob demanded the dismissal of the chief of police. Sykes's despatch continued the story:

> An appeal was made to me and, as the Chief of Police alone stood between Meshed and anarchy tempered by Russian administration, I took the unusual step of intervening and informed the Governor-General that the crisis was over and that it was unjust to dismiss the official who had saved the situation. As I threatened to agree with Prince Dabizha on the next occasion that he complained [to Tehran] of the Rukn ud-Dowleh's weakness, the Chief of Police was duly reinstated . . . I have dwelt at length on these disturbances which, but for British influence, would undoubtedly have culminated in an attack on the Constitutionalists.

On 16th February Dabizha's motives became clear. Sykes cabled to Barclay:

> Agitation under Yusef Herati has again become more serious than before. My colleague is still openly encouraging it by allowing use of Russian telegraph line. I asked him to notify Khorasan conjointly that ex-Shah had agreed to leave Persia, but he states that he has no such information. I can hardly expect to restrain the Constitutionalists from retaliating much longer. <u>I understand that he is promised large sum</u> [by the ex-Shah's party] <u>for his support.</u>

The last sentence was heavily underlined by Barclay.

Following a sudden reversal of official Russian policy at the highest level in St Petersburg, brought about by a general wish to improve relations with Britain, Barclay replied: 'Russian Minister instructing Russian colleague [Dabizha] to make the change of attitude towards ex-Shah known as widely as possible. He is to say that agitation on ex-Shah's behalf is useless and unwelcome.' Sykes responded:

Yesterday upon receiving your telegram I communicated with my Russian colleague, who has just written a letter that he has received no instructions whatever. This confirms my view that there is double dealing. Huge armed mob is assembling at mosque in favour of the ex-Shah and bloodshed which would justify occupation by Russian troops may occur any minute. Muhammad Ali was proclaimed in mosque last night and unless you can arrange for my colleague to be instructed to join me in joint message to the Karguzar as previously suggested by me it is improbable that I can save the situation much longer. The Constitution party subscribed 900 tomans to have Yusef Herati murdered. I dissuaded them on the grounds that this would create the situation they wanted to avoid.

What had happened was that one Muhammad of Nishapur, a notorious brigand in the pay of Muhammad Ali, had arrived in Meshed with a band of twenty followers and had taken *bast* in the shrine. There he and Yusef Herati arranged demonstrations in favour of the ex-Shah, who then sent a telegram to Dabizha asking him to inform the mujtahids, merchants and people that he would 'soon be in Meshed, will bow before the grave of the holy Imam and, together with you, will march on Tehran'. Dabizha, ignoring the change in Russian policy towards Muhammad Ali, asked St Petersburg for instructions. Sazonov, the Minister of Foreign Affairs, told him not to transmit the ex-Shah's telegram but to co-operate with Sykes and take all measures to stop the activities in favour of Muhammad Ali. He also told him to let the ex-Shah's partisans know that the Russian troops in Meshed were there to maintain order and that any act of violence would be put down by military force.

Muhammad Ali, bereft of support, left Persia once more but his supporters in Meshed, to the embarrassment of the Russian government, installed themselves in *bast* in the Shrine. Dabizha, with breathtaking disingenuousness, claimed that he had done his best to prevent ferment at Meshed and that he had expelled Yusef from the Consulate on becoming aware of his connection with the agitation. He also declared that he had ordered the Russian Muslim subjects to desist from troublemaking, but 'I cannot, nor do I have the right to, prohibit them from visiting mosques'. Dabizha knew how to play by the book.

Sykes sent another cable:

Position is that my colleague acknowledges receipt by telegraph on 20th February of instructions to change his attitude and wrote letter in this sense to a leading agitator. Secretly however, he is supporting the royalists and on 21st February delivered telegram from the brother of the ex–Shah to the effect that Muhammad Ali was coming to Meshed and this has encouraged them considerably. I have secured a copy. Royalists are fortified in the shrine. My Russian colleague refused to act with me as he had had no special instructions to that effect. Has the ex-Shah left Persia? This would strengthen my hand against double dealing.

Barclay, taking this extremely seriously, cabled back: 'I am asking Secretary of State to urge Russian Government to instruct your colleague categorically to concert with you to announce jointly attitude of Powers towards ex-Shah.' It was becoming impossible to have any rational discussion with the crazed Dabizha. On 29th February Sykes cabled: 'Surgeon considers my Russian colleague suffering from incipient senile decay. I find him quite unable to discuss questions and his staff hint much the same.' On 13th March Muhammad Ali left Ashurada for Baku.

Amid all this Sykes came in for severe criticism from Barclay for compromising security by sending the Legation clear copies of his cipher telegrams through the post, without altering the text. The cipher had to be changed. While the Russians may or may not have been reading Sykes's letters, he was having Dabizha's telephone tapped from the Consulate, and Redl, the military attaché, was listening to the conversations. On 18th March Sykes cabled to Barclay: 'My Russian colleague instigating attack on IBP [Imperial Bank of Persia] in order to force me to agree to Russian troops dispersing the royalists. I am advising manager to close the bank.' The next day he cabled: 'Dabizha urging Tehran for permission to declare martial law. This was refused, presumably owing to your representations. To disperse royalists by force would necessitate violation of shrine and this would start immense wave of fanaticism throughout Shia world and would cause attacks on Russians and downfall of Persia.'

On 24th March 1912 Sykes reported a conversation between Dabizha and Yusef Herati. Yusef had told Dabizha that he had captured the Sir-i Shur ['Pickled Garlic'] police station and was now ready to seize the Telegraph Office when instructed to do so. Dabizha told him to wait a little. Over the next three days Sykes, under pressure from all sides, bombarded Barclay with cables of transcripts of conversations between the Russian Consulate and various religious agitators, to the frustration of the Legation. ('I wish Sykes had a more lucid manner of describing a situation. For this he is the slackest or perhaps the most incompetent of our Consuls; I defy anyone to form a picture in his mind of what is passing in Meshed from Sykes's telegrams', Barclay commented.) Yet Sykes's reports were unclear because the situation itself was confused. However much they may have frustrated Barclay, Sykes's diaries conveyed the feeling of events far more vividly than a more traditional civil servant's writing would have done.

On 28th March Dabizha panicked and filled the city with troops. The Shrine rapidly filled with terrified townspeople, who turned it into a fortress. Sykes cabled: 'Dabizha declared martial law. Leaders of ex-Shah party now realise they have been deceived by him and if he could be instructed to take leave, which his mental health requires, and Consulate-General to be placed in hands of Grigoriev, order could be restored in a few days . . . Thousands of villagers have entered shrine to join in holy war.' (Barclay noted: 'It is rather a pity Sykes ever worried about Dabizha's mental state. At one time he considers him in "senile decay" and at another a wily old man full of intrigue. He can hardly be both.')

Sykes sent in the native attaché, who persuaded the religious leaders to declare that to bear arms in the shrine was disrespectful and that the bazaar should be reopened. A few shops were opened and the crowd decreased, but the leading agitators remained inside with their armed followers.

At 2.30 p.m. on 31st March 1912 Dabizha telephoned Sykes and informed him that he had given Yusef an ultimatum to leave the shrine. At 4.45 p.m. the Russian artillery bombardment of the shrine began. *The Near East* reported it in detail:

The Russians had planted a field battery of four big guns about half a mile outside the city and one big gun in the main thoroughfare leading to the Shrine. At four points around it they placed Maxim guns and surrounded the whole place with a strong line of infantry. The bombardment lasted for two hours and about two hundred heavy shells were thrown, with constant firing from the Maxims and the infantry. Serious damage was done to the gold dome and to the blue-tiled dome. Shortly after sunset one of the Maxims was brought forward and installed on the roof of a caravanserai overlooking the main courtyard of the Shrine, into which it fired indiscriminately. The Russian infantry then entered, shooting and bayoneting all those who could not find cover. Another Maxim was emptied into the tomb chamber itself, the holiest part of the Shrine, killing several. Some women, trying to escape, jumped into a lavatory well and others were pushed in. The soldiers stripped both the dead and the living of all their valuables. In all, some two hundred of the crowd were killed, but none of the agitators was touched. The Shrine itself was looted of most of its valuables, carpets and manuscripts and it was sealed by the Russians for two days.

Sykes arranged for a local artist to produce a cartoon drawing in vernacular Persian style to show the carnage. The borders were framed with verses expressing horror at the slaughter of the innocents by the Russians. The cartoonist was arrested by the Russians and accused of sedition but he protested astutely that the cartoon was intended to demonstrate how futile it was to argue with Russian military might. The cartoon was sent to India and published in the press, to show the Indian Muslims what they could expect if they ever fell for Russian blandishments.

Yusef Herati eventually left the shrine under arrest in a covered wagon bound for Ashgabad, escorted by Russian Cossacks. Persia reacted with stunned silence. The extreme power and violence of the Russian action had knocked the spirit out of the people and the government made only a feeble protest. Sykes sent photo-

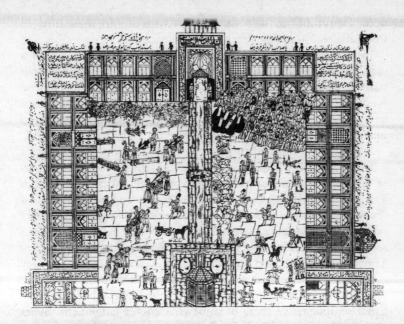

graphs of the damage to India, where they were widely distributed as anti-Russian propaganda, which was so effective that the All-India Muslim League, based at Lucknow, wrote to the Government of India 'respectfully urging them to take steps for the removal of Russian troops from Meshed to prevent the recurrence of such sacrilege, which must necessarily touch the hearts of His Majesty's Mussulman subjects'.

The following day the Shrine authorities, in an unprecedented gesture to a non-Muslim, invited Sykes to enter the sacred precinct and inspect the damage, which he agreed to do, provided that Dabizha accompanied him. This led to subsequent legends in the bazaars that Dabizha had been forced by Sykes to leave his carriage and enter the Shrine on foot and that, having thus publicly humbled him, Sykes forced him to restore the Shrine property. It was also said that Sykes had obliged the Russians to return the Shrine to the Persians. These legends spread to Afghanistan and India, where it was reported that the British Consulate had done everything to help the Persian Muslims in their time of trouble.

In the aftermath of the bombardment Major Redl 'acquired' a copy of the full Russian military orders issued the day before it started, suggesting that it had been planned all along. General Redko also told 'an informant' of Redl's that British policy had bested the Russians in the matter of the return of the ex-Shah and that the bombardment was their reply.

Sykes had maintained throughout to the Legation that Dabizha was far from being a loose cannon and that his actions were all part of Russian government policy. Despite all the official instructions sent to him to co-operate with the British and to abandon his support for Muhammad Ali, he had received, Sykes insisted, 'other orders' under separate cover. If not, then why had he not been removed? He wrote at length to Sir Walter Townley, the new Minister at Tehran, expounding this unwelcome view. Townley minuted: 'These reports are interesting and the conclusions to be drawn are not adverse to Major Sykes' general view, but I wish we had a representative there of somewhat cooler judgement.' Sykes sent another report that the Russian garrison at Nishapur had handed over four Maxim guns and twenty thousand rounds for distribution to supporters of the ex-Shah's younger brother Salar ud-Dowleh, who had recently started a rebellion in the west and went on to say that Muhammad Ali had signed a secret treaty with the Russian government in which he agreed to hand over the whole of Khorasan to them.

Townley was unimpressed by Sykes's constant demonizing of the Russians and minuted: 'Sykes must be an uncomfortable colleague with his monomania . . . Now that Salar has been broken, any intrigues on his behalf must fall to the ground.' Salar ud-Dowleh's movement had been broken by Amir A'zam, the Governor of Shahrud and ruthless suppressor of the Turkoman raiders. Sykes later reported that he had

invited Musaib Khan, chief of the followers of the Salar, pretending to be a partisan of his. The four hundred-strong party were persuaded to leave their arms outside the town and were promptly seized and relieved of 33,000 tomans, five hundred rifles and two hundred horses and mules. He reported his success to Tehran and asked for funds to maintain the prisoners and in reply to Tehran's suggestion that he use the money he had seized for this purpose, he swore that he had not found more than 100 tomans. The Persian Government finally said that no money would be sent, so the prisoners were stripped and released to earn their living as brigands.

Sykes was eventually proved right about Dabizha, but not until June, when the native attaché 'acquired' copies of correspondence, which he forwarded to the Legation, between Yusef Herati and the Persian prime minister, Muhammad Vali Sepahdar, showing that there had undoubtedly been official Russian government complicity in the bombardment and proving that they had been engaged in double-dealing throughout.

Townley's minuted comment on this despatch – 'This looks pretty damning' – was grudging. The Convention was a creature of the Foreign Office and Sykes, a creature of the Government of India, by exposing the Russians' persistent disregard for it, was an irritating bearer of unwelcome news. But Sykes – rather than playing the Foreign Office game – saw it as his duty to serve not only the Empire but also Persia, a country that had been his home since 1893. He was one of those people who could often be forgiven for being wrong, but never for being right.

Yusef Herati escaped and for seven weeks was on the run both from the Persian authorities and from Dabizha, who wanted him silenced. At one point, realizing that he had been disowned by his Russian masters, he even sent a message to Sykes, complaining that the Russians had not even paid him for all his trouble and asking for British protection. On 23rd May he was arrested by the Meshed authorities, acting under Russian orders, and, before he could tell any tales, was promptly shot. His corpse was paraded through Meshed in a carriage full of roses and then hung on display in the main square.

Meanwhile the poor old Rukn ud-Dowleh had again been dismissed, to be replaced by his old rival the Nayir ud-Dowleh, who was about to make his official entry into Meshed. The diary shows the height to which British prestige had now risen:

The Nayir ud-Dowleh telegraphed to the Chief Astrologer to inquire what day would be most suitable for entry in to Meshed. The Chief Astrologer, hearing that 4th June was the King's birthday, replied that this was especially auspicious and the Governor-General arranged to take advantage of that fact. I pointed out that this date was only auspicious for Emperors and Kings and that if he arrived on that date I could not send out to meet him. The Chief Astrologer has kindly laid down that 5th June is even more auspicious and His Highness will accordingly make his state entry on that day.

This he duly did, 'reaching Meshed at exactly 42 minutes before noon. The Chief Astrologer had insisted on this exact minute.'

To demonstrate that the ex-Shah Muhammad Ali was finished, the new Governor-General gave a reception to celebrate the birthday of the young Ahmad Shah. At dinner the band omitted to play the Russian national anthem. Sykes, who had noticed the omission, sent a discreet warning to the bandmaster and then whispered to the Nayir that he might care to propose a second health to the Tsar. This time the band responded and the next day Sykes 'received a grateful note from His Highness for saving the situation'.

Dabizha was now recalled to St Petersburg, despite sending presents of looted emeralds in the hope of inducing government officials to rescind his recall. On 23rd August he and General Redko left Meshed, although Redko, who had always been on good terms with Sykes, made a point of leaving separately. In September 1912 the Russian Foreign Minister, Sazonov, visited Britain to resolve a number of Anglo-Russian disputes that had arisen in Central Asia. King George V invited him and Sir Edward Grey to Balmoral, where they could settle matters in more informal surroundings. Among other things, Sazonov told Grey that Afghanistan was a hotbed of pan-Islamic fanaticism and propaganda that was penetrating into both British and Russian possessions, which was equally dangerous to both Powers. Sazonov's notes made in preparation for this meeting show that he intended to make an official complaint about Sykes's behaviour and demand that he be replaced by a Foreign Office man, who would not be tainted with the Anti-Russian attitudes of the Indian Political Service.[6]

This was not, however, the last of Dabizha, who was to reappear in Meshed on 30th December, to be given an *istiqbal* by the Russian garrison and the Persian authorities, as if he were arriving for the first time. Rumour among the Russians in Meshed had it that he had begged to be allowed to return to Meshed to end his days there and had been finally allowed to do so, but with instructions to be quick about it.

In September 1912 Sykes went on a month's tour along the border to Bojnurd and the Turkoman country. There were two things that concerned him. The first was the question of where the border with Russia lay. The internationally agreed border lay along the western end of the Atrak river but the Russians were claiming that the natural border was the Gorgan river, which would have taken a large slice of fertile Persian territory away. There is a story in Henry Smyth's family that Sykes confronted a Russian officer at one point along the disputed border and took him to task. The Russian stood his ground, claiming that he was in Russian territory. When the argument looked as though it was going to lead to war both men decided that, to save lives, they would settle the question with a duel. Being gentlemen, they each fired into the air and retreated gracefully. The border remained where it was on the map. Unusually for Sykes, this incident did not figure in his official report.

The other question that concerned him was the increase in Turkoman raiding across the border, which was becoming a serious problem. The Governor of Nardin showed Sykes where the last *alaman* had passed on its way home only two days before. There were still tracks of five hundred horsemen and thousands of stolen sheep, camels and mules. He was lucky to have missed them. The Governor had managed to recover some of the sheep but, with only sixty men, he had been unable to tackle the robbers. Sykes discovered that the Russian commissioners at Gonbad-i Kavus had been instigating these *alamans* and were paying the

---

[6] I am indebted to Jennifer Siegel for this information.

Turkoman on a per capita basis to join them, in an effort to make the country so unstable that the Persian government would be forced to cede territory to Russia.

During Sykes's absence on this tour the consulate was run by Captain Wilson, the Indian Medical Service doctor, who had none of Sykes's understanding of Persian affairs. At one point he cabled to Tehran: 'Meshed rumour that Persian Ministers have taken sanctuary in British Legation. Would be obliged for any news'. Townley commented, 'Sykes is on tour; if he had been at his post little credence, I imagine, would have been placed in such a silly rumour.' 'Napoleon' was being missed.

Some light on Russian views of British players of the Great Game and of Sykes's good relations with the Russians emerges from a brief report on a visit to Ashgabad by Captain Blair, the acting British military attaché during Major Redl's absence on leave. He went to visit the Russian garrison commander.

> In answer to a remark of mine that it was rare for an English officer to have the honour of being entertained at Ashgabad, General Shostak laughed and said, 'Well, it is not all English officers who pass through here who call on me. I have recently heard of three English officers travelling through Transcaspia in disguise. They had however, crossed into Afghanistan before I received the report.' I endeavoured to persuade my host that he must be entirely misinformed, but was merely met by polite smiles.

Sykes added a footnote to this report: 'I subsequently repeated this remark of the General's to a senior staff officer whom I knew well. He replied that some senior Russian officers still had an exaggerated suspicion of the British, a legacy from the period of Anglo-Russian hostility. He himself believed that the suspicious characters were in fact Turkish officers.'

In December the Russians declared an outbreak of plague along the Afghan border, which gave them an excuse to close the frontier and set up quarantine posts, disrupting trade with India. There was no plague; in fact, some peasants had died after eating a poisoned camel. The 18th Turkistan Rifle Regiment was reported to have sent a mapping party across the border to survey the region between Quchan and Bojnurd, and reports came in that the Russians were building barges on the Oxus at Charjui, which could be used for carrying troops and supplies up to the Afghan border, only a few days march from Kabul and the Khyber Pass.

By the beginning of 1913, Sykes's last year as Consul-General in Meshed, the life of Khorasan had returned to normal, with nothing for him to report other than routine brigandry and border raiding. At the end of May he recorded that the bandit Timur Khan, who had been giving trouble for years, had been arrested in Yazd but had 'paid large sums to the mullas, who are arranging for his release. He is protected by the Governor of Tabas and its leading mujtahids. It is facts like these which make one despair of Persia.'

The consular cavalry escort, returning to Meshed from leave in India, made itself useful when it took a large caravan under its protection. Between Birjand and Torbat-i Haidari a gang of robbers emerged from a fortified tower and demanded money from them. The cavalry arrested the robbers and took them to Meshed, where they were kept in the Consulate prison. When they protested that their chief was working in league with Adil ud-Dowleh ('Just Man of the State'), the Governor of Torbat-i Haidari, Sykes in turn protested to the Governor-General of Meshed. The latter sent him a message saying that, since Sykes had been in Persia for some twenty years, he must have known that this was the way things were, but that nevertheless he would do as Sykes wished and have them flogged before releasing them. A twist to the story was that the Russian Consulate, who had their own dealings with the Adil, insisted on suppressing the story about the latter's patronage of the robber gang.

Another robber gang working for the same Adil ud-Dowleh was led by a seyyid, a descendant of the Prophet. This gang broke into a merchant's house, forced his safe and stole 4,700 tomans, of which it sent 3,000 tomans to the Adil, of which the Governor-General also took his own share. There were so many demands for the Adil to make compensation that he had to do something. He told the seyyid to threaten to attack a large village. The Adil then collected a large sum of money from the villagers to protect it from the seyyid's gang and with the proceeds paid the merchant back

1,000 tomans, pocketed the balance and paid off the seyyid by giving him a pardon.

On a more peaceful note, Sykes went fishing and sent some specimens to the Natural History Museum in London. He wrote to Townley to say that the museum would also like some specimens of trout from the Lar river, above Tehran. The Legation maintained a fishing camp equipped with magnificent Indian marquees in the high valley of the Lar, the summer grazing grounds of the Persian cavalry, and used it as a summer fishing resort. Townley minuted: 'The Legation staff might be prevailed upon to oblige!'

The military attaché, in a comment on the improved state of relations with the local Russians, reported that many of the soldiers in the Russian garrison at Meshed were in trouble. They were under strict orders not to touch Persian women, but the temptation of the many prostitutes who swarmed around the shrine had been too much for them and large numbers were contracting venereal disease. Rather than report sick to their own army doctors, they were coming to the British military hospital for treatment.

With Meshed now at peace, 4th June 1913 saw the 'most successful King's Birthday ever', which was followed shortly afterwards by a wild boar shooting party which Sykes organized for the Russian Colonel Khakandokov with two other officers and twelve Cossacks at his country retreat at Jagharq. Four boar were bagged, including a monster weighing 300 lb. dressed. This was a record, and everyone returned happily to Meshed. Relations with the Russians had become thoroughly cordial.

The clouds of the Great War were building up over Europe, however, and Germany was now extending its feelers towards the East. The diary reports blandly that on 13th May a certain German Lieutenant Oskar Niedermayer, accompanied by an Austrian, Dr Ernst Dietz, had arrived at Meshed.[7] Niedermayer and Dietz claimed to have been travelling widely in north Persia, studying

---

[7] This was the same Niedermayer who later led the German expedition with Wassmuss and Zugmayer from Berlin via Baghdad and Persia to Kabul with the aim of rousing an Islamic jihad against the British Empire in India. In 1910 there had been lengthy correspondence between the India Office and the Foreign Office concerning Zugmayer's application, supported by the Bavarian Academy of Sciences, to travel in Baluchistan engaged in zoology, botany and palaeontology. He had also made an expedition to Central Asia in 1906.

geology, archaeology, anthropology and history, and to be heading for Sistan. Two months later they were still in Meshed and Sykes invited them to Jagharq, where Niedermayer mentioned that he had managed, by disguising himself as a Persian, to enter the forbidden shrine. Sykes said nothing and the explorers went on their way.

In September Sykes telegraphed to Townley: 'Niedermayer robbed of everything near Turshiz.[8] Am instructing British agent at Turshiz to assist.' Ten days later he cabled with lapidary brevity: 'Governor-General has repaid Niedermayer stolen cash, but his surveying instruments were taken. Local sub-governor was involved.' The Great Game was still on, albeit with a new player, and Sykes was enjoying himself.

Sykes's long tour in Meshed was at last over and on 20th November 1913 he and his family left for the long journey home, with Evelyn already expecting her fourth son, Geoffrey, who was later born in Jersey. The acting Consul-General, Captain Thorburn of the IMS, wrote in the diary:

> The departure of Major Sykes is much regretted by all classes at Meshed. He has for the past eight and a half years been associated with Meshed and the friendly relations that have been established on all sides must be most gratifying to him. Before his departure Major Sykes was dined by Prince Dabizha in the Russian Consulate-General and by the officers of the Semirechnia Cossack regiment in the Officers' Club. From the speeches, which were of the most friendly nature, the Entente Cordiale appears to be well established in Meshed.
>
> On the morning of Major Sykes's departure Colonel Kulikoff and all the officers of the Russian garrison and the regimental band came to the Consulate and escorted his carriage for about two miles along the road to a place where they had provided a stirrup cup. After suitable compliments had been exchanged Major Sykes drove off amid cheers.

Sykes was rewarded for his services with the award of a KCIE from the Government of India, but he received little public

---

[8] Present-day Kashmar.

recognition in Britain. Sir Edward Grey announced to Parliament on 3rd July 1913, four years after the Anglo–Russian Convention, that there were 17,500 Russian troops in Persia and none had been withdrawn, except from Meshed. Possibly out of diplomatic propriety, he gave no credit to Sykes for this. According to Sykes's daughter Elinor, 'In 1913 my father did not receive the promotion that he expected and decided to retire from service. He told me that Lord Curzon was jealous of him.' He was offered the Residency of a minor Indian princely state, but turned it down. The *Times of India* ran an article, obviously written by himself, saying what a waste of Sykes's talent this would be.

Although his consular duties were at an end, Sykes had not finished exploring. On his way home he fitted in a short tour of some unsurveyed country between Radkan and the frequently disturbed district of Dareh Gaz. He wanted to find the source of the Atrak, which formed part of the border with Russia, and to visit the birthplace of Nadir Shah, the eighteenth-century conqueror of Delhi. He was escorted on this trip by Russian Cossacks, proving, as he said in his final despatch, 'that the entente cordiale had taken firm root in Meshed'.

He was met at Chenaran by Zabbardast Khan, cousin of the Governor of Dareh Gaz, and camped by the Royal Meadow, doing some duck shooting in the morning. His historical curiosity aroused, Sykes acquired the accounts of Dareh Gaz for 1746, showing the charges for the upkeep of the grave of Nadir Shah's father, Imam Quli, at Kapkan, which he gave to the Royal Asiatic Society. He also acquired a prehistoric bowl, which he donated to the British Museum.

I recognized with delight that it was similar to one discovered below the stratum of earliest Elamite civilisation by De Morgan in the great mound at Susa. Similar pottery has been found at Annau [outside Ashgabad] by an American mission under Pumpelly. This pottery, which is of a yellow colour . . . is believed to date from perhaps the sixth millennium BC. It proves the existence at Dareh Gaz of a culture earlier than the historical cultures of Sumer and Akkad, of Elam or of Babylon.

On this note Sykes took leave of Khorasan and set off home by train from Ashgabad, through Merv, Bokhara and Samarqand.

After he had gone, his final despatch reached the Legation at Tehran. The last entry read: 'The young widow of the very wealthy Muntasir ul-Mulk is receiving offers of marriage from every quarter. Among her would-be husbands are the Governor-General, an old man of over seventy, and the noted ruffian Kardash Bala. The Sepahdar [the prime minister] has also proposed to her by telegram. The lady is said to reply in caustic strain.' Townley noted, 'We shall miss the Sykes diaries!'

Shortly after he returned home, Sykes published his massive two-volume *History of Persia*, which went into several reprints and subsequent revisions and was the standard work on the country for years. The only comparable work was Sir John Malcolm's history, written in 1815. Sykes describes the period before his arrival in heavy-handed Victorian style, but his account becomes much more lively thereafter. Indeed, a disproportionate amount of the two volumes is devoted to the 'Sykes period'.

Colonel Haig, who took over from Sykes as Consul at Meshed, recorded in his memoirs a story of the Russian bombardment of 1912. An enormous religious painting, showing scenes from the martyrdom of the Imam Hussein, had been looted from the Shrine:

> Later an Englishman, whose name I was not permitted to disclose, discovered this picture in a shop and bought it. It was sent to me with a request that I would send it to the Mutawalli-Bashi, and inform him that it was returned by an Englishman who was a friend of Persia. The Mutawalli-Bashi exhibited it in the Great Court of the Shrine and . . . the people said, 'See the difference between our two neighbours – one takes away and the other gives back.'

This could be a rare occasion when Sykes did not blow his own trumpet.

16

Kashgar and the Pamirs

At the outbreak of the First World War in August 1914 the British army did not have enough trained and equipped troops available in England to send to France to halt the German attack. Three days after war was declared, the Lahore Division from the Indian Army was shipped off via Suez and Marseilles to assist the French army to hold the line until English forces could be built up.

At the beginning of the war Sykes was posted to Southampton as City Commandant, a glorified baggage-master for the troops on their way to France. When the Lahore Division arrived in the south of France at the end of the autumn, the Indian officers and soldiers spoke no French and not much English, and were therefore practically paralysed, unable to find their way anywhere or discover what they were meant to do. The call went out in Britain for interpreters who could speak Indian languages as well as French, and Sykes, who was not enjoying being bogged down with administration behind a desk in Southampton, jumped at the chance to join them and get closer to the fight.

The interpreters were a curious group, by no means all of them military men. When they got to France it turned out that not only were they required to liaise between the French army and the Indians over joint operations but, since sepoy and *poilu* spoke not a word of each other's language, the interpreters had to arrange their billets with the local mayors, lay on food supplies for them and issue them with their orders. They had to do everything for the Indians, including finding a supply of nappy pins to pull in the waists of the British winter underwear which had been issued to the shivering and skinny sepoys.

The long-suffering Indians were unsung and virtually unpaid heroes who held the line until the British were able to muster their army and take over. They were involved in the First Ypres Campaign from September to November 1914, resisting the German push towards the Channel ports. At this stage the war was conducted in basic slit trenches only; the real horror of deep trench warfare came later. By Christmas the line had settled and the Indians, especially the martial and resourceful Sikhs and Pathans, had picked up enough French to survive without the interpreters, who were sent home.

To the north of India, on the other side of the Karakoram Pass in Chinese Turkistan,[1] was the city of Kashgar. Controlled by China but peopled largely by Muslim Turki-speaking Uighurs, Kashgar stood at the foot of the Pamirs – 'the roof of the world' – beyond which, to the west, lay Russian Turkistan. The hub at the centre of Russia, China and India and the gateway from Russia into India, Kashgar was for many years a sensitive point in the Great Game and a focus of intrigue between all three Powers. It had long been thought that the Russians could march a force there over the Pamirs and then, albeit with some difficulty, make their way over the Karakorams into India. At the end of 1890 Francis Younghusband and the half-Chinese George Macartney, his young assistant, were sent to establish a consulate at Kashgar to keep a watch on Russian moves in the mountains. Younghusband moved on but Macartney settled into the now famous Chini Bagh (Chinese garden) and stayed there as Consul until 1918. By 1915 he had been there for twenty-four years, with only two home leaves, on the first of which he had found a good Scottish wife robust enough to accompany him on the journey back out over the Pamirs. The Government of India felt that, twelve years after his second leave, he and his wife might by now need another short break.

---

[1] Modern Xinjiang or Sinkiang.

China had regained control of Sinkiang from the native Turkic khans in 1877. However, the town was so remote from central China that all its trade was across the Pamirs with neighbouring Russia, making it a tempting morsel for St Petersburg. So bad were internal communications in China that Chinese goods from Peking had to be sent by sea all the way round to Batumi on the Black Sea and then via Baku, across the Caspian to Krasnovodsk and by rail overland through Russian Turkistan to Andijan.

At the end of 1911 Sun Yat-Sen's republican revolt against the corrupt Manchu emperors had thrown the country into turmoil. Sinkiang was split between the republicans and the supporters of the Manchus. Stray packs of unpaid disbanded soldiers added to the violence of the upheavals and, on top of that, there was a local native nationalist movement to secede from Chinese tutelage. Such was the level of disturbance in Kashgar that the Russians, on the usual pretext of protecting foreign subjects in danger, sent in a thousand Cossacks and four hundred riflemen, which the Chinese were unable to resist. Macartney, fearing that the Russians might attempt an annexation of Kashgar, reported the matter via Kashmir to the Government of India. Sir Edward Grey immediately took the matter up with Sazonov, the Russian Foreign Minister, who assured him, as he had done over the Meshed business, that their sole purpose was to protect the European community (which, apart from the inflated Russian presence, amounted to a handful of teetotal Swedish missionaries and the Macartneys, who did not feel particularly threatened). Since the Anglo-Russian Convention of 1907 had included an agreement that Russia would not interfere in Tibet as long as Britain kept out of Sinkiang, the situation was delicate.

With the outbreak of war in Europe the Russians, now uneasily allied to Britain against Germany, had withdrawn most of their troops and the Chinese, sensing that both Russians and British were weakening under the German attack, had become noticeably aggressive towards the old imperialists. The spread of the war had made the Turki-speaking province of Sinkiang of interest to the Germans and their Turkish allies, who were dreaming of 'setting the East ablaze' with a fire of Islamic pan-Turkism which would sweep all the way to India and destroy the British Empire. In

February 1915 a party of five Turks appeared in Kashgar. China was neutral and had no reason for excluding them, but Macartney learned from his informers that in the spring they intended to travel to Afghanistan and attempt to incite the Afghans to join the fight against the British. Other Turkish agents were also using Sinkiang as a base from which to stir up the tribes on the borders of India and in Russian Turkistan.

In April 1915 Macartney, whose overdue leave had been cancelled because of the war, was at last able to take his children home to go to school in England, and Sykes, who had made a name for himself as a self-sufficient man able to make himself at home in the most inhospitable of places, was the obvious choice to go out and replace him until his return. Evelyn, however, put her foot down. Catherine Macartney's journey out as a young bride, without children, had been hard enough. The easy part had been the train ride to Samarqand, after which the train had plodded along to the end of the line at Andijan at walking pace, with frequent picnic stops. There they had taken to a springless four-wheeled *tarantass* drawn by three horses for a whole day's dusty journey to the end of the road at Osh. Here, now in winter, they had assembled a caravan of ponies, camels and yaks for the week's march to Kashgar through the Kirghiz country and over the Tian Shan mountains by the frozen 13,000 feet Terek pass, carrying with them a harmonium bought from some Russians at Osh.

Sykes's sister Ella was now in her fifties. She knew about Kashgar from Younghusband and, keen for more adventure, volunteered to come out in Evelyn's place and keep house for her brother, as she had done at Kerman. On 5th March 1915 they set off for St Petersburg. Since it was wartime they had to take a neutral Norwegian vessel to Norway and then, as it was unsafe to cross the Gulf of Bothnia to St Petersburg, they had to make their way overland northwards through Sweden to the Finnish border just below the Arctic Circle before turning south into Russia. There they met Sykes's old colleague de Klemme, the former Russian Consul-General at Meshed, who was now head of the Central Asian section of the Russian Foreign Office. He was all friendliness and, saying that he knew that Sykes would want to travel in the Pamirs, arranged for him to meet various Russians who knew the area and would give him advice. Sykes and Ella spent two days in Moscow collecting supplies, followed by five days on an uncomfortable train to Tashkent.

At Tashkent he made a formal call on the Governor-General, who remarked that Sykes must indeed have been *persona grata* in St Petersburg, since it normally took six months to get a permit to travel in the Pamirs. In fact the permit reached Kashgar before he did. As a matter of courtesy, or perhaps of old Russian habit, the chief of the Tashkent police accompanied Sykes and Ella to Andijan, from where they found a victoria to take them to Osh, covering the thirty miles in five hours. At Osh they were invited to dine at the Russian Officers' Club, where they were given a most friendly reception. In his official report on the journey Sykes noted drily that 'the Tsar's prohibition on alcohol had not yet reached Osh'. He was able to stock up with wine to take with him. Osh was the end of the road and he hired ponies for the twelve marches across country to Kashgar. A Kirghiz *min-bashi*, or major (literally 'head of a thousand [men]'), accompanied them to the border, looking a magnificent sight in his velvet cummerbund set with bosses and clasps of Bokharan silver work and, on his head, a tall conical white felt hat with a black tassel. He found them accommodation in the villages that they passed through and, as Ella remarked in her account of the journey,[2] was particularly useful in securing right of way over oncoming caravans on the narrow mountain tracks.

> This was a privilege that I keenly appreciated, as the track, when it skirted the flanks of the mountains, was hardly ever wide enough for one animal to pass another, and I had no wish to be pushed out of my saddle over the precipice by the great bales of cotton that formed the load of most of the ponies that we met.

By the time they reached the Pamirs there were no more villages and they had to take shelter with some Kirghiz nomads in their yurts before attempting the Terek pass. It was cold and the

---

[2] *Through Deserts and Oases of Central Asia* (London, 1920), written jointly by Ella and Percy Sykes.

snow was frozen hard on the Russian side, which made the going not too difficult, but on their descent into Chinese Turkistan the snow was melting and the ponies floundered as they broke through it. Inside China they were met by Jafar Bai, the highly respected *chaprassi* (uniformed messenger) from the Kashgar consulate, who escorted them in, receiving salutes from all the passing horsemen, to arrive on 10th April, thirty-six days after leaving London. They were welcomed by the Macartneys, who introduced them to the Swedish missionaries and the senior Russians. After a suitable interval Sykes made his official calls on the Chinese authorities and reported afterwards that he had been able to speak to the Chinese Governor-General and his Secretary in the Russian that he had learned at Meshed. The Macartneys, after a brief handover, left two days later.

Kashgar was the most isolated of all the British consulates. It took a runner three weeks to take despatches, which were necessarily brief, to the British Resident at Kashmir for forwarding to the Government of India. For urgent messages there was an extremely unreliable telegraph connection through Russia. The Consul therefore needed to be self-sufficient and able to act on his own initiative. As it was wartime, Sykes's first recommendation was to install a powerful wireless.

Out in the vast Taklamakan[3] desert to the east of Kashgar, Aurel Stein, the great Anglo-Hungarian archaeologist, had been for years excavating ancient cities buried under the sands and sending his finds back to Europe. Almost immediately after Sykes's arrival in Kashgar 149 boxes of antiquities from his dig reached the city for onward dispatch. The Governor of Sinkiang was incensed at this pillage and wrote from his capital at Urumchi, eight hundred miles and fifty days' journey away on the other side of the Taklamakan, to query Stein's right to make excavations and carry off the proceeds. The artefacts that Stein had looted – for, in that he had no permit to export his finds, that is what it amounted to in Chinese eyes – were kept in Kashgar until July, when he loaded them up on a caravan headed for Leh and India. Rumours

---

[3] Almost every travel book on this area repeats the error that 'Taklamakan' means 'he who enters never leaves.' It doesn't. It means 'empty place'.

abounded that the Chinese planned to seize the caravan before it could leave the country but Sykes was 'watching the matter' and the antiquities are now in various museums in Europe, where their legitimacy is still questioned by the Chinese.

Another matter that Sykes was watching was another party of Turks heading for Afghanistan. Kashgar was a small place in which there were few secrets, and Sykes and the Russian Consul, acting together, arranged for the Taoyin, the local governor, to cancel the visas of the Turks and detain them. This tiny move in the Great Game amounted to no more than swatting a passing fly which might just possibly have led to an anti-British uprising in India. These Turks were certainly not horse-traders.

A more welcome visitor to Kashgar was Nicholas Romanov, a Russian authority on Islamic architecture and art, who had been on tour in Yarkand. Sykes had met him in Bokhara in 1913 and had later arranged for his election to the Royal Geographical Society. Romanov told him that Russians had bought enormous tracts of land near Gonbad-i Kavus, in north-east Persia, to grow cotton – just as Sykes had predicted when he was travelling through the area from Meshed.

In May 1915 another party of Turks appeared and was arrested by the Russian Cossacks on the border. The Chinese diplomatically decided that they were outside Chinese territory when they were arrested and allowed the Russians to deal with them. Two months later the Turks tried again. This time a number of them came to open a school,[4] but the Kashgar merchants were opposed to the idea of uncontrolled education and paid the mullas to denounce it and force the Chinese to close it. There were many rumours in the bazaars of Turkish plots.

Among the European community all was not harmony. The Lutheran Swedish medical missionaries did not get on with the boisterous Russians, outwardly because of Russian treatment of the Finns, but no doubt for other reasons which could not be so readily admitted. Sykes and Ella had to invite them to social occasions at the Chini Bagh separately, while the Russians would invite the

---

[4] Turks have been opening Qoranic schools all over Central Asia recently, in an updated version of the Great Game.

Swedes to their Consulate only on the Tsar's name day. Social life among the expatriates was therefore limited. 'Society' was made up of a dozen of the Russians, headed by Prince Mestchersky, the Consul-General. They were convivial but exhausting, since their idea of the proper hour to end a dinner party was five in the morning.

Ella was helped in her entertaining by the domestic staff left by the Macartneys but was troubled by the butler, who had once made rock cakes that, no matter how much baking powder he used, had refused to rise. It turned out that he had been using the stock of arsenic kept for curing animal skins.

Life in the Kashgar oasis, when not a matter of moves in the Great Game, revolved around the culture of raisins and water-melons. To seek relief from the tedium of irrigated country Sykes and Ella left the oppressive heat of June on an expedition to the high Pamirs, where there was sport to be had in the wild open spaces. However, it was not just adventure that they sought; there were mountain passes to be mapped. Russia was an ally for the moment, but might not always remain so.

Ella was again in charge of supplies, for nothing other than meat and yak milk would be available in the mountains. Eighteen pack ponies were loaded with boxes of tea, sugar, rice, tinned food, compressed vegetables, dried fruit, jam, biscuits, candles, horse-shoes and nails, sacks of barley and bed rolls. Ella decided that on rough going she would ride astride her Badakhshani horse on a native saddle rather than on her side-saddle, which was not safe on the tricky mountain tracks. Since the Kirghiz women rode astride, no scandal would be caused.

Their journey took them across the fast-flowing Gez river up to Lake Bulangul and the country of the hospitable Kirghiz nomads, who welcomed them into their felt *ak-oys*,[5] which were much more comfortable than the small and draughty campaign tents which they had brought. As they climbed, they changed their pack ponies for yaks and reached the 16,000 foot crest of the Katta Dawan pass, on the Roof of the World, with its spectacular view of the Great Karakul Lake on the Russian side. They visited the

---

[5] Literally 'white house', the proper word for a yurt.

Pamirski Post, the Russian military outpost at the head of the Murghab valley, which forms one of the headwaters of the Oxus. Here they were travelling in high country; the bottoms of the valleys were 12,000 feet high, the same as the top of the Alps. Here ranged the *Ovis Poli*, the Marco Polo sheep. When caught spying out the land in these hidden mountain passes leading to Russian territory, Indian Army officers explained their presence by saying that they were sportsmen in pursuit of this great trophy beast, with its massive head of horns. In this big-game country Sykes's shikari (ghillie) Nadir came into his own. He took over the running of the camp and started ordering the servants about in a most masterful way, turning his own hand to anything, and showed himself to be an excellent singer when in the hills and on form. Proud of his martial appearance, he sought to add to it by adorning his hat with a bunch of primulas. For three days he and Sykes disappeared up a valley recommended by the local Russian commandant; they returned with a pile of *Poli* strapped to their yaks, having left Ella in camp to pursue edelweiss and gentians.

Crossing back into Chinese territory at Tagharma, with its astounding view of the Muztagh Ata (Father Ice) mountain, they were treated to a display of *olak tartush*, the Kirghiz equivalent of the Afghan *bozkashi* and roughly equivalent to a mounted rugby game. A goat or calf is beheaded, gralloched, stuffed with sand and stitched up, to be picked up from the ground and carried off under the thigh to a distant post, while the other riders try to snatch it away.

They made an excursion to the Sarikol valley, populated by Ismaili Muslims, followers of the Aga Khan, who spoke Sogdian, a very ancient form of Persian. The Aga Khan, who lived in India, was thereby a British subject and thus, by extension, the Sarikol Ismailis considered themselves similarly tied. Their priest insisted on making them wait while his invisible womenfolk prepared a feast in their honour. Although they declined the offer of food, Elle remarked that their visit did some good, for two brothers, rich landowners who had long been at enmity with one another, became reconciled that morning when they came to pay their respects to the Consul.

They continued up to the foot of the glacier of Muztagh Ata on their grumbling and grunting yaks, led by their Kirghiz guide in his long red leather riding boots, fur cap and padded coat of many colours. Further than this he refused to go, for the Kirghiz believed Muztagh Ata to be haunted by fairies, camels of supernatural whiteness and mysterious drummers, which were probably just the sound of rocks splitting in the cold. The guide was keen to get down and, heedless of her protestations, led Ella's yak in a series of headlong and terrifying slides down precipitous scree to the bottom of the valley. The normally imperturbable Ella this time knew real fear that her yak would fall and hurl itself and her to destruction, but it never lost its footing and took her safely down to the glacier stream at the bottom, where she found some wild rhubarb. Mindful that the Russian rhubarb jam that she had brought from Kashgar had exploded in its bottles, she told the guide to gather it for their supper. Yaks had gone up in her estimation.

The Gez river being now flooded with snow melt, they had to return by way of the difficult Ulutagh (Great Mountain) pass, which was open only in summer and was always dangerous for animals. Ella quailed when she saw what was ahead:

> A long stony valley led us past great glaciers hollowed into caves, the entrances to which were fringed with stalactites of ice, and the mountains seemed to close in more and more forbiddingly. I confess that my heart almost failed me when we reached the foot of the pass and I saw a series of zigzag tracks faintly marked on what seemed to me to be the face of a precipice. It would have been impossible to negotiate such a place on horseback; but yaks were in readiness and I mounted mine thankfully, with a grateful remembrance of the shaggy bull that had carried me down from Muztagh Ata.
>
> But I was now to learn that there are yaks and yaks. These animals strongly objected to the job. They jibbed constantly and took to backing off the path and sliding in perilous fashion on to the long slopes of shifting rubble. I became nervous on my brother's account, because the fastenings of his saddle broke twice, and if he had not realized that he was sitting on the yak's tail instead of the middle of its back, he would have fallen right

over the precipice. He had fastened the thong of his hunting crop round the horns of the yak, thereby saving himself from disaster.

Once over the pass and on level ground they exchanged their yaks for camels and rode the last thirty miles back into the stifling July heat of Kashgar and the comforts of life at Chini Bagh.

In September they set off once more on tour, this time along the southern edge of the Taklamakan desert to the oasis cities of Yarkand and Khotan (present-day Shache and Hotan). They hired high-wheeled wagons to carry their baggage and, although highway robbery was almost unknown in Sinkiang and the protection of a caravan was not necessary, various characters attached themselves to their party in order to enjoy the reflected consular glory: the Master of the Horse of the Rajah of Punyal and his groom, on a mission to buy Badakhshani horses for their master; the Chief Falconer to the Mehtar of Chitral, looking for a pair of the extremely rare white hawks found in only in the district of Sarikol; and finally a Hindu trader with a wooden leg, who saluted Sykes in military fashion whenever occasion offered. There were many British subjects in south-western Sinkiang, mostly Indian merchants bringing goods[6] over the Himalayan passes, to whom the visit of the Consul was welcome, and as Sykes's caravan proceeded, its tail grew longer and longer.

Yarkand they found to be the most fertile and prosperous of the southern oases, apart from the famous prevalence of goitre among the Yarkandis, who did not boil their drinking water. At each town they received the respect of the *Ak Sakal* ('White Beard'), or British agent, who was usually the senior Indian merchant. Under Chinese capitulations the Indians were subject to British law and it was the Consul's duty to settle their disputes with the Chinese authorities.

To reach Khotan they had to ferry the horses across the wide Yarkand river, which carried melting snow-water northwards to disappear in the desert. Khotan was famous for jade and for its silk:

---

[6] They exported high-quality cannabis and raw silk and imported English and Indian printed cottons and muslins, spices and Lipton tea.

it was from there in AD 550 that silkworm eggs had been stolen and taken to Byzantium to break the Chinese monopoly on the trade. Sykes settled consular cases, some of which had been outstanding for years, and they returned by the way they had come. In November 1915 the Macartneys arrived back in Kashgar, and Ella and her brother made their way back through Russia to England and the war.

17

South Persia Rifles

P ERSIA HAD NO wish to be involved in the war that broke out in 1914, but since three of the protagonists were her neighbouring countries of Russia, British India and Ottoman Turkey (which then included Mesopotamia, present-day Iraq), it was caught in the middle. The Persian government was under pressure from the nationalists and Democrats to keep out of it, but neutrality is only ever an option for strong countries, which Persia was not. They waited to see what would happen. They did not have to wait long.

In 1913 the Ottoman government had given command of its army to the German Liman von Sanders, who had begun to train it in modern methods of warfare. In Berlin General von der Goltz had been appointed head of all activity in Turkey and Persia. By November the German consul at Erzurum, in the far east of Turkey, was spreading bellicose propaganda and in early 1914 at Tabriz, the capital of Persian Azerbaijan, the German consul was arming the tribes. At the outbreak of war the Russians passed through Persian Azerbaijan and pushed the Turks back to Lake Van. For most of the rest of the war the north-west of Persia saw a back-and-forth campaign of Russian and Turkish troops attacking and counter-attacking each other. To the south-west, India sent an expeditionary force to Mesopotamia in November 1914, which occupied the river port of Basra and began to advance up the Tigris towards Baghdad.

The south-west of Persia was vital to the British. In 1909 the ships of the Royal Navy had started to burn oil and in 1914 the government, at Winston Churchill's insistence, had become the largest shareholder in the Anglo–Persian Oil Company (which later became BP). According to the terms of the Anglo–Russian Convention of 1907, the area in which the oil fields were later developed was in the neutral zone, but by 1914 this had become a fiction and the oil fields, where Persian government writ did not run, had become a British protectorate in all but name. In 1915 the British had made a secret agreement with their new Russian allies by which, in exchange for free access to the neutral zone of Persia, Britain would later allow the Russians to take Constantinople and the Dardanelles from Turkey.[1]

To safeguard their oil operations the British had contracted agreements both with Sheikh Khazal, the chief of the Arab tribes near the coast at Muhammerah, and with the Bakhtiari khans, in whose mountains lay the oil. They were generously subsidized to keep the peace and guarantee the safety of the pipeline down to the coast. This was not an easy job, for when in 1907 a detachment of Central Indian Horse was sent up to protect the early oil drillers they found the Qashqai and Tangistani tribes to be better armed than the Persian government forces and even the Bakhtiaris. The Muscat arms smugglers were still very much in business.

Long before the war the Germans had been working with the Turks on a plot to stir up an Islamic revolt against the British in India. They were supported by a group of exiled Persian Popular Democrats, who planned to use the Germans as a lever to free Persia from the combined control of the Russians and the British. In *Greenmantle* John Buchan gives a thrilling, if coloured, account of this colossal conspiracy, but Peter Hopkirk gives the full story of the affair in his *On Secret Service East of Constantinople*. The plan was to send a group of agents – Wilhelm Wassmuss, Oskar Niedermayer, Erich Zugmayer, Walter Griesinger, Fritz Seiler and Otto von Hentig – from Constantinople into Persia and from there into Afghanistan, where they would persuade the Amir to join cause with the Kaiser and launch an uprising among the Muslims in India, who would throw the British out of the Raj. To

---

[1] This agreement was made public and then repudiated by the Bolsheviks in 1917.

impress the Muslims the Germans carried an impressive scroll declaring that the Kaiser had converted to Islam – and had also made the pilgrimage to Mecca – and was ready to lead them in the jihad which the Turks had declared against the British. When British agents captured this document they found that it had been written in impressive Turkish calligraphy, on vellum made of German pigskin – a small detail that, if the document had been allowed to reach India, would have landed the Kaiser and all his works in ridicule.

Niedermayer and Hentig, after a game of hide-and-seek with the British forces guarding the eastern Persian frontier, reached Kabul in September 1915. There the Amir, mindful of the subsidies that he was receiving from the Government of India, detained them hospitably at his pleasure and would not allow them to proceed further. Zugmayer and Griesinger, carrying huge bundles of propaganda leaflets in Persian and Urdu declaring great German victories, went to Kerman, where they attempted to set up a German consulate, which the Persian government refused to recognize. There they were later joined by Seiler. There was an astonishing naïvety and arrogance about the German command, who thought that by distributing money, a few rifles, some rounds of ammunition and picture postcards of the Kaiser they could rouse the Persians to do their bidding. 'They were indiscreet, and prone to neglect important details and incapable of understanding the people with whom they had to deal.'[2] One very prominent and apparently pro–German landlord, the Nizam us–Saltaneh, extracted a vast sum of money from von Kanitz, the German military attaché, to raise a regiment and, when the German came to inspect it, paraded in front of him a dozen of his unemployable farm labourers.

Wassmuss, however, was altogether of a different calibre, and knew how to play on the Persians. He persuaded one of the leading merchants of Shiraz that he was in direct touch with the Kaiser via radio telegraphy and tapped out messages of greeting purporting to come from the Kaiser. The merchant was duly flattered and, when Wassmuss told him that it was customary to offer the Kaiser a substantial gift in return for this honour – as indeed

---

[2] Lt.-Col. Haig, *Memoirs*.

was the Persian custom – he gave Wassmuss the enormous sum of £10,000.

Niedermayer, after two months in Persia, began to have doubts about the project. He had succeeded in getting support only from some of the mullas in the provincial towns, while the chief mullas of Qom had no intention of risking the loss of their considerable wealth in a jihad of uncertain outcome. Wassmuss, the most successful of the German agents in Persia, remained with the tribes in the hinterland of Bushire, where he established himself with the outlaw Tangistanis and the Qashqai khans. A visionary, quasi-mystic character, he lived with the tribes in their villages and, combining his great charm with the distribution of gold and rifle ammunition, inspired them to rise up against the British in a great war to restore their liberty and honour. This was music to their ears, for they liked nothing better than a fight with the prospect of some loot at the end of it.

Before the war the only German presence in the Persian Gulf had been the trading house of Wonckhaus, which dealt in pearls. In 1906 Wonckhaus had been appointed agents of the Hamburg-America Line and had established branches up and down the Gulf. Since the Hamburg-America Line had little business in these waters, the German government paid Wonckhaus a generous subsidy to maintain its presence and, in return, was allowed to staff the company with its intelligence agents. Back-up for the jihad mission was provided by these branch offices and by the branches of the German Persian Carpet Company, which had factories and representatives throughout the country. For several years before the war a series of 'scientific' and 'commercial' German travellers and agents had been gathering information about every aspect of national life and establishing relations with practically every person and group of any importance, particularly with the Swedish officers of the recently formed Persian Gendarmerie, many of whom had received military training in Germany and were naturally sympathetic to the German cause. All of this had been noted by British Intelligence, but there was little they could do about it. Frederick O'Connor, an old Persian consular hand, had pointed out that, since the central government was weak and governors-general came and went, real power lay with the tribes and the British should therefore try to come to terms with the more powerful of these, to make each of them responsible for maintaining order on their territory. However, this modest proposal was overlooked.

Public order in the countryside, particularly in the south, where there were no Cossacks, had more or less broken down, to the extent that it was unsafe to travel on the roads or send merchandise by caravan without a sizeable escort, which few could afford. Bandits were rife and powerful. In 1905 Sykes had recommended the formation of a British-officered mounted regiment to guard the roads in the south of Persia but, out of fear of provoking the Russians, this idea had been turned down. Discussions with the Persian government on this subject were renewed between 1908 and 1910, but the Russians objected, saying that if such a force were raised in the south they would increase their own Cossack presence in the north. After a number of particularly serious incidents the British government insisted that if order were not restored on the Bushire–Shiraz road they would go ahead anyway and send in a force to keep it open. At the end of 1910 the Persian government finally agreed to form a force of Gendarmerie, to be largely paid for by the British but officered by Swedes who, being neutral, would be acceptable to the nationalists. Many of the Persian officers were from prominent Qajar families and were well educated, having been trained in military academies in Turkey and Europe. Most of them came from the north of Persia, which meant that they had little in common with the more dreamy and anarchic southerners. The Swedes were ignorant of Persia and Persian ways and thus ended up as puppets of their Persian officers, on whom they were totally dependent. They also caused much bad feeling among the merchants by banning travel by night, the traditional time for travelling in the summer, when it was too hot to travel by day. The ordinary Gendarmerie recruits tended to be semi-criminal riff-raff.

The only other force for the maintenance of order was the Amniyeh police force, which was supposed to guard the roads but effectively made them safe only for the robbers. One of the causes of the highway robbery was the series of bad harvests and plagues of locusts, which led to serious shortages of bread. These were exacerbated by the hoarding of grain by many of the landlords, resulting in intolerably high prices for basic food. Destitute villagers were thus forced into banditry.

In March 1911, before the Gendarmerie had been fully established, there were serious bread riots in Isfahan and Shiraz. The vital road from Shiraz to the coast at Bushire was closed by the tribes for months, and all imports and exports were stopped. Four hundred soldiers of the Persian army, who had not been paid for months, attempted to take *bast* in the British Consulate at Shiraz, but were refused entry. Three of them were shot by the Indian escort. To protect the small British colony of consuls, bankers, missionaries, doctors, merchants and telegraph engineers, two squadrons of the Central India Horse were sent up to Shiraz, but they had orders never to fire first, a fact the bandits quickly took advantage of.

In December 1912 Frederick O'Connor, who had previously been Consul at Sistan and knew the country well, had become Consul at Shiraz. He found that the Fars provincial treasury was bankrupt and that the salaries of most of the officials, soldiers and police were months in arrears. At this stage the British government made an advance of £30,000 (about £1 million today) to the Persian government, specially for the use of the Fars administration. This money was remitted to the Imperial Bank of Persia at Shiraz, and was paid over by the British Consul, who thus kept some kind of control over how it was spent. One of the first advances was made to Qavam ul-Molk, a leading citizen of Shiraz and chief of the Arab Khamseh tribe,[3] to enable him to undertake a punitive expedition against a section of his own tribesmen. Qavam successfully reduced the malcontents to submission and hanged their leader.

In 1913 Wassmuss appeared in Shiraz, where he stayed for three months, meeting the tribal khans and village headmen. O'Connor met him, offered him hospitality and took him shooting. He reported that he was a 'friendly, manly, blond Saxon' but did not take seriously the idea that the Germans might be planning to

---

[3] The Khamseh tribe numbered about 70,000 at the time and migrated from their winter quarters near Bandar Abbas and Lar up to Niriz and Dehbid for the summer. The five clans (*Khamseh* is Arabic for 'five') were made up of Arabs, Turks and Luris and spoke a patois of mixed Arabic, Persian and Turkish.

penetrate into inland Persia. In 1915 Wassmuss was back in Fars on his way to Afghanistan. He was arrested by tribes friendly to the British but escaped in the night, leaving behind his German diplomatic code book, which was the one used by the German Foreign Ministry to communicate with their embassy in America. Unknown to Wassmuss, this useful book was duly handed over to the British. After his escape he went up to Shiraz, protected by the Swedish gendarmes, and moved in with the new German consul. The situation then became more serious. The Germans financed a scurrilous anti-British press and suborned the mullas. Backed by German money, the Governor-General turned pro-German. The Democratic Party, chaired by the Governor-General, controlled a society of several hundred members, through various committees, each in charge of a separate cell or lodge, who agitated against the British. All this activity was carried out in the name of patriotism, but it was in fact a German-funded operation.

In September 1915 the British vice-consul was shot outside the consulate. The Governor-General failed to react and, after protests from the Legation, was replaced by the pro-British Qavam ul-Molk. In October the Consulate secretary was wounded and one of the *ghulams*, the local mounted escort, was shot dead. The Qavam was unable to make an arrest and the British colony lived in terror. In November the Swedish gendarmes, acting under German orders, surrounded the consulate and gave those inside three hours to surrender the entire British colony to the National Committee for the Protection of Persian Independence.[4] O'Connor just had time to burn his documents and bury £2,000 of consular gold in the garden. About twenty of the British were marched off by the Gendarmerie and the Qashqai towards Bushire. Some way down the road they were met by Wassmuss, who handed the men over to the Tangistanis and sent the women to the British consulate at Bushire. The men were kept for nine months in the mud fort of Ahram, thirty miles from Bushire, by Zair Khidhar, the local bandit chief. The prisoners were eventually exchanged for some Tangistani prisoners held by the British at

---

[4] This committee funded itself by exacting donations from the merchants, and even from the Armenian bishop of Isfahan (Haig, *Memoirs*).

Bushire but, while they were languishing in the bandit chief's fort, the Foreign Office and the Government of India decided that 'something had to be done'.

The difficulty was to decide what. It was felt that the Germans and their agents were everywhere and that, unless action were taken, they would overrun first Persia and then India. Many Persian historians have said that the British misread the situation, and that the German threat was never very serious. (The implication is that the Persians were only too happy to accept the German money being offered them, but they did not intend to do much in return for it.) However, the Foreign Office and Government of India files are full of reports about German activity at this time.

According to one of these, written in 1915, Germany was attempting to organize a general revolt in Persia, chiefly in the west at Kermanshah and at Borujerd, in order to secure Hamadan, an important town on the main route from Baghdad to Tehran. They were expecting assistance from the Kurds, the Lurs and some Bakhtiari chiefs. The Vali of Posht-i Kuh (the hereditary governor of the 'Ultramontane' region of Luri and Bakhtiari tribes) had been persuaded by von Kanitz to attack the British with 30,000 men in the Karun valley, carry the Arab tribes with him and sweep the British from Iraq. The main German effort, however, was now directed at getting Indian agents to work in Sistan and Baluchistan in the south-east. Indian revolutionaries returning to India from the USA were to call at Persian ports and spread the word along the Afghan and Baluchi frontiers. Seiler was advancing from Khorasan with a party of five Germans and thirty Austrians to Afghanistan.

All these reports purported to have come from 'totally reliable sources' in Persia. However, a cautious official in the India Office in London minuted that he thought it was possible that some of them could have been planted rumours, intended to frighten the British as they advanced towards Baghdad and make them divert some of their troops away from the front.

In April 1915 the Turks occupied Kermanshah and drove out the Russian and British consuls. German agents, supported by large numbers of Austrian prisoners of war who had escaped from Russian captivity in the Caucasus, began to swarm over central and southern Persia, raising local levies as they went, and drove the British colonies out of Isfahan, Yazd and Kerman. Seiler organized an attack in Isfahan which wounded the British Consul and killed the Russian Consul. The British consular agent at Lengeh and his two brothers had been murdered by German agents, and the Bushire–Tehran telegraph line, which in wartime was the principal means of communication between Britain and Russia, was in enemy hands. Until a new line was laid from India up the eastern side of Persia the only other line went through China.

The British had a picture of several parties of German agents covering the country, stirring up the tribes and breathing jihad against the Raj. The Germans were also giving money, some of it silver Persian currency minted in Germany, to the various Persian Democrat Committees in an attempt to destabilize the bankrupt Persian government, which itself was now totally dependent for its finances on British and Russian loans. To counter the threat, the Russians, at British urging, landed more troops at Enzeli on the Caspian, but the Germans and Turks nearly succeeded in persuading the young Ahmad Shah that these troops intended to capture Tehran and he should leave at once. Realizing that, if this happened, the Persian government would collapse completely, the British and Russian Ministers with great difficulty and at some expense persuaded the Shah to stay put.

The German agents Max Otto Schoenemann in Kermanshah, Pugin[5] and Seiler in Isfahan, Zugmayer and Griesinger in Kerman, and Wassmuss in Fars were all active in raising, arming and drilling levies and local mujahideen. The German and Austrian Ministers, who left Tehran at the outbreak of war in 1914, had returned with arms and money to finance them, but things did not turn out as they expected. Von Kanitz, the German military attaché, set out to recruit support among some of the tribes and found that they were ready to accept his liberal distribution of gold. They led him to believe that they would be valuable allies against the Russians. However, the moment the Russian troops approached the tribes

---

[5] Pugin was a Chilean Jew who sold German carpet dyes. He became a very active agent for Germany.

vanished, taking the attaché's gold with them, and the wretched German blew his brains out.

In February 1915 British forces at Bushire had arrested the Wonckhaus staff, along with the German Consul Listerman, and deported them to India. In retaliation Wassmuss organized a Tangistani attack against the cavalry escort of the British Residency, in which two officers were killed. After a long argument between the Foreign Office and India, the British responded in August by occupying Bushire from the sea, raising the Union Flag over the custom house, arresting Persian ships and their cargo and imposing martial law. Wassmuss immediately organized another Tangistani attack, which caused heavy casualties to the Indian cavalry. India insisted on pulling the force out of Bushire before it got further involved in expensive punitive raids, and the British decided to maintain order by installing Sykes's old friend the Darya Begi as Governor and by 'making arrangements' with the Bakhtiari khans around Isfahan, with Qavam ul-Molk and his tribes around Shiraz, and with two of the principal landowning khans of Kerman. They also temporarily bought off the Qashqai tribes of Shiraz, who had been taking Wassmuss's gold.[6]

In November 1915 the British were badly defeated in Mesopotamia by the Turks at the battle of Ctesiphon, and General Townshend, who was in command of the British forces, retreated to Kut al-Amarah on the Tigris, where he and his army were besieged for five months before finally surrendering to the Turks in April 1916. This disaster led to the end of the myth of British invincibility and a collapse of the prestige on which they depended to preserve their position throughout the Middle East and India. It gave heart to the Persian nationalists, and a large part of the Gendarmerie, encouraged by the pro-German faction, combined with them in a bid to push the Persian government into joining the Central Powers.

In November and December 1915 the British communities at Hamadan, Sultanabad (present-day Arak) Kerman and Yazd were

---

[6] The Bakhtiari to this day reproach the Qashqai for their 'temporary' sense of loyalty. While the Bakhtiari are indigenous Persians speaking a dialect of Persian, the Qashqai are Turkish speakers who came down from Central Asia in the Middle Ages.

all pushed out by the Germans or Turks. They had already been forced out of Ahvaz, Isfahan and Shiraz. By mid-December the Legation was cabling to London: 'The Germans are master of all Persia south of Yazd, Qom, Sultanabad and Kermanshah.' Allied intervention had become inevitable.

In January 1915 the Marquess of Crewe at the India Office in London had suggested to the Viceroy, Lord (Charles) Hardinge (Sykes's old enemy from the Tehran Legation), 'In case the Swedes are quietly got rid of and the Foreign Office should favour employment of British officers for the southern Gendarmerie, have you considered whether two senior officers like Sykes and Kennion . . . could not be lent for organization and administration?' Hardinge was not keen on the idea: they would need to be supported by junior officers, who were needed in Mesopotamia and could not be spared.

Meanwhile in Persia the government was in total confusion and the cabinet was constantly changing. During the war there were to be eight prime ministers and sixteen different cabinets, which changed whenever the government was faced with an intractable problem or too much pressure from inside or outside the country. The military situation was changing daily and the government, although it had declared neutrality in 1914, was powerless to enforce it. In December 1915 the Prime Minister, Mostowfi ul-Mamalik, made a proposal: 'Persia is to adopt a position of benevolent neutrality and in order to have a force capable of putting down German agitation, the Cossack Brigade is to be increased to ten thousand men with Russian officers.' The Shah proposed a new prime minister, Sepahdar-i A'zam, but Sir Charles Marling, the new British Minister, asked to have Farman Farma installed. Farman Farma had been making overtures to the Russians, who believed him to be sympathetic to them, and so the appointment was agreed. The Russians lost no time in adding to their forces in the north and Marling pointed out to Farman Farma, now in office, that the British ought to be allowed to have a similar force in the south. He also pointed out that, as the Gendarmerie was by now ineffective, it would be better to raise a new force with British officers. The Foreign Office and India Office in London agreed, albeit in the face of opposition from the Government of India, which was hard pressed in Mesopotamia and in no mood to embark on a new and risky adventure.

In London the government was lurching from crisis to crisis. The fall of Kut al-Amarah had released 18,000 Turkish troops, who had promptly invaded the north-west of Persia. London's main concern was that the new Russian forces in the north would succeed in pushing the Germans and Turks down to the south, where there was a power vacuum, and that the latter would be able to push the British off the oil. This new factor was now of far more serious concern than the existing activity of the German agents in the south.

London was now in a hurry to send in the new force, irrespective of the wishes of the Persian government, which, they thought, would probably treat its existence as an insult to what remained of Persia's sovereignty. The British therefore decided to confuse the Persians by declaring that the purpose of the new force was to reinforce the existing Anglo–Russian East Persia Cordon, which had been set up to protect the Indian and Afghan frontiers against German incursions. They would move fast and put in the force without waiting for official Persian consent. Sykes was appointed as its head, principally on the grounds that he was the best person to work with Farman Farma, the new prime minister. But this overlooked the fact that, although his political knowledge of Persia was unmatched, Sykes's only experience of active military service had been in South Africa. Sir Percy Cox, the wise and experienced Resident of the Persian Gulf, with whom Sykes and Ella had stayed when passing through Muscat, had written to Marling and the Government of India in February 1916 suggesting that Sykes be instead appointed Consul at Shiraz to act as political officer to the force, and that a man with military experience be put in command of it. This was by far the most sensible suggestion as to how the force should be run, but it was not heeded.

The Persia of 1916 was very different from the country that Sykes had left in 1913. The nationalists had become a powerful force and had formed revolutionary 'Committees for the Protection of

Persian Independence' in the important cities of Isfahan, Yazd, Shiraz, Kermanshah, Hamadan and Qom, all of which reported to the National Defence Committee. The members were mostly Democrats and were minor officials, merchants, mullas or Gendarmerie officers – the sort of people who resented the corrupt and grasping central government, which they believed to be in the pockets of the British and the Russians. There was still plenty of nationalist spirit about, but it was noticeable that the activities of these Committees had ceased when the German subsidies to them ran out after 1915. The Democrats were secularist and anti-clerical; they favoured military action with German support against the government but they had been naturally reluctant to combine in a jihad with the reactionary mullas. It was not until late 1915 that the Democrats were to present a united front with the mullas against the government.

The government was bankrupt and the Germans had made an attractive offer to relieve the debts of the Persian government to the Russians and the British. The Turks had invaded from the west. Were they attacking Persia itself or just the British? The young Ahmad Shah was dizzy with conflicting advice.

Now that Russia and Britain were allied against Germany, there was no longer room for the old antagonism between the two Legations. Townley and Sazonov had both been recalled and replaced, by Marling and de Etter respectively, who got on well and successfully foiled the old Persian government game of playing the two Powers off against each other.

From the beginning, Sykes's position was awkward. The Government of India, concerned only for its own interests, expected him to go to Sistan, where there was a small consulate just across the border, and recruit a police force to march down to Kerman to restore the British position there. The Foreign Office and the War Office had far more ambitious plans and wanted the force to land at Bandar Abbas and proceed to Shiraz to support Qavam ul-Molk, who had been pushed out by Wassmuss. While India saw the operation as a simple policing job on the frontier, the Foreign Office saw it as a much larger military and political exercise. The War Office, knowing the difficulties of tangling with the Tangistanis in the mountains, put its foot down and refused to sanction 'any operations of an extended nature and limited the sphere of action 'to the low country only'. This was pointless, for the coastal plain around Bushire was very narrow. Marling, for his part, insisted that Sykes should be sent to support Qavam ul-Molk with a supply of arms and money. He was not interested in a petty police force, but in establishing pro-British rule throughout the south. Qavam, well aware that visible British support would alienate the nationalists among his supporters, did not welcome this proposal. The Viceroy, who was going to have to provide the troops and finance for the force, was obstructive, for India had plenty of experience of such expeditions getting out of hand.

Sykes's force needed a name, and months of discussion were devoted to finding one. For six months it was referred to as the South Persia Military Police, until Sykes pointed out that a mere police force would neither attract the sort of officers that he needed nor impress the robber tribes. He wanted the force to be called an army and proposed the name Qoshun i Jonub i Iran ('South Persia Army'). The Viceroy preferred the South Persia Militia, which the India Office in London thought sounded feeble. Finally, Major Steel at the India Office came up with the inspired name of the South Persia Rifles. However, since the nearest Persian word for 'Rifles' (*tofangchi*, meaning a local village guard) was not dignified enough, when this was translated back into Persian, it came out as Qoshun-i Jenub, which by suggesting that the SPR was an army of occupation similar to the Cossacks, entirely defeated the object. The British tried to dress the SPR up as a force acting on behalf of the Persian government but with British officers, and Marling told the Persian government that its object was the 'maintenance of their independence and authority and the restoration of order in South Persia under their auspices'. It was to be understood that, while the British would pay for the force, the money was to be treated as a loan to the Persian government. Lord Grey, the Foreign Secretary,[7] requested documents to confirm Persian official approval of the force, but these were never given.

In March 1916 Sykes sailed from Karachi and landed at Bandar

---

[7] Sir Edward Grey had been made a viscount in 1916.

Abbas. He had three masters – the Government of India, the Home Government and the Persian government – and his little force consisted of three British officers, three Indian officers, twenty Indian NCOs and a cavalry escort of twenty-five Central India Horse.

Small though his force was, Sykes made an impressive show of his landing. He paraded the Royal Navy bluejackets and held a durbar to celebrate the arrival of the mission, with the Governor of Bandar Abbas as the principal guest. His reception, however, was mixed. While the Armenians and Christians were 'elated and welcoming, most of the others looked on quietly'. The Germans had been very successful in undermining the British position, but Sykes wasted no time and immediately started recruiting. On his first day fifty-four men presented themselves, but the next day they all returned their advance pay, saying that they were not prepared to go and fight the Germans in Mesopotamia. The crisis was solved by the Governor of the Gulf ports swearing on the Qoran that the men were engaged to serve in Persia only. On the first pay day there was more trouble but the very capable Deputy Governor, a staunch ally to Sykes, summarily punished and dismissed the ringleaders. The little force, now purged of trouble-makers, set up camp a short way inland of Minab at Neyband and within a month three hundred men had enlisted. Recruits were well paid and were introduced by guarantors who stood surety for their good behaviour. Various government officials brought men in but most of them were sent in by village landlords who had spare labour. Some of the village headmen were taken on as recruiting sergeants, charged with bringing in fifty men a month each. The best recruits came from the village of Jallabi, which had supplied many of the camels that Sykes had used on his expedition to avenge the murder of Graves. The headman was an old friend of Sykes, who had travelled throughout this part of the country in his years at Kerman and was known and trusted by practically every landlord and head man. Word spread quickly that 'the Great Consul' Sykes was recruiting and, each time the story was repeated, the teller thought to impress his hearers by increasing the size of the force. In no time at all the 300 men were reported as 30,000 and the 4,000 rifles were multiplied by the Deputy

Governor, as he took a convivial pipe of opium in the evening with his friends from the town, to 10,000, and by his son the Governor of Minab to 20,000. It was a superb bluff.

Meanwhile Qavam ul-Molk was at Bushire, seeking money and arms from Sir Percy Cox, the Resident, to support his return to Shiraz to remove the pro-Germans who had taken it over. The rumours of a 'huge British force at Bandar Abbas' were reaching the ears of the Qashqai, who were now disposed to change sides. There had been a plan for Sykes to come and join him, but Qavam told Cox that he had to make a start for Shiraz before the north-ward spring migration of the Qashqai got under way or they would be too far ahead of him. He went on to say that, in order not to give 'hostile elements' any excuse for accusing him of being a British puppet, he would prefer not to be accompanied by any British forces at all. All he needed was guns and money, which he got. Not long after Qavam had set off for Shiraz he was killed when his horse fell while he was chasing a gazelle, but he was succeeded immediately by his son, who was travelling with him.

At Shiraz German subsidies had run out and support for Germany was waning. The gendarmes had gone unpaid for months and were fed up. One of their bolder Persian officers,[8] with money sent to him by O'Connor, took over the city and imprisoned the troublemakers, locking up Persians, Germans, Swedes and Turks without fear or favour. Among the German papers discovered was a watercolour sketch of a Persian with a vulture for his mother and any one of a pig, a fox and a hyena for his father, an illustration of the Germans' real attitude to the Persians and their democratic aspirations.

Shortly afterwards the new Qavam ul-Molk, chief of the Khamseh, entered Shiraz with Saulat ud-Dowleh, the chief of the Qashqai tribe, and took the city over in the name of the Persian government. To cement this unlikely alliance between the rival tribes, the two chiefs promptly betrothed their sons and daughters to each other. The situation appeared to be improving. Marling, however, did not trust Qavam ul-Molk or the Qashqai and arranged for Farman Farma to be appointed Governor-General of

---

[8] Fath ul-Molk.

Fars, with a view to his working with Sykes and the South Persia
Rifles. Sykes was delighted to be collaborating with his old friend
and sent him a very apposite quotation from a Persian poem:

> *Biyâ be-khorrami bar ru-yi Takht-i Jam bensheen*
> *Ke man do-asbeh biyâyam barâye didâret.*
> ('Come with joy and sit on Jamshid's Throne[9]
> And I shall ride post-haste to see you there.')

Even the very anti-British Persian historian who quoted this
letter[10] acknowledged an ungrudging respect for Sykes's knowledge of Persian literature, which set the writer apart from the other
British politicians and diplomats.

The young Qavam's loyalty to the British tended to depend on
which way the wind was blowing. Although he was a man of the
city, he was also the head of the Khamseh tribe of Arab semi-
nomads. He was about twenty-eight and Sykes described him as:

> . . . well educated and knowing a good deal of English, but
> immature and easily swayed. He is fond of shooting and shoots
> well; he is also fond of wine and women. He is extravagant and
> badly off, partly because he has five sisters, who received their
> shares of the family estates after the death of his father. He is
> fond of the society of Englishmen and should be influenced
> considerably thereby. He is also influenced by his brother-in-
> law [Nizam ul-Molk], who was educated at Bedford College.
> He, however, is not a satisfactory product of English education,
> being a bosom friend of Mirza Mustafa Khan, a noted
> Democrat, who was removed by us from Shiraz as his extraordi-
> nary influence over the Qavam ul-Molk was being exerted
> against us.

After spending two months recruiting local villagers at Bandar
Abbas, Sykes was sent a force of five hundred rifles from the 124th
Baluchi Regiment, with a squadron of 15th Lancers and a moun-

---

[9] Persepolis, just outside Shiraz.
[10] Abu'l Fazl Qasemi.

tain gun section as support. It was time to take his force inland, but again the Foreign Office was at odds with India as to where it should go. Marling wanted him to go west to Shiraz to join Farman Farma, while the Viceroy wanted him to go north to Kerman. Telegrams between London, India, Tehran and Bandar Abbas got delayed and muddle ensued. Sykes had been put into the impossible position of trying to serve at least two masters. He had become used to working on his own and acting on his own initiative, but now he was under wartime orders — not just orders, but counter-orders and the consequent disorder. In the end it was agreed that he should go to Kerman, where it would be much easier to get supplies, and establish himself there to strengthen the hand of the pro-British Sardar Nosrat against the German agents and their Democrat allies. He would await developments there before proceeding to Shiraz. On 16th June 1916 he reached Kerman and established his force in the old Gendarmerie head-quarters. The German and Austrian agents at Kerman and Bam fled with their supporters towards Shiraz, where Qavam ul-Molk duly arrested them.

Sykes was given a warm welcome by his old friends in Kerman, and the Telegraph and the Imperial Bank of Persia reopened their doors for business. Recruitment to the SPR now began in earnest under Major Farran. The original plan was to raise a body of eleven thousand men, but the actual figure never exceeded eight thousand. The landowners and merchants, who had had enough of Buchaqchi raids and highway robbery, were delighted and offered their support. Farran believed that it would take a year to make a useful force and thought it would be better to subsidize the local tribes, as the Germans had been doing, and train them later. However, the men poured in, attracted by the generous pay, and the force built up rapidly. One of their first actions was a successful skirmish with a party of Buchaqchi and twenty-five escaped Germans and their Persian agents. India ordered Sykes to send the Germans, who were involved in the jihad plot, under escort of British officers to Bandar Abbas, where they would be taken over and sent to India. Having no officers to spare, he entrusted them to the son of a Kermani prince, Shahzadeh Hussein, whom he knew and trusted, who would hand them over to an Indian escort coming up from the coast. Sykes's trust, however, was misplaced and the young nobleman, unnerved by news of a Turkish advance, let the prisoners escape to Sirjan, where the Buchaqchi chief Hossein Khan gave them refuge in his fort. Sykes sent an officer in pursuit but the Germans got away to Shiraz. This early fiasco raised serious doubts in India as to Sykes's reliability and long official memos of criticism were filed against him. These, in their restrained prose, were damning enough, but a letter from the young Clarmont Skrine,[11] who became Vice-Consul at Kerman the following autumn and wrote many long letters home to his mother about Sykes and the SPR, spells out what Sykes's colleagues thought of him at the time:

> Then came a most extraordinarily stupid bit of muddling on Sykes's part. Everyone knows that Sykes is an utter humbug, a man of shallow judgement and capacity, combined with inordinate vanity, who has only got the position he has because he has got a good Press at home – but this business of the prisoners really takes the cake. Would you believe it, he sent twenty-seven men, several of them exceedingly clever and unscrupulous Europeans, on their way to Bandar Abbas with nothing but a handful of venal and disaffected Persian sowars to look after them. And not only that, instead of sending them by one of the nearer and safer routes he sent them via Sirjan, the very heart of the anti-English tribes (Afshars and Buchaqchis). . . . The prisoners escaped on 22nd August and I reached Simla on 3rd September, when the news was still fresh and the harassed Foreign Office and General Staff were putting their heads together as to how to deal with this new piece of Sykesian strategy. I tell you, I heard some pretty strong language about Sykes at Simla, and opinion here in Persia, alike among Europeans and Persian partisans of the British, is even stronger about him than at HQ. . . . And this is the man who is hailed . . . as the best man we've got in Persia. 'What Sykes doesn't know about Persia isn't worth knowing etc'. *The Near East*, I am sorry to say, joins in the ridiculous chorus of praise: it actually stated in a recent

---

[11] Pronounced 'Clairmont Screen'.

number, in criticizing Sykes's mission, that although General Sykes was of course the best possible man for the job etc, most of his officers were badly chosen, being largely without Persian experience. Great Scott!! They're all Indian Army men[12] – Sykes was given his pick among the best confidential files at AHQ at Simla. As everyone knows, it's his chief Staff Officer, Major Hunter, a most brilliant man, who has kept the General safe and has secured (up to date) the success of the mission. In nearly everything he twists the General round his finger and it's only in cases like that of the prisoners, when the General goes against Hunter, that there's bad trouble.

Marling was now pushing for Sykes to go directly to Shiraz, but India was dithering. With higher command sending him conflicting sets of instructions, it was not surprising that he should eventually go his own way and decide that, since the direct way to Shiraz was infested with well-armed Buchaqchi bandits, and there was no telegraph line to keep him in touch, he would do better to take the long way round and march the 220 miles along the telegraph line to Yazd. There he made a triumphal entry. The British community had returned and, ever the showman, Sykes organized a ceremony to celebrate the occasion by raising the Union Flag over the British Vice-Consulate, where Mr Merriman of the Imperial Bank of Persia was able to resume his post.

At Yazd there was more delay while Sykes's different masters argued about his next move. According to the final chapters of his *History of Persia*, which give a rather self-serving account of how he won the war in Persia single-handed, the original intention was that he should go straight to Shiraz, 'the storm-centre of southern Persia', but that by this time a large force of Turks, with German officers and artillery, was moving fast towards Isfahan, nearly two hundred miles to the west of Yazd, which was defended by 'only six hundred Russian Cossacks with two field guns'. He arrived in August and the Turks, who had received suitably exaggerated accounts of the size of his force, melted away to the west. Sykes's tiny force of Indian lancers and newly recruited South Persia Rifles

---

[12] Thirteen of them spoke Persian.

entered the city, where they received a particularly warm welcome from the large Armenian community, who had been terrified of being massacred by the Turks.

Sykes's constant self-congratulation and his instinct for the grand gesture were anathema to people such as Skrine. It has to be remembered that Skrine had not been at Kerman at the time in question and was just repeating what he had heard from others. Nor was he aware of the conflicting instructions with which London and India were bombarding Sykes at the time. But it was clear that Skrine spoke for many.

I tell you, *everyone*, the Gov't of India, SPR, Political élite, is thoroughly sick of Sykes. The universal opinion is that neither the SPR nor the peace of Southern Persia has a proper chance to get established until he's outed. He's literally nothing but a man of words and d....d dull words at that. He's never *done* a thing in his life, except write a few inferior books, nor has he an idea in his head beyond flattering and getting popular with Persians and advertising himself. The secret of his success is that he's got a good Press at home and forms a mutual admiration society with certain gentlemen whom I could name but won't. Thanks to this, he got put in by the Home Gov't (against the wishes of the Indian Gov't) to raise the SPR and 'restore order in Southern Persia . . .

Meanwhile Sykes, having left the hard work of starting the SPR here entirely to his officers — while here he did nothing but buck his 'old friends', as he always called them – off he marches to Isfahan via Yazd, turning his back on the difficult situation in Kerman and Sirjan. While the column was at Yazd, it was wired to him that the prisoners had escaped and the situation was dangerous. What he ought to have done of course was to march on Sirjan, either attack the Buchaqchis and Baharlus or at the very least make a much-needed demonstration in force and if possible round up the escaped prisoners; and then march to Shiraz (his ultimate objective) via Niriz. Instead of which he wires, 'Hope you are taking all necessary steps to recapture prisoners. Situation obscure – I'm off to Isfahan.'!! Thanks entirely to the good luck of British arms, and against all the chances, the rebels failed to score any decisive success and the Democrats failed to re-establish themselves in Kerman, so we pulled through . . .

Why did Sykes insist on going to Isfahan, right out of his way? Simply swank; he wanted to have a triumphal entry into the ancient capital of Persia: he wanted to pow-wow with the Russians there and get an Order or two out of the Russian government (this he succeeded in doing). For this purpose, he delayed his arrival at Shiraz – the most important thing to be done – for several weeks, and shirked marching through the rougher and more dangerous country of Laristan and Fars.

Sykes did indeed make a triumphal entry into Isfahan. The magnificent main square, the Meidan-i Shah, is 560 yards long and 180 yards wide, with the original stone polo goalposts put there by the Safavid Shah Abbas in the early seventeenth century. In the middle of the west side is the Âli Qapu – the Lofty Gateway or Sublime Porte – with its pillared viewing platform on the roof looking out over the Meidan in which, in Safavid times, gladiatorial contests, fights between wild beasts and polo matches were staged. The south side is dominated by the façade of the blue-tiled Masjid-i Shah mosque, built by Shah Abbas in 1611, with its stunning turquoise-blue dome, and on the east side is the pale caramel-coloured dome of the smaller Lutfullah mosque which Shah Abbas built to honour his father-in-law. The whole square is surrounded by a covered bazaar and is rivalled only by Tamerlane's Registan square in Samarqand.

The Russian Commandant Bielomestinov, who had arrived in Isfahan a short while before, invited Sykes as the senior officer to review a parade of both forces. From under the Âli Qapu the South Persia Rifles, the Bengal cavalry and the Kuban Cossacks entered the Meidan. The infantry marched past first, followed by the squadron of lancers at the gallop past and then followed the three squadrons of Cossacks. The first squadron went by at the walk, the second artillery squadron fired a salute and the third squadron galloped past. The night before, a year to the day after the British colony had been forced by the Germans to leave Isfahan, the Russians had laid on a great celebratory dinner to honour their return, with toast after toast and Cossack dancing. Sykes offered a return dinner the following night and worked hard on the Russian that he had learned at Meshed so that he could reply suitably to all the speeches and toasts. There was much fraternizing between the British and Russian officers, but sadly the Indians, who did not share the Russian love of alcohol, were rather left out. Not since Tsar Alexander and his troops entered Paris at the time of Waterloo had such a joint Anglo-Russian parade been held.

'Swank' it may have been, but Sykes's purpose was to produce the first public demonstration that the Russians and the British, whom the Persians had been playing off against each other for nearly a hundred years, were now united against the invading Turks and Germans. 'Swank' was required to mark such a radical change and to impress on the Persians that German victory, of which the nationalists and Democrats were so sure, was by no means certain.

Skrine, however, along with many of his colleagues, was not impressed and wanted to cut Sykes down to size. He wrote to his mother again:

> He is a big man in no one's estimation but his own. He's con-
> vinced he's one of the big men of the age, and views himself
> theatrically as a second Alexander, with a dash of Kitchener. He
> has a remarkable capacity for self-deception which makes him
> liable to appalling mistakes, but he's a good hand at bluff and
> manages to carry off his mistakes.

Sykes and his force halted at Isfahan for five weeks. The Russians set about clearing the bandits from the road north to Tehran, but to the south-west the British-built Lynch road from Ahwaz was blocked at a point fifty miles from Isfahan by the presence of a large gang of robbers and all trade had ceased. Sixteen thousand loads of goods destined for the bazaars of Isfahan had been dumped in the open by merchants unable to move any further because of the danger of bandits. With the merchants unpaid, the goods deteriorating and the Russians not prepared to act, Sykes gathered three thousand camels and sent them under strong escort to collect the merchandise. As the first loaded caravan emerged from a very difficult pass on its way back it was attacked by three hundred mounted robbers, but the escort managed to drive them off and the rest of the loads were brought in over the next few days. Business in the bazaar resumed, the merchants were grateful and the bandits kept away from that road for some months to come.

The situation at Shiraz, which had only recently stabilized, had once again deteriorated, however, and there were serious disturbances brought on by high bread prices. Farman Farma, with his own personal guard of two hundred men and two Maxim guns, accompanied by Colonel Gough, the new British Consul, set off from Isfahan for Shiraz to take up his new post as Governor-General of Fars. Contemporary Iranian historians consider that it was a mistake for the British to have insisted on installing the by now notoriously grasping and avaricious Farman Farma as Governor, for his greed had made him many enemies. Not far from Shiraz, at the village of Dehbid, Farman Farma and Gough were stopped by a large body of men from Qavam ul-Molk and Saulat. These two former rivals were now united in their opposition to Farman Farma's presence in Fars. While in Tehran, the Prince had arranged for Saulat to be officially recognized by the government as Il-Khan or supreme chief of the Qashqai, but was insisting on a massive 'squeeze' of 50,000 tomans (about £10,000 at that time). Saulat regarded this as extortionate and had persuaded Qavam ul-Molk, who could see that the same demands would be made on him, to join him in resisting Farman Farma's appointment. Telegrams flew back and forth to Tehran until the Persian government persuaded Saulat and Qavam to back down and allow Farman Farma and Gough to proceed.[13]

As soon as Farman Farma had established himself in his new Governorship, Sykes and his column followed on, and in November 1916, after a march of 320 miles from Isfahan and a total roundabout march of a thousand miles from Kerman, twenty-three years after their first meeting in the desert, Sykes and Farman Farma entered Shiraz together. What followed was the most difficult and trying period of Sykes's career.

---

[13] It later turned out that Zill us-Sultan, who wanted to be Governor of Fars, was also involved (Haig, *Memoirs*).

18

Under attack

SHIRAZ WAS ONE of the most beautiful cities of Persia, renowned for its roses and its poets. Coming from the north, after passing the ruins of Persepolis and the tomb of Cyrus the Great, the traveller crossed a range of barren mountains running east–west some 1,500 to 2,000 feet above the plain until, in a narrow defile, there rose a stone archway across the road, through which there suddenly appeared a view of the city and the mountains behind. The view from here was so stunning and unexpected that it was called the Allah-u Akbar ('God is Greatest') pass.

The city was surrounded by walled gardens and orchards, ablaze with blossom in the clear air of spring, but this apparent peacefulness was deceptive. The long fertile valley in which the city lies was dotted with fortified villages. The mud-brick forts, now crumbling away, were built to protect the settled villagers from the nomad tribes, particularly the Qashqai, who in the spring brought their huge flocks of sheep and goats from their winter grazing in the warm southern plains up to their summer quarters in the mountains to the north. On their way through the settled villages they tended to help themselves to whatever they could find and, like locusts, let their flocks graze on the young wheat and barley until the fields were bare. The tribe itself numbered about 130,000 and, over the length of their 200-mile migration route, it controlled settled villages with a population of another 100,000. At any one time the Qashqai could field a force of 5,000 horsemen with ease. Their chief, Saulat ud-Dowleh ('Ferocity of the State'), was the uncrowned king of Fars and immensely rich from the revenue that he collected from the village landowners and from the booty or blackmail that his men collected on the roads. He had no interest in the British or the Persians imposing their law on his territory, which he wished to be allowed to enjoy unmolested.

With the beginning of the winter of 1916 the Qashqai had migrated south and there was a respite from their raiding. Sykes had until the spring, when they would be moving north again, to establish a force that would put an end to their banditry and make the roads safe. The first problem he faced was what to do with the three thousand members of the Gendarmerie spread over three hundred miles in the province. They had no Swedish officers, many of the Persian officers were pro-German, and they were half-starved, unpaid and undisciplined. Only a year earlier they had arrested the British Consul O'Connor and had driven Qavam ul-Molk out of Shiraz, as well as signing an agreement with Saulat by which the Gendarmerie and the Qashqai would unite against the British and the Russians. They possessed field guns and machine-guns, and they had strength in numbers. Sykes had a choice of either disbanding them or taking them over. He did not have enough staff officers to take them over, but if they were disbanded they would either take to banditry or go over to the Germans. Sykes could not wait for decisions to be made for him by London or India, so the day after his arrival in Shiraz he addressed the officers and told them that he was raising the South Persia Rifles for the Persian government and that he had decided to take over the Gendarmerie in Fars. It was a bold step and although many of the men, happy at the prospect of regular pay, accepted the take-over, a large number of the best officers, who were patriots and Democrats, refused to serve under British command. Sykes was later frequently criticized for his decision, but none of his critics suggested a better alternative.

Sykes was desperately understaffed and under pressure. He had not only to recruit and train his new force but also to produce a budget. He raised some eyebrows in London and India by listing his initial modest requirement for 'the most modern instruments of war such as aeroplanes, armoured cars and a tank'. 'Ye gods!!!'

minuted the Military Secretary at the India Office, and 'Tanks to deal with tribesmen!', minuted someone in the Foreign Office. The comment on the first budget that Sykes sent to India was that it was 'so inaccurate and unintelligible as to be useless'. When reproached for its inadequacy, he asked India to ignore it, writing that it had been 'prepared under circumstances of sickness and constant changes of staff, and in the stress of organizing the move to Kerman'.

More pressure came from the Persian government. The Prime Minister, although he had given verbal approval to Marling for the formation of the SPR, was most reluctant to do so officially for fear of the nationalists. And Sykes had not been given official approval for taking over the Gendarmerie on his own initiative. Marling reported that there were 'the usual intrigues on foot at Tehran to overthrow the government' and that 'the Prime Minister was afraid to furnish further material for anti-government agitation by taking any open step in execution of the August agreement'. The Prime Minister did, however, promise Marling to find some formula to convey the necessary instructions to Farman Farma to co-operate with Sykes. Meanwhile Sykes was instructed to act as if the position had been regularized. Ten days later Farman Farma received a long telegram from Tehran which, while ostensibly censuring him for allowing Sykes to exercise greater powers than were admissible under the August agreement, was really intended, and accepted by everyone concerned, as tantamount to official recognition of the SPR. Throughout his time at Shiraz, Sykes was bedevilled by the refusal of the Persian government, in whose name he was supposed to be acting, to give his existence its open and official approval. Although amenable to British influence at the highest level, the government was under heavy pressure from the nationalists and, when this pressure became particularly pressing, it not only instructed the officials in Fars to be as obstructive as possible towards the SPR, but encouraged the tribes to attack the SPR, and its members to desert. When under pressure from the Legation it would send instructions to its officials to support Sykes, but under separate cover it would send a private letter telling them to ignore the official document.

Sykes's position was not enviable, but in spite of everything the recruiting carried on. The target was to raise forces in three areas:

Fars Brigade	800 cavalry, 1,600 infantry, 18 guns and 6 machine-guns
Kerman Brigade	400 cavalry, 800 infantry, 12 guns
Bandar Abbas area	400 cavalry, 800 infantry, 6 guns

By December 1916 he was doing well and he reported that the strength of the SPR, including levies and ex-Gendarmerie, was:

Fars	450 cavalry, 2,000 infantry, 2 guns and 1 machine-gun
Kerman	550 cavalry, 550 infantry, 4 guns
Bandar Abbas	50 cavalry, 100 infantry

The SPR, who were all locally raised troops, were backed up by Indian troops with British officers, who did the training and, initially, most of the fighting. These troops were not part of the SPR. They were made up of:

Shiraz:	15th Lancers	146 sabres
	3rd Mountain Battery	2 guns
	6th Rajputs	539 rifles
	3/124th Baluchis	18 rifles
Saidabad/Sirjan:	16th Rajputs	78 rifles
	Burma Mounted Infantry	110 rifles
On convoy duty between Saidabad and Bandar Abbas or Shiraz:		
	16th Rajputs	233 rifles
Dehbid:	3/124th Baluchis	395 rifles
	Burma Mounted Infantry	123 rifles

Although it was relatively easy to recruit ordinary soldiers, it was far more difficult to recruit suitable officers. Most of the former Gendarmerie officers were well-educated Tehranis, nationalistic and independent-minded and therefore unlikely to take kindly to receiving orders from the invading English, still less from the far less well-educated Indian NCOs. Sykes's solution was to recruit junior Persian officers with no previous European training, who would be easier to assimilate into the Indian Army way of doing things. Colonel Orton, a thoroughly competent British officer of the old school, took a dim view of the 'well born Persians, who were too full of vices, too lazy to learn and inordinately conceited, always quick to think they knew everything there was to learn'. Major Frazer-Hunter, a very successful and popular officer, who appreciated Persian sensibilities and was sensitive to their national pride, pointed out that one 'could not treat the Persians like Indians. British officers should instruct the Persian soldiers, not command them.' W.A.K. Fraser, who took over command of the SPR after the war, wrote in his diary: 'The Persian officers were a most pleasant surprise to me. They are energetic and keen and men of a good class and breeding. They put up with a lot of rough handling . . . They look fit and strong and well set up.' He did not however, take to Qavam ul-Molk, whom he described as 'an unimpressive and pimply young man. 'However', he went on, 'he is our friend.'

The British officers of the SPR were divided: some thought that they could get away with kicking the Persians around like Indians, while others, more enlightened, realized that they had to treat the Persians with proper respect. The Persians held equally racist attitudes: the young trainee officers did not take to being ordered about by the Indian NCOs, whom they regarded as being inferior to them in every possible way.

A contemporary Iranian historian, when asked what his compatriots thought of Sykes and the SPR at the time, mentioned that what they resented most about them was not so much the raising of the local regiment or the presence of British officers as the fact that the troops who backed up the force were Indian: 'We would not have minded so much if you had sent English soldiers, but when you sent those Indians to occupy us we felt really insulted.'

This racism was played on by the German propagandists, who put about a story that the duplicitous English, in order to make the Persians believe that they were on the side of Islam, had told the Hindu soldiers to pretend to be Muslims. When they disembarked at Bushire in 1915, the Hindus were said to have been clutching their idols while, at the same time, chanting the Shia Muslim imprecation 'Ya Ali'. This story appealed to the Persians who, because it was a good one, believed it and repeated it. But while some of the Persians resented the Indians, others pitied them, seeing them as being made to fight far from home for a cause in which they could have no interest.

British officers rapidly built up the strength of the SPR by recruiting around Bandar Abbas, Kerman and Shiraz, but it was not an easy job, and progress was uneven. Major Merrill reported that the two hundred levies recruited to the cause at Bam were useless: 'No discipline, cannot even be turned out for parade at any given time.' Locals would not fight other locals and left all the fighting to the Indians. Another British officer, Major Wagstaff, declared that they were 'more interested in taking in money than in taking on the Germans, Austrians and Swedes or the Persian robbers, bandits, agitators and Russophiles'. To avoid making them face people who were known to them, he proposed moving the recruits to serve away from home, but they hated leaving their families. The useless ones, he said, could not be disbanded because 'they would be lost to the enemy'.

Clarmont Skrine, writing to his mother from Kerman in a more uninhibited style, described the three thousand members of the Shiraz Gendarmerie enrolled by Sykes as:

> A set of bog-rats as mutinous as they are syphilitic, who have to be paid extra bonuses to make them attend drills. These are the '5,000 troops' Sykes is supposed to have raised. Not a word is said about the splendid work that three or four officers have done here, raising 1,000 infantry and 400 cavalry, only sixty of whom belonged to the old Gendarmerie, and in less than one year have already licked them into shape.

Although much of the material was unpromising, it was surprising how quickly Sykes and his officers managed to create a disciplined force such as – apart from the Russian Cossack Brigade – had never been seen in Persia before. Quite apart from the question of their military effectiveness, however, was the fact that the sheer existence of the SPR in such numbers was sufficient to create an effective British 'bluff' in south Persia. It was easy for

Skrine, venting his spleen in Kerman, to be critical of Sykes as he struggled away in the much more populated province of Fars, which was dominated by two large and well-armed tribes who considered that they had a natural right to prey on farmers, merchants and travellers, a right of which they were constantly reminded by Wassmuss from his lair at Ahram.

The SPR established posts along the main roads to deal with the many tribal robbers. In December 1916 the post at Kazerun, on the vital road from Shiraz to Bushire, was attacked and the former gendarmes who manned it were stripped and turned out. At first it was thought that Wassmuss was behind the attack but it later turned out to be an act of retaliation by Saulat against Farman Farma, who had been trying to undermine Saulat's tribal position. The situation was further complicated by the 'arrangement' that the British had made with one of Saulat's rivals to deal with the Kazerunis.

Later that month a force of tribesmen captured the SPR post at Dasht-i Arjan, about thirty miles west of Shiraz, and took its garrison prisoners. Sykes telegraphed to India to call for strong support from Bushire, which, although in Persia, came under Mesopotamian command. General Maude, the commander-in-chief in Mesopotamia, replied icily that he could of course send the necessary troops, but only at the expense of the operation against the Turks that he had just commenced on the Tigris. It was to be regretted, he said, that Sykes should have sent out detachments in a partially unsettled country and so invited their capture. Sykes concluded that Qavam ul-Molk had been involved in the attack, and decided to stay in Shiraz to deal with him. He sent a column out in the Kazerun direction under Colonel Twigg, which met with considerable opposition. The country was mountainous and the ammunition for the old and inadequate 7-pounder mountain guns was defective. The local guides misguided the column up the very rocky, dry and narrow Kotal-i Pir-i Zan ('Pass of the Old Hag'); the Persian troops were reluctant to face the tribesmen and many of them either ran off or went over to the enemy. In the very difficult country the force became split, and when the enemy counter-attacked the muleteers fled, leaving them without transport. The Indian troops behaved splendidly but two-thirds of the

SPR shirked the fighting, although the remaining third showed considerable gallantry. It was a fiasco and the remains of the force straggled home with great loss of face.

Sykes had misjudged the quality and number of enemy. In the space of five days he had demanded first two hundred support troops from General Maude, then four hundred and finally, in a tone of panic, a total of six hundred men. Trying to put a brave face on it, in his subsequent report he described the failed operation as an exercise of 'reconnaissance in strength', while admitting that 'politically, the result of retirement was unfavourable'. However, apart from loss of face, the SPR had not suffered too great a setback. Heavy snow set in and sent the tribes back down to Kazerun, on the other side of the mountains from Shiraz, where they remained for the rest of the winter.

In early 1917 Sykes began to receive some recognition for his achievement. On 20th February 1917 Lord Curzon, replying to a question in the House of Lords about the situation in Persia, paid tribute to Sykes's long march to Shiraz and remarked that there had been about a hundred groups of German agents active in Persia. According to *The Times*:

> The Marquess of Crewe replied that the long march of Sir Percy Sykes was very remarkable and he hoped that the nature of his task and of the obstacles which Sir Percy had to surmount would receive greater recognition than they had done hitherto in the pressure of news concerning the war. (*Cheers*) It was clear that some progress had been made in Persia and it might be said with some confidence that the situation tended to improve.

In Shiraz, Farman Farma had arrested a number of German agents, including Zugmayer, whose diary raised some eyebrows. In it he had surreally recorded that the Turks had captured Tehran; Sweden and Norway had joined the Germans; the Bakhtiari tribes had defeated the SPR; and Sykes himself had been captured near Dehbid. In fact, the Germans were only under house arrest in the *Arg*, from where they were still able to conduct their anti-British campaign. In March 1917 Farman Farma handed the agents over to Sykes, who decided to get them away from Shiraz and hand them on to the Russian Consul at Isfahan. The question arose of how they should be conveyed on the 200-mile journey. Sykes did not wish to lose any more prisoners. Since they could hardly be dragged there in chains, it was decided to send the officers in carriages and the men in *kajavehs*, which was almost worse than being made to walk.

In March 1917 the Prime Minister, Vossouq ud-Dowleh ('Confidence of the State'), officially recognized the SPR and Farman Farma held a reception for the officers, where he made a speech emphasizing that England and Persia were old friends with common interests. This greatly eased Sykes's position and gave the tribes pause for thought.

Since Saulat and his tribe exercised complete control over the Shiraz end of the Bushire road, the British had to come to terms with him. In May Sykes and Gough went out to meet Saulat in his summer quarters and arrived at a 'friendly agreement', partly financial, that promised to improve matters. Farman Farma, however, who had not been included in this distribution of bounty, denounced Saulat to the Democrats as being in the pay of the British and protested to the Persian government against Saulat's presumption. When Gough took him to task for this, Farman Farma reconsidered his attitude. After paying a friendly visit to Saulat he came to an arrangement with him for the maintenance of security on the Kazerun–Shiraz road, in return for a very large British subsidy which he would arrange and from which both of them could benefit. When the British refused to fall in with this neat stitch-up, it was, to say the least, a disappointment to the pair of them. As it turned out, it might have saved a great deal of British money if the deal had been accepted.

By the early summer of 1917 the SPR had established small posts along the road to Isfahan to deal with the tribal robbers, who made their appearance after the spring migration from the hot country in the south. In May a section of forty-five of the SPR based at Abadeh pursued a band of about eighty Qashqai sheep- and donkey-stealers for ten miles, recovering all the stolen livestock and causing ten casualties. Then in June a caravan of donkeys carrying wheat for Shiraz, escorted by the SPR, was attacked and captured by the Qashqai. Captain Lilly, with sixty SPR cavalry, pursued them for fifty miles before catching them up and recovering a good many of the donkeys and their cargo. His only casualties were one horse wounded and two dead from exhaustion. A week later the Burma Mounted Infantry took on a gang of robbers who had looted a caravan. They killed nine of them and captured another eighteen, as well as recovering much of the stolen property, 'which had an excellent effect on the neighbourhood'.

In June the Persian government fell and the pro-British Vossouq was replaced as Prime Minister. The first act of the new government was to rescind its recognition of the SPR, which led to an immediate increase in trouble in Fars. In July a squadron of the Burma Mounted Infantry, supporting 150 men of the 124th Baluchi infantry and a machine-gun section, attacked a particularly troublesome Qashqai clan which had a long list of robberies to its name. The Qashqai spies got news of the raid, which gave them time to organize their defence. They scattered themselves among some innocent Basseri[1] camps before retreating to a large fort on a hill, from where they started to fire at the Indians. To the astonishment of the Qashqai, the 'skinny-legged' Indians advanced in a steady line straight into their fire and, when they were a hundred yards away, fixed bayonets and charged. The five hundred Qashqai, who had never faced such a disciplined attack and were certainly not expecting to see such bravery from the 'timid Indians', fled into the hills, leaving all the stolen cattle and property behind. This was a substantial victory, and news of the impressive performance of the Indians spread rapidly round the villages and camp fires of Fars.

The settled villagers, whose crops and livestock were being raided by the Qashqai, might have been expected to welcome and assist the SPR, but their view was that, while gendarmes came and went, the robbers were always with them and would take reprisals if the villagers co-operated with the SPR. The tribal women were particularly effective in support of their men, and often drove their huge flocks of sheep and goats in front of the SPR to block their way.

Kerman, although much more peaceful than Fars, still had occasional trouble with the Baharlu and Buchaqchi tribes. In August a

---

[1] A clan of the Khamseh tribe.

detachment of SPR escorting a caravan travelling from Tehran to Kerman had been attacked near Anar by a large group of bandits and, although the Persian officers had escaped, the whole caravan with them had been captured. The bandits were reported to be attacking another large caravan and to be planning a raid on Anar. Colonel Farran set off from Kerman with a squadron of SPR cavalry and a mountain gun on the 128-mile ride to Anar, where he immediately set about rounding them up. In this he was reasonably successful: he killed or captured ten of the bandits and recovering four hundred of the stolen camels, while SPR casualties totalled two men and seven horses. Like their counterparts in Fars, the Kerman bandits were unused to such firm treatment and thereafter ventured out less. Farran reported that 'the local effect was excellent', meaning that the Persian soldiery, new to being led from the front by competent officers, began to have faith in their British officers and to feel confident enough to follow them.

Transport was a problem for the SPR. Most of the roads in south Persia were no more than tracks worn down by the passage of camels and donkeys over the centuries and were impassable to wheeled vehicles of any kind. There was a serious shortage of horses in Fars, and at Bandar Abbas the SPR had taken over so many camels that the merchants were objecting.

The donkeys had suppurating sores, but had to be used. The government caravans with mixed donkeys and camels were bad for both. In rocky places the camels held up the donkeys and on the flat plain vice versa. All the animals were exhausted.

Forage for the animals was also scarce and expensive, so it was decided to bring in motor vehicles and to build roads for them. By the autumn of 1917 the Kerman–Bandar Abbas main road was passable to motor traffic and a further 385 miles of motorable road had been built between Kerman and Shiraz. By the end of the war the SPR engineers had built a thousand miles of motorable road. However, although the Bandar Abbas road was open in 1917, the Kazerun–Shiraz road, with its narrow mountain passes, was still in the hands of the Qashqai, under their chief Saulat ud-Dowleh, who extorted heavy sums to allow cargo to be carried up it, thus effectively closing it.

In the summer and autumn of 1917 the punishment being dealt

out to various robber tribes by the Indian troops and the SPR was having an effect on Saulat and apparently leading him to pay attention to the anti-British emanations from Tehran and the machinations of Wassmuss. The hostile attitude of the Persian government to the SPR, followed by news from France that Germany was winning the war, had an immediate and great anti-British effect in South Persia. Saulat, seeing an opportunity both to get the better of his enemies and to gain power and influence, decided to fall in with the instructions coming secretly from Tehran to destroy the SPR and drive the British out of Persia. The constant assurances by Wassmuss of the inevitability of German success and of the consequent immunity of their Persian friends from British reprisals contributed, no doubt, to this decision.

A particular success for British intelligence at this time was the capture of Gustav Bruggmann by Captain Reginald Teague-Jones, the Intelligence Officer for the Persian Gulf, based at Bushire.[2] A copy of the report of his interrogation is among Sykes's private papers; it tells much about the activities of the German agents in Persia. Bruggmann was a Swiss who had been working in Persia since 1909 as the representative of the Oriental Carpet Manufacturers company, spending time in all the important carpet-weaving towns of western Persia. In 1913 he had gone to Kerman to act as the agent for the German Carpet Company. When Zugmayer had left for Baluchistan he was appointed as German Consul, in that he represented a German firm. However, he fell ill and Seiler, who was on his way to Kabul, took over from him until, hearing of Sykes's approach, he packed up his camels and followed Zugmayer. Bruggmann was arrested by the SPR and sent down to Bandar Abbas as part of the group under the disastrous escort of Shahzadeh Hussein. His version of the story was that, when they were in the hands of the chief of the Baharlu, who formed part of Qavam ul-Molk's confederacy, an official letter came from Qavam to the chief telling him to hand the prisoners over, followed by a private letter telling him to do no such thing. Later on, clearly under heavy British pressure, Qavam gave him

---

[2] See *The Spy who Disappeared*, in which Teague-Jones tells the astonishing story of his role in the post-war fighting between British forces and the Bolsheviks in Baku and Transcaspia.

firm orders to hand them over, but still gave them time to depart. On the way Bruggmann met Saulat, who told him that Baghdad had fallen to the British and that circumstances did not permit him to assist the Germans. However, Saulat said that if the situation improved, he would be ready to help them. He sent Bruggmann off to Wassmuss down at Ahram.

There he developed severe pain in his back and, unable to get a local doctor to come out from Bushire, decided after a while to slip into the town under cover. He paid a fisherman a large sum of money to ferry him up the coast but bad weather made the boatman put ashore close to the British military camp, where he took him to the house of a friend. The friend promptly handed Bruggmann over to the British, who arrested him. He protested that he carried a Swiss passport and was in a neutral country; it was only circumstances that had made him accept the position of German Consul at Kerman, he said. He was prepared to talk, however, and told Teague-Jones much about Wassmuss:

> Bruggmann has a great admiration for Wassmuss, to whom he attributes considerable influence throughout Fars. He cannot clearly explain this influence, but admits that it is not personal, nor is it due to monetary considerations . . . [but] chiefly due to the fact that Wassmuss still maintains the dignity of a representative, in fact *the* representative, in southern Persia of the German Government. [He has] a considerable correspondence, the bulk of which consists in the exchange of letters with his Persian friends, but much of which comes from sympathizers in Shiraz and Tehran and he is occasionally in correspondence with Turkish Army Headquarters . . . Wassmuss has so many influential friends that the sending of letters without fear of detection or capture is not difficult. He has a regular office, typewriter etc. and three Persian clerks. He has writers [i.e., reporters] in most of the important places and is well posted as to the latest political developments, particularly the Democratic movement and Wassmuss is undoubtedly in touch with the leaders of this movement . . . [He has] cordial relations with all the leading men of Fars, who come to him for advice . . . Zair Khidhar will do anything for him . . . Both Saulat and Qavam ul-Molk are in

frequent correspondence with him, although Qavam is more cautious than Saulat. Both of them in their hearts are very anti-British and would turn on us at once were circumstances to become sufficiently favourable. The same applies to Farman Farma, who realizes the necessity of associating himself with the progressive party in Tehran . . . It is for no particular love for Germany that Wassmuss stands high in popular opinion, but simply that he is an enemy of the British and ipso facto a friend of the Persians . . .

Referring to the SPR, Bruggmann does not prophesy much success for them and thinks they will prove a danger rather than a safeguard . . . He considers General Sykes's position a most difficult one, surrounded as he is by very influential enemies.

Sykes, while trying to raise and train the SPR as well as deal with the robber tribes on the road, was caught up in an argument between London, Delhi and Tehran about his position in the new force and the very nature of the force itself. It had been started by the fiasco of the Dasht-i Arjan incident, which had made his masters aware that the SPR might prove very expensive if it required troops from Mesopotamia to get it out of trouble. The correspondence, which went on for months, boiled down to the argument as to whether the SPR was to be a police force, limited to preventing robbery on the roads, or a military force, taking a much more aggressive role in pursuing the tribes and launching punitive raids against them. The next question revolved around who was to control the SPR. The Foreign Office took the view that the SPR was a Persian regiment with British officers, which was serving the Persian government and assisting it to establish order in the south. As such, it should be under the control of Marling at the Legation. Not surprisingly, few Persians shared this view! The War Office, agreeing that it was politically impossible to have the force controlled by General Maude in Mesopotamia, suggested that the Government of India should be made responsible for staffing and supplying the SPR, and should also have control of it. India was asked for its opinion.

The reply, based on the view that the Turks intended to advance towards Afghanistan, recommended that the SPR should be placed under the command of the C–in–C India, who would nominate an experienced General Officer to exercise command in South Persia, with supreme control of operations in the area. He should receive his instructions from the Government of India, and act under the orders of London after consultation with the British Minister at Tehran. Sykes, it was suggested, should be appointed as his chief political adviser. The Government of India emphasized the importance of avoiding anything in the nature of dual control, apparently oblivious to the fact that its proposal would create exactly this problem. It also recommended that trade should be encouraged on the Bushire–Shiraz road and that for this purpose the rebel khans should be permitted quietly to re-establish relations with the British, without promises being made to them of anything in the future.

Marling, from his Foreign Office position with responsibility for political relations with Persia, replied that because the tribal chiefs in Fars were in close touch with Tehran and susceptible to government influence, the much more political nature of the Fars Brigade's job meant that he himself should be closely involved in the operation of the SPR. Kerman, where there were no powerful tribes or political complications, was a different matter. He added that, in his opinion, the unrest in South Persia was due less to German influence than to the dislike of all the local chiefs of the prospect of an efficient authority that would limit their own opportunities for brigandry and blackmail. In this he was right, in that all that Saulat and the Qashqai wanted was to be left alone to make their living by extracting tolls from the merchant caravans on their way up from the coast. Saulat could not understand what business it was of the British to interfere in his long-established livelihood, and this was what defined his nationalism.

The War Cabinet in London was reluctant to replace Sykes with a General Officer from the Indian Army. Sykes had an exceptional knowledge of the country and was very much liked by Persians generally and by Farman Farma in particular. It was also felt that a General Officer would give the SPR a military appearance, which would justly excite the suspicions of the Persian government. They asked Marling and the Government of India to review the question again. India, already responsible for reinforcements, munitions and supplies for the SPR, considered that logically it should also be responsible for operations. It doubted whether Sykes had sufficient military experience and still wanted a military man in command. Although the Chief of Staff in London agreed, the War Cabinet, thinking more of the post-war political implications, was not convinced and decided that unless the Turks advanced into Persia in force, the existing arrangements should continue. Sykes, they said, should remain in charge of the combined Indian and Persian forces and India should send him a military field officer as an adviser. India, ever with its feet on the ground and seeing the sort of mess that would ensue if this were agreed, pointed out that it would be inequitable and unsound to make this officer responsible for operations without giving him the corresponding authority – the nightmare of all military men to this day. It therefore preferred to leave Sykes in full charge. In the meantime, however, it would send a qualified general staff officer and a highly experienced senior administrative staff officer to serve under him.

There were many in India who wanted to get rid of Sykes altogether, as he knew. He had come under heavy criticism from the Viceroy and now relations between him and Gough, as also with Marling, were severely strained. He had reacted strongly to Marling's instructions that he should steer clear of political decisions concerning the operation of the force, arguing that this was in direct opposition to what was laid down for a GOC in charge of a force in the field in time of war. Feeling shunned and persecuted by both British and Persian quarters, he became even more bellicose in his attitude to those around him. He began to see conspiracy against him everywhere and on one occasion, when he was in Tehran, told Marling that there was a plot to murder him and Colonel Frazer-Hunter. Marling investigated but could find no evidence for such a plot. He reported the incident and said that he 'believed that Sykes's imagination had had a part in informing his notion' since at that time, with the activities of the Komité-ye Mojazat (Punishment Committee), talk of murder and assassination was everywhere in the air. The military secretary felt that 'this rigmarole is a sufficient commentary on Sykes's methods to make it more desirable than ever to find a good officer to command the SPR'.

The circus of debate continued under its own ponderous momentum. The War Cabinet informed India that, now that the Turks had retired from Persia and Mesopotamia, Sykes ought to be able to deal with the situation if he had a good financial adviser. He was to remain under the orders of Marling and India would be responsible for supplying him with his needs. Meanwhile, inspired no doubt by the unexpected British success in Mesopotamia, the Persian government finally gave official recognition to Sir Percy Sykes's appointment to the SPR and informed Farman Farma accordingly. London thought that it had won the battle with India, which, it said, would be fully responsible for keeping the SPR operational while Marling and the Foreign Office would decide how the force was to be used. With all the appearance of reasoned courtesy, London told India that when any proposal made by one authority was likely to affect the other, the two would consult. The Government of India was not prepared to accept this poisoned chalice and replied saying that the C–in–C India could not agree.

Marling, who was occasionally a firm supporter of Sykes, had not received copies of all this correspondence. He had urged that Sykes should be given a free hand in the running of the SPR, without any need to bog himself down with Indian red tape and regulations, and he was opposed to the appointment of a GOC for the SPR, which would be unacceptable to the Persians. The only possible way of making the SPR a success was to make it a truly Persian force, to be used by the Persian government and not in a way that would make it an adjunct to British forces. Sykes thoroughly understood this, Marling said, and for this reason he trusted that there would be no question of replacing him. Moreover, the results that Sykes had hitherto achieved, for a long time with insufficient means, reflected the greatest credit on him and his staff.

The civilian Marling's opinion of Sykes's capabilities was not shared by India. A long paper considering his position refers to his having 'lack of political insight . . . doubtful competence as a military leader . . . tendencies to draw hasty conclusions which makes for his highly optimistic or deeply gloomy reports at short intervals . . . [a] mercurial temperament which is difficult to deal with . . . no sense of humour'. It also drew attention to his demand for the supply of aeroplanes and a tank. Damningly, it attributed most of the chaos surrounding the organization of the force to his incompetence in not producing a plan at an early date. It also detailed at length the escape of the Sirjan prisoners and the fiasco of the Kotal-i Pir-i Zan expedition. In reply, his supporters in London exonerated him from most of all this, except for his failure to produce a proper plan. 'Whether that is because he is incompetent or because he had so much else to do . . . is uncertain.'

Sykes protested at the pressure from India to produce a plan and robustly responded to all the criticism that was heaped on him. It was easy enough for Indian army commanders, with a battery of staff officers to assist them, to produce plans and detailed budgets. Until May 1917, however, he had had only one clerk, borrowed from the Kerman consulate, and two staff officers. All three had quickly broken down through overwork. For nine months he had had no Indian superintendent of accounts, and for thirteen months no British treasury officer. He was still waiting for a financial adviser. His officers did not know their rates of pay, their allowances or their conditions of service. He complained bitterly of the red tape with which he was being strangled. As W.A.K. Fraser wrote in his diary: 'The office was in an appalling condition of muddle and the accounts in a dreadful mess.'

The Viceroy, Lord Chelmsford, denied that there was an excess of red tape and said that Sykes had been given a free hand but had still failed to produce a budget. There followed much acrimonious correspondence which ended only when Colonel Orton, an experienced administrator, produced an acceptable plan. One of Sykes's contributions to this concerned the welfare of the men's dependants. The Swedish Gendarmerie officers had kept the names of their casualties on the payroll, which enabled the men's heirs or family to continue to subsist quite comfortably but, since the SPR could not afford to set such a precedent, he insisted that some sort of provision should be made to cover death or injury on active service. Without such a provision the men, he said, would go into action knowing that if they were killed their families would be destitute, their wives would be reduced to prostitution and the children would starve. This offered little inducement to the men to become good fighting soldiers. Morale in the new force, he said, was being badly affected by the sight of widows and dependants constantly appealing for aid at the barrack gates.

While India and London corresponded in the restrained and elegant prose of officialdom, Clarmont Skrine wrote to his mother again, leaving nothing unsaid:

> When I was at Simla in September I saw quite plainly that they had no opinion of Sykes, but that he had the confidence of the Home Government. India is longing to kick him out of this job, but they can't; their policy is now to give him as much rope as possible in the hope that he'll hang himself with it. That's why they're refusing him nothing, in fact are pouring out money like water in the SPR show – the roads, the telegraphs, military expeditions from India etc. They know that if they refused him anything and then he came smash, he'd say it was their fault.

Despite all the criticism, by the end of August 1917 Sykes's force, which had begun with a mission of three British officers just over a year earlier, was now up to a strength of 6,000 Persians, 70 British officers and 84 British NCO instructors. Since the Persian officers, unlike their British counterparts at Sandhurst, were not accustomed to taking instruction from mere sergeants or corporals, the NCOs wore no badges of rank and were addressed as 'Mister'. The rapid expansion of the force and the reputation that it soon won for firm action proved a strong deterrent to the habitual robbers and there was a great improvement in security. It could have made even more rapid progress if it had not been hampered by the obstructive attitude of the central government and the general feeling of uncertainty arising from the state of near anarchy caused by the Democratic movement in the north of Persia. None the less, by the end of 1917 the SPR had imposed a security on south Persia that was greater than at any period in the previous decade.

19

Triumph or fiasco?

THE DEMOCRATS, BACKED up by some of the mullas, and
encouraged by the return of the German Legation and later
by the Bolsheviks, who also promised them support against the
British, had been making constant attempts to undermine the
SPR by inciting the Persian ranks to desert, and were having
some success. Farman Farma invoked these facts, and the fact
that the Persian government still refused to recognize the force,
to discourage Sykes from dealing too firmly with the robber
tribes. Sykes, however, took the view that his old friend's real
reasons were of a more 'personal' nature. He also felt that both
Saulat and Qavam ul-Molk, at the head of their large tribes, saw
the establishment of order under the British-led SPR as a threat
to their own power and influence and that they were at heart
hostile to the Sykes mission. He had been given an almost
impossible task.

In the spring of 1917, following the revolution in their country,
the Russian Cossacks had ceased to salute their officers and by the
winter most of the Russian troops were making their way home,
selling their arms and ammunition as they went in order to feed
themselves. The Russian collapse had suddenly opened the
German road to India via the Caucasus and Transcaspia.

In January 1918 the British position in Persia looked extremely
perilous. The combination of Persian 'extremists' with Muslim

'fanatics', Bolsheviks and the great numbers of escaped Austro-German prisoners of war[1] who were constantly moving from Transcaspia into Persia, where they were joining up with the Jangali movement of Communist revolutionaries operating in the forests, was seen by the British government as the ingredients of a world revolution, a holy war and a pan-Turkish rising. Although they were probably incapable of organized or prolonged hostilities, the anarchy these forces would produce in Persia meant potential danger to Afghanistan and India.

In March 1918 Marling delivered a Note to the Persian government, reminding it that the British had offered aid for the establishment of a national Persian army after the war, into which the SPR would be incorporated, and that it also offered to abrogate the Anglo-Russian Convention of 1907. These offers, which were still open, had so far not been accepted by the Persian government. The Persians rejected the presence of British troops, but not the financial assistance.

Lawlessness was rife. The Turks had entered western Azerbaijan. The Jangalis had practically cut the road between Tehran and Enzeli and had arrested the British Consul at Rasht. In fact, northwest Persia from the Caspian to the Turkish border was either in a state of active disorder or exposed to hostile movements that threatened the neutrality of the Persian government and the interests which the British were endeavouring with Persia to defend. In view of this situation, daily growing worse, the British government had been reluctantly forced to conclude that it must make itself responsible for measures of protection against a common danger which the Persian government were either unable or unwilling to adopt.

When Marling presented this Note it at once became apparent that the 'extremists' – expecting, it was said, an event in about five weeks' time that would enable them to defy the British – were urging a policy of stubbornness. To this end they were resorting to force to crush all opposition, going so far as to assassinate the

---

[1] There were 150,000 German and Austrian prisoners of war in Transcaspia. Many of them escaped to Meshed, where the Karguzar, who was in the pay of the Germans, helped them on their way (Haig, *Memoirs*).

editor of a pro-British newspaper. By the beginning of April information was received that made it clear that the Turks were actively working for the formation of a new Muslim state, which would include both Persian and Russian Azerbaijan. Turkish agents were negotiating with the Persian 'extremists' and with the Jangalis but, finding that they objected strongly to any cession of Persian territory, were concealing their real aims under the guise of an intention to resist British attempts to intervene in Persia and Trans-Caucasia. The Germans had occupied Odessa, were likely to obtain control of the Black Sea and obviously meant to move into Georgia. Their agents were skilfully playing on the anti-British faction in Persia, where they hoped to bring about a revolution; *Greenmantle* was still alive.

The Persian government regarded the Note as an empty threat and replied accordingly. The upshot was that the British dispatched another force to Persia – this time from Mesopotamia – to fill the gap in the north-west left by the departure of the Russian troops and to keep a line open to Baku. This force was led by General Dunsterville (the inspiration for Kipling's *Stalky*) and known as Dunsterforce.

The situation in South Persia was also becoming serious and Sykes went to India to speak directly to the army command and request increased supplies of heavy arms, with motor vehicles, which could now be used on the roads that the SPR had built. On his way from Shiraz to Bandar Abbas he called in to inspect all the SPR outposts, staffed by lonely young British officers.

One of these was Captain Tommy Sherwood at the SPR headquarters at Kerman, whose letters (now in the Imperial War Museum) to his very new and pregnant wife give a vivid picture of the lives led by the junior British officers of the SPR. Before being sent to Kerman, Sherwood had served in the disastrous Gallipoli campaign, then in Serbia and Bulgaria. In November 1917 he wrote home, complaining that the mail, which came up by donkey from Bandar Abbas, four hundred miles away, took three months to arrive. He was very distressed that it was taking six months to get replies to his requests for news about his child to be and where his wife was going to live.

Sherwood was just out of Cambridge, where he had been sent

with a number of other young officers to learn Persian. Although a serious and hard-working soldier, he had a public schoolboy's arrogance about 'the natives' and talked cheerfully of whipping his servants. As for women, there were 'only two white women' in Kerman, the wives of the managers of the Imperial Bank of Persia and of the Indian Telegraph Service, who had been in Kerman since before the war and had got stuck there for the duration. These good ladies occasionally entertained the young officers to tea, but their company was not lively. More entertaining had been a lunch with 'The Prince', who was half-brother to the Shah and Governor of Kerman. 'He is very keen on tennis but refuses to take off his frock coat and *kolah* [hat] when he plays. His retainers rush up to him and brush his clothes and shoes after each set . . . He is only friendly 'cos he's afraid of us.' Major Fraser, an older and less arrogant man than Sherwood, had more to say about the Prince in his diary:

> The Governor is Prince Nosrat us-Saltaneh ['Triumph of the Realm'], an educated and civilized Persian with European tastes who has been in Europe and talks French fairly well. He hates his exile here and is, I think, rather a puppet in the hands of . . . his . . . confidential adviser, a very clever, genial and probably quite unscrupulous blackguard. The Prince has also an ADC, an extremely pleasant Persian of the same type as the Prince.
>
> The other camp is headed by Sardar Nosrat, a Persian gentleman of the old stamp, formally courteous, narrow-minded, a born intriguer. He was at one time Deputy Governor, but being in a continuously hostile state against the Prince, the latter got him kicked out. The Sardar is a local Kermani – much the wealthiest man in the district. He has a big local following and outdoes the Prince in charities in the town. He is assisted by his brother Adl us-Saltaneh, who is head of the road guards. The Adl was in with the Boche when they were here. There is tremendous rivalry between the two camps. When Sardar Nosrat gives a lunch to Europeans the Prince gives a bigger one. Anything that goes wrong in Kerman is put down by each side to intrigue by the other.

Sherwood kept up a correspondence with a friend from Cambridge, Harry Newton, who was 'all on his own' at Niriz, in charge of three hundred troops. Newton wrote that life was: 'somewhat lonely, but the Governor is not a bad sort. I now go out shooting once a week with him . . . Fearful amount of work here . . . My other diversion is horses and tent-pegging. I have bought a horse and hope to make a star of him . . . You people at Kerman are much better provided for than us at Shiraz. Smokes and drinks cost a small fortune.' The Shiraz contingent were fed up with a new brigade commander: 'numberless returns and silly orders are making things rather intolerable'.

By January 1918 the young Sherwood was in command of five hundred men and fifteen Persian officers, who spoke not a word of English. The days were monotonous and filled with 'work', followed by a bath, dinner in the mess at 7.30, then bridge with his fellow officers and bed. He began to like the country, however, and described the joy of clear, frosty winter mornings followed by warm sunshine. He did not talk about his 'work' to his wife, but he mentioned once – quite casually – that there had been a rising in the town and that they had had to suppress it. Shots had been exchanged but there were no casualties. They soon restored order, arrested the ringleaders and had a bath before dinner, bridge and bed.

Clarmont Skrine wrote to his mother in February 1918 to say that Sykes, about whom he had been writing such scathing comments, had arrived in Kerman. It is astonishing to see how his opinion of Sykes had changed:

> I like him, as I expected I should. I gathered from all I've heard about him during the last year and a half (and that's a good deal) that he is a very human and likeable person for all his faults. He is as vain as a peacock . . . He's not a soldier except in name, having been in political employ practically all his career, and it takes some blarney to carry off all the military howlers he perpetrates. However, he's got the faculty for choosing his men, and the sense to defer to them in most – if not all – of the military decisions he makes, with the result that really, so far, in the

work he was sent to do in June 1916 – the pacification of South Persia and the raising of the SPR – he has made excellent progress up to date . . . There's a good chunk of humbug in Sykes – his real jobs are diplomacy of an honest, open, sympathetic sort, and exploring. But the humbug in him has secured, mainly by advertising and mutual admiration society means, a much higher position and better chances than either diplomacy or exploring or both together would have brought him. As for the soldiers, his military shortcomings, together with his absurd vanity and his un-English love of theatrical display, speechifying, flattery etc., put them off a good deal. But that, after all, is mainly concerned with work. As a man, he is extremely good-natured and human, his faults being all on the surface and (unless one is a bad listener) very easy to get on with. So he's much more liked than disliked . . .

Skrine had understood that, in accordance with the practice of public life in Persia, Sykes was expected to go in for theatrical display, speechifying and flattery. The occasion when Farman Farma had kissed him at the gallop had taught Sykes how to behave 'when in Rome' and he duly made a grand triumphal entry into Kerman. The streets were lined with troops and gay with flags and a salute of thirteen guns was fired by the 2nd SPR Artillery as the General entered by the Yazd Gate. As Skrine ungrudgingly wrote, 'there were huge crowds of Kermanis and altogether it was a great *tamasha* [spectacle].' The parade was followed by a military tattoo, with an attack by the SPR on a wooden fort built specially on the parade ground, and was followed by the by now customary gymkhana and displays of tent-pegging by the cavalry. The occasion had been, as usual, a success.

From Kerman, Sykes went on to Army Headquarters at Simla, bearing with him Colonel Orton's scheme for the organization and development of the SPR. On his way to Bandar Abbas he called on the Governor, Sardar Mojallal, who promised to raise a Camel Corps of Baluchi levies. He also set up a strong intelligence unit in the coastal region around Fin, to the north-west of Bandar Abbas.

Orton's scheme was regarded as sound, but its expense disturbed the Army Command, particularly as it included a full-blown band.

In the previous year the entire cost of the Sykes mission had been £600,000 (about £23 million today), which the India Office in London found 'incredible'. Not only had the SPR been fleeced by the local provision merchants and contractors but the British had also had to spend huge sums of money on importing flour from India to keep the local price within reach of the people, who would otherwise have rioted. Sykes was told that he had to reduce the cost of his force, not least because the plan was to hand it over to the Persian government at the end of the war and they had to be able to afford it. There was limited scope, however, for making economies. He could close down some of the outlying SPR posts; he could get rid of the *tofangchis* or village levies, who kept on either losing or selling their rifles and ammunition; or he could delegate road security to the Persian authorities and the guilds of merchants. None of these options was satisfactory. Most of the money went to the profiteering merchants who supplied the SPR, together with the local authorities, who were official robbers, and the (unofficial) bandits on the roads. The bandits frequently turned out to be in cahoots with the authorities who were supposed to be suppressing them. The Viceroy had already written to London pointing out that if the force was not reduced the government would be faced with endless expense, but by now the SPR was committed and India was compelled to continue paying up.

Sykes's force was in trouble. News was coming through that the Germans were winning in Europe and the pro-German Persian Minister of the Interior[2] had publicly repudiated the SPR and was inciting the Qashqai to attack them. Saulat, who the previous summer had come to an agreement with Gough to keep the Fars roads open in exchange for a contribution to his expenses, was perplexed to be now receiving orders from Tehran to harry the SPR. The former gendarmes in the SPR mutinied and five hundred of them had to be dismissed.

Sykes told India all this and, that in order to deal with it, he had to have more arms and transport before the tribes moved up again

---

[2] Mukhbir us-Saltaneh. He had been educated in Germany and had been Governor-General of Shiraz in 1915 before being replaced by Qavam ul-Molk. He stayed in Shiraz and worked for the German Consul Wustrow (Haig, *Memoirs*).

in the spring. He succeeded in getting hold of thirty-five Lewis guns and thirty Ford lorries and some cars, together with agreement to build more barracks, and headed straight back to Shiraz.

In his book *World War in Iran* Clarmont Skrine described Sykes's return to Kerman towards the end of February 1918 on a visit of inspection from Shiraz. There was now a good road, and the journey from Shiraz via Niriz and Sirjan in the new four-cylinder Hup tourers had taken only three days. By now the growing influence of the nationalists had caused a distinct public cooling towards Sykes in Kerman, and his old friends did not wish to be seen turning out to welcome him.

In spite of mutterings from the Fifth Column in Kerman, nothing untoward marred the visit, but the great parade ground or Maidan in the middle of town was suspiciously bare of spectators when the cavalry and infantry of the brigade marched across it past the General and next day only a handful of Aghas watched a parade and polo match on the plain behind the Bagh–i Zirisf. General Sykes recognized and talked to several of the Persians present as old friends, for he had a flair for people, spoke Persian fluently, and kept the ball rolling with a skill that I envied. His visit was important also as a boost to the morale of the rank and file of the SPR, to whom the highlight of the programme was a feast in the big Drill Hall of the Gendarmerie. This was an occasion I shall never forget. Eight hundred men stood to attention in long ranks, each with a mound of mutton and rice pilau covering a flat Persian loaf at his feet. At a megaphoned word of command all eight hundred literally fell on the food as one man . . .

Not content with showing the flag at Kerman, the General took us all a hundred and forty miles further south east to Bam, a town guarded by a towering medieval fortress renowned in the history of the province. Here a company of SPR was stationed to keep an eye on the marauding Perso-Baluch tribes. Two thousand feet lower than the Kerman plain Bam, with its orchards of luscious mandarin oranges, is warm and sunny in early spring when the wind is not blowing and the General had pleasant memories of it from the days of his Kerman consulship twenty years before. The Governor, Sardar Mojallal, a son in law of Sardar Nosrat, was friendly and could be relied upon to welcome us hospitably.

Next day the party split up, for the General had to return to Shiraz . . .

On their way back to Shiraz, Sykes and Colonel Grant, the Quartermaster-General of the SPR, were ambushed by robbers in one of the passes. They brought the new Lewis gun to bear but after firing one round it jammed. Grant seized a service rifle from an orderly and fired two quick shots at a range of about three hundred yards. With the first he killed one man and with the second he fatally wounded another. The rest of the gang fled.

Shortly after he had returned to Shiraz the trouble that Sykes had feared started. On 18th April a number of the SPR deserted from the Abadeh post, explaining in a letter that they were doing so for political reasons and denouncing their colleagues for selling their country to the British. Many of Sykes's Persian friends warned him that he could no longer rely on the loyalty of the SPR Fars Brigade to their British officers. Six of the deserters were caught near Isfahan and were due to be sent down to Shiraz, escorted by a young British officer. The general agreement was that the officer was unlikely to reach Shiraz alive, so Sykes sent an order to Colonel Haig, who was now Consul at Isfahan, to 'deal with them' there, which he reluctantly obeyed. Marling, at the Legation in Tehran, felt that this was too strong and pointed out that even the Russians did not execute their deserters. In late May the first signs of the expected tribal revolt against the British came when a force of Kazerunis rode over the mountains to occupy Dasht-i Arjan and, at the same time, several senior Persian officers of the SPR resigned.

To head off the trouble that would come when the main body of the Qashqai moved up to Shiraz for the summer and could combine with the Arab tribes to the south-east, Sykes sent Colonel Grant to attack two of these tribes, who had been raiding the villages round about. Grant took a sizeable force composed of a squadron of 15th Lancers, two squadrons of Burma Mounted Rifles, one section of the 33rd Mountain Battery, the half-battalion 3/124th Baluchis from Shiraz, a bombing and demolition section of 16th Rajputs, an Indian field ambulance and a Persian demolition section – a total fighting strength of 100 sabres, 2 mountain guns and 600 rifles, of which 200 were mounted. The Shiraz SPR, who were by now considered unreliable, were left behind. The cavalry covered the thirty-eight miles from the starting-point to Chah Haq in eight hours and at once surrounded its group of three forts. Two of the forts had been evacuated the previous evening, when the chief of the Labu Mohammedi had arrived. The third fort was still occupied by thirty riflemen. Some of them escaped through a *qanat* with most of the arms and ammunition, but the rest finally surrendered. The tribesmen lost five killed or wounded and twenty-seven captured. All three forts were demolished the next day.

Grant then set off in pursuit of the Labu Mohammedi. When he caught up with them, he found that they had joined forces with a group of Chehar Rahi tribesmen, three hundred of them armed and thirty of them mounted. Major Dyer with two troops advanced boldly on the Labu Mohammedi and, led by scouts who charged mounted with bayonets fixed, drove them into the high hills. Meanwhile the Chehar Rahi, who had seen the dust of the approaching British column and were trying to escape with their flocks, were pursued and finally driven off, without their animals. The tribes suffered over sixty casualties, while the Burma Mounted Rifles, who recovered a large number of animals and stolen property, had only two men wounded. They had been nineteen hours on the move and had covered about fifty miles. When the action was over, the local villagers came to thank them for relieving them from the depredations of these robbers. The fleeing Chehar Rahi were subsequently tracked down to their stronghold in very difficult mountainous country to the north. Thirty of them were taken prisoner and a large number were killed, for three Baluchis wounded. Grant attributed his success to the accuracy of his intelligence, the fitness of all his troops, the brilliant tactics of the BMR and the presence of the new Lewis guns. Farman Farma was greatly pleased with the success of these operations, not only because they had made the district secure but also because it was now possible for him to collect revenues, 10 per cent of which were his recognized perquisite as the Governor-General.

Meanwhile the situation to the west of Shiraz had become critical. On 7th May 1918 Sykes telegraphed that Saulat was trying to induce Qavam ul-Molk to join him in attacking the British and that there were further signs of disaffection among the SPR. Three days later the British scored a disastrous 'own goal' that led to a full-scale tribal war.

At the village of Khan-i Zenyan, nineteen miles west of Shiraz, there was an SPR garrison of seventy men under the command of Captain Will. This was the last SPR post on the road to Bushire; the territory beyond was in the hands of the Qashqai and the Tangistanis. On 10th May Will arrested a small party of Dareh-Shuri, one of the larger Qashqai clans, famous for their excellent horses, thinking they had stolen two SPR donkeys. Their khan, according to custom, sent a courteous message asking for them to be released, which Captain Will, ignorant of local custom, discourteously refused. The Dareh-Shuri then attacked the post to rescue their kinsmen. A large force of SPR under Colonel Williams came out from Shiraz in defence and ambushed the Dareh-Shuri, inflicting fifteen casualties and taking thirty-six prisoners, including the khan's two nephews and four *katkhodas* (headmen), which the Dareh-Shuri regarded as a serious lack of respect. The SPR doubled the Khan-i Zenyan garrison from seventy to a hundred and forty men and returned to Shiraz.

This was too much for the Qashqai. Ten days later Saulat moved camp from Firuzabad to Khan-i Khabis, nearer Shiraz. A thousand more Kazerunis moved across the mountains into Dasht-i Arjan, where they were joined by three hundred assorted *tofangchis*. Altogether about 3,000 armed men were now surrounding Khan-i Zenyan. In Shiraz itself the Democrats, together with some of the mullas, started serious anti-British disturbances, proclaiming through the mosques, the tea houses and the bazaars that the Qashqai had defeated the British, and Saulat informed Farman Farma that he had the backing of Tehran to fight the British. To the south-east, the Sheikh of Firuzabad declared a jihad.

Sykes, facing the worst crisis of his career, mobilized a force of 1,600 Baluchi Infantry and Burma Mounted Rifles and then demanded aeroplanes from the base at Bushire to be sent up to assist him. The Bushire command, exasperated by Sykes's habit of continually being in trouble, refused him the aircraft on the grounds that they could not operate at the altitude of the mountains round Shiraz. Near Deh Sheikh the Indian troops fought for fourteen hours against 4,500 Qashqai and 300 Khamseh of the Baharlu, nearly half of whom were mounted on very nimble mountain ponies, and pushed them back to Saulat's camp at Khan–i Khabis, which they shelled. Saulat retreated, having lost 200 dead and up to 700 wounded. Two British officers and eighteen Indians were killed. On the same day the SPR at Khan-i Zenyan mutinied and murdered Captain Will and his sergeant. Seven hundred troops were sent to rescue them, but they were too late. The tribes withdrew.

As always in Persia, there are several explanations for this extraordinary incident. Sykes maintained that the attack had been premeditated and that Tehran was behind it. He saw the hand of the Minister of the Interior, who was believed to be on the German payroll, behind several other tribal raids and also behind the Karguzar's extravagant claims for compensation for British damage to property and crops, most of it imaginary. He also believed that Saulat wanted to frighten the British into paying him a large subsidy to put him in sole charge of the security of the Bushire–Shiraz road, which he would share with certain 'highly placed Persians' (Farman Farma and Qavam ul-Molk).

Some fifty years later, in a private interview, one of Saulat's sons gave a quite different explanation. He maintained that the Dareh–Shuri were on migration with their women and flocks and were clearly not a raiding party. Far from stealing the donkeys, one of the arrested *katkhodas* was in fact returning them. If the English captain had come to an arrangement with the *katkhodas* over the donkeys and treated the khan with respect, there would never have been any trouble. However, far more serious than the insult to the khans was that the SPR had laid hands on some of the Dareh–Shuri women and that women had been killed in the following attack. Saulat's wife had then taken an oath to divorce him unless he took up arms to avenge them. Saulat himself complained that the women and the tribal hotheads had been pushing him into action, but that he could have restrained them if the British had just left him and his territory alone.[3]

Sykes now started firing off telegrams to India, reminiscent of those he had sent from Meshed when events were coming thick and fast. He trumpeted that the situation was serious and that there was a widespread plot against the British, fanned by strong fanatical feeling. Saulat might soon assemble another force; the SPR were either disaffected or frightened and, given the turbulent state of the city, it would be risky to send the Indian troops more than five or six miles out of Shiraz. Shiraz was about to be surrounded and a strong column should be marched inland from Bushire to relieve him. Just to hear word of the arrival of reinforcements coming up from Bushire, he said, would be enough to improve the position.

He estimated that Saulat could collect ten thousand well-armed Qashqai and a thousand Kazerunis, whom he might be able to hold together for a month. They had plenty of rifle ammunition and had, besides, captured sixty thousand rounds from the SPR at Khan-i Zenyan. Farman Farma was now working well with him; Qavam was also on side, and had provided seven hundred of his Khamseh tribesmen to protect Shiraz, but could be relied on only if things went well. In fact, a contingent of the Baharlu, one of Qavam's Khamseh clans, was fighting on the other side with Saulat.

General Marshall, now in command in Mesopotamia, when asked if he could send Sykes two infantry brigades with pack transport, replied that he had no forces to spare and certainly not enough pack mules. To rescue Sykes, India had to divert to Bushire a large force that was on its way to Egypt. Two companies of 3rd Brahmans were also ordered to move from Muscat to Bandar Abbas to secure the base there.

No sooner had these arrangements been made for him, however, than Sykes cabled that, on reconsideration, he thought an advance from Bushire would take too long to organize. He recommended instead that a force of two squadrons of cavalry, a mountain battery and two infantry battalions should be sent to

---

[3] I am indebted to Floreeda Safiri for this explanation of the incident.

advance on Shiraz from Bandar Abbas. British ranks were recalled from all SPR posts that did not have Indian Army units to back them up, and even in Shiraz all the artillery, machine-guns and ammunition were kept in the hands of the British officers.

The Government of India pointed out the gravity of the situation to London and said that, since Sykes's position was now far more military than political, they insisted that he should come under the orders of the Commander-in-Chief, India, rather than the Foreign Office: the soldiers saw that the politicians were making a mess. India now considered the SPR in Fars to be a liability and were considering disbanding it: as a focus for so much nationalist and anti-British sentiment, it was a political millstone around their necks. Marling also agreed that it would be best to disband it but keep on the Indian troops for as long as necessary.

The situation was indeed serious, since the Germans had now taken over the Black Sea and the Turks were about to take the Caucasus. They were also again spending money freely in Persia and Wassmuss was on his way to join Saulat and try to start a jihad which, if successful, would divert a great number of British troops away from the main effort.

On 13th June 1918 the tribes outside Shiraz cut the river that not only supplied water to the city but also powered the flour mills. This did more damage to the townspeople than it did to the British, who had good wells in their quarters. In preparation for an expected attack by Saulat the mullas in the town began to incite the people against the British and anyone who helped them. The next day Colonel Orton took the initiative by leading a pre-emptive strike on the tribes. His force killed about two hundred of them, losing two of his officers and three men. The mullas continued their agitation, partly encouraged, as Sykes said, by Farman Farma and Qavam ul-Molk, who were both pressing the British to grant them substantial pensions and compensation for any losses that they might incur through siding openly with the British. When the mob got out of hand, cut the telegraph and then began to plunder the property of anyone who had worked for the British, the Persian ranks of the SPR, who were the prime targets of the rioters, turned against the mullas. Farman Farma, seeing that the wind was now blowing from another direction, agreed at last to

take measures to restore order and arrested some of the leading
Democrats. The townspeople furious with Saulat for having cut
off their water then turned against him and the Qashqai began to
quarrel among themselves. At this point Gough and Sykes persuaded Farman Farma to make Saulat's rival half-brother Sardar
Ihtisham into the Il-Khan; he then led his men against Saulat. The
tables had been turned on Saulat. Wassmuss, who by now had run
out of money and was borrowing heavily from the Tangistani
chiefs, had fallen out with him. With the eight hundred men left
to him, Saulat fled back to his winter quarters at Firuzabad,
seventy miles south of Shiraz. On 23rd October Sardar Ihtisham,
with a small force of SPR, pursued him there and Saulat fled once
more. To crown his defeat, the SPR set up a post in Firuzabad,
which had previously been a no-go area for them.

At Abadeh, on the road north to Isfahan, was the largest SPR
post outside Shiraz, with a garrison of 600 Persian troops, supported by two hundred Indians. In July 1918 Saulat ud-Dowleh
told the local Qashqai khan to collect a force of six hundred men
from the local tribes and to announce that the Persian government
had ordered him to remove the 'infidel foreigners'. Saulat ud-
Dowleh's full-brother Saulat us-Saltaneh[4] then heard that a caravan
carrying silver for the Imperial Bank of Persia had arrived and the
two of them attacked the garrison, whereupon all but two
hundred of the SPR contingent mutinied,[5] leaving the British and
the Indians to defend it on their own. The Qashqai diverted a
water channel to the foot of the mud walls, hoping to wash it away,
but two of the officers came out under heavy fire to mend the
breach; one of them lost his life. The situation was now desperate
and Colonel Haig, with no Russian troops near enough to assist,
resorted to dissimulation. He concocted a letter from himself to
Saulat us-Saltaneh in which he acknowledged receipt of a letter
from him, thanked him for his services in drawing the Qashqai
into the trap that he had prepared for them and begged him to
hold on and keep them there until a force sent by Sykes could

---

[4] Saulat us-Saltaneh 'had been at the Church Missionary Society Hospital at Isfahan with liver disease, aggravated by excess. He was a wreck' (Haig, *Memoirs*).
[5] Haig was convinced that this mutiny had been organized by the Persian Cabinet.

surround them. He also hinted at a promise of British support for his claim to the Il-Khanship. He attached a large consular seal to this letter and arranged for it to 'fall into' the hands of the non-Qashqai tribes surrounding Abadeh, who were curious to see what the Consul might have to say to Saulat and predictably opened the letter. 'I have no means of knowing the details of what followed,' he wrote in his memoirs, 'but Saulat us-Saltaneh's protestations were evidently not believed, for he immediately fled from Abadeh and the besieging force was diminished in numbers.' Meanwhile, Sykes had sent a relief force up from Shiraz which, in the intense heat of July, managed to complete the forced march of the hundred and eighty miles to Abadeh in sixty-nine hours. It is characteristic of Sykes that he later claimed in his *History* that it was this march which saved Abadeh and even Isfahan itself, which he said was under threat from the Bakhtiari. Haig felt moved to point out in his memoirs that the threat to Isfahan had been removed some time beforehand.

Despite the improvement in the situation in Fars, London had had enough of Sykes running the military operations. Since the Shiraz telegraph had been cut Sykes could not communicate with the Kerman Brigade of the SPR, which gave India the excuse it had been looking for to put Colonel Farran in command of it. London also wanted to send out a brigadier-general from India to take over all the Indian and British troops, leaving Sykes in command of the Persian troops, but India opposed doing this until the situation in Shiraz had been cleared up. It was also opposed to having command split between the political and the military, and yet again, a long triangular argument ensued about command and responsibility for the British forces and the SPR. Sykes then demanded that Gough should hand over the political control to him, since he was the commander of a military force in the field, but India refused, saying that as a military situation no longer existed, political control should revert to Gough and, through him, to Farman Farma. It was ironic that Sykes, whose experience was largely political, had been put in charge of the soldiery while Gough, whose background was military, should have been given the political job. The argument was further complicated by the new Persian government under the Vossouq ud Dowleh, who suggested that he could recognize the SPR officially if it were put under the command of neutral officers from Sweden or Switzerland.

At this point some friction finally arose between Sykes and Farman Farma, whose friendship went back to 1893. This was prompted by the fact that Gough wanted to pay Farman Farma a subsidy to arrange for guards on the road to Isfahan, which he regarded as a lot cheaper than putting in the SPR. Sykes, who felt that the SPR should be responsible, suspected that Farman Farma was profiting extravagantly from Gough's arrangement, although he accepted that it was perfectly natural for a Persian grandee to intrigue and look after his own safety and his own pocket. In addition, the Prince's lack of principle could be a source of danger to the British if he was not watched carefully. In fact, Farman Farma, as he wrote to his eldest son, Nosrat ud-Dowleh, who was then in the Cabinet at Tehran, had been paying the road guards' wages out of his own pocket while waiting for the agreed subsidy to come from the British, and the road was much safer than it had ever been under the protection of the SPR, who cost ten times as much.

Gough, in a later report to India, urged the abolition of the SPR on the grounds that they were untrustworthy, useless, expensive and dangerous. It was costing the colossal sum of over £1 million a year to feed and pay them, and they required a permanent escort of British troops to control them. The Viceroy complained that the SPR were 'chasing elusive tribesmen' instead of damaging Turks and Germans, the real enemy. 'We should be prepared to give up the SPR . . . We do not wish to shed further Persian blood or drift into a rupture with Persia, with whom we have no quarrel . . . By releasing South and Central Persia we shall lose nothing.'[6]

Marling, who for a long time had been defending Sykes against the various attacks made on him, now openly criticized him in a telegram to the Chief of the General Staff at Simla for failing to act against the tribes in timely fashion:

---

[6] Viceroy to Secretary of State for India, Cabinet Papers, EC 487 CAB 27/27, 6th June 1918.

It seems inexplicable how Sir Percy Sykes had to remain inactive at Shiraz with a considerable force of regular Indian troops after the combination worked up by the Consul, Farman Farma and Qavam had broken up Saulat's forces. From private accounts[7] I have little doubt that the danger from Saulat was enormously exaggerated . . . One private letter observes that our troops were rarely outnumbered and that for three days 1200 or 1500 tribesmen besieged Shiraz [when there were] 2500 Indian troops [to defend it].

In the scrupulously fair manner of the army, this telegram was relayed back from India to Sykes to give him an opportunity to justify himself. He sent back a long telegram to point out that, of his Indian troops, seven hundred were raw recruits, who had not even been taught musketry and needed to be trained, and a further one hundred were sick. Two thousand of the SPR troops were close to mutiny, the tribes were gathering in strength and Qavam ul-Molk's attitude was 'doubtful'. Neither Marling nor Gough was taking political steps to counter the anti-British agitation from the mullas and Democrats. Sykes described the attitude of these two as 'unhelpful' and said that the tone of their telegrams showed 'continual and ungenerous animosity towards myself and SPR'. He had himself taken the initiative of cutting the telegraph line from Tehran to Shiraz to prevent the Persian government from inciting Saulat and had then occupied the city of Shiraz, assuming political control and forcing Gough and Farman Farma to take the 'political measures' that he had been urging for the last three months – making Saulat's half-brother Sardar Ihtisham the Il-Khan of the Qashqai and encouraging the tribesmen to go over to him.

The Chief of the General Staff, sympathetic to a soldier under attack from the politicians, wrote in Sykes's defence:

We consider that it must be placed to Sykes's credit from a purely military point of view that, taking into account all the circumstances of the case, the quality of the troops at his disposal,

---

[7] As Sykes penned on his own copy of this telegram, 'A drunken Persian revenue official who had been dismissed!'

the indefinite extent of the potential tribal opposition, and the
unreliability of the SPR, he was successful in avoiding disaster.

In October 1918 the British decided to open once and for all
the Bushire–Shiraz road, which had been practically closed by the
various tribes along it for the entire war. Troops moved out of
Bushire[8] in force across the coastal plain and up into the hills,
improving the road as they went, while Colonel Orton set out
from Shiraz to meet them with a force of Indian troops. Saulat,
hearing that these troops had gone to the west, decided to attack
Sardar Ihtisham, who was in the south-east at Firuzabad. There
Saulat gathered some two thousand men, who had gone back to
him from Ihtisham, and surrounded him. Sykes sent Orton back to
deal with this reverse. The Qashqai stood and fought bravely,
losing over a hundred men before fleeing to the hills once more.
Orton entered Firuzabad and reinforced the SPR post before suc-
cumbing to an attack of Spanish influenza, which prostrated him.

The influenza epidemic spread all over the south of Persia (and
over most of Europe), killing hundreds of the troops and thousands
of the local people, and putting a stop to all further military operations. Eighteen per cent of the Indian troops in south Persia were
lost to it. Captain Sherwood at Kerman wrote a long letter to his
wife describing the epidemic. The Kerman Brigade of the SPR,
he said, had had a hundred and fifty cases in twenty-four hours,
with thirty deaths. All three of the doctors had gone down with it,
as had half the British officers. No Persian officers were left on
their feet. For three days Sherwood ran the hospital himself,
looking after all the men before collapsing. He was unconscious
for a whole day but was saved by the wife of the manager of the
Imperial Bank of Persia, a Mrs Taylor, who took over and fed all
the patients in the SPR hospital herself. All the servants were ill, so
she worked on her own. She had been stranded in Kerman by the
war – and Sherwood had thought her 'rather dull'.

With the Allied victory in Europe, the British had to do something about Wassmuss. On 20th November 1918, after the

---

[8] These troops came under the Mesopotamian command, not under Sykes.

Armistice, the British commanding officer in Bushire sent a messenger to him at his hiding place up in the hills to say that if he surrendered he would be given safe conduct and repatriated to Germany. Wassmuss refused to submit to this indignity and travelled in disguise northwards towards the Turkish border, begging forgiveness from his Tangistani and Qashqai friends for not having brought them victory. The closer he got to Tehran the bolder he became, and he threw off his tribesmen's clothes and put on European dress, telling the puzzled tribesmen who were accompanying him that he did not wish to dishonour them by travelling as a fugitive in their clothes. An Armenian telegraph clerk spotted him in Kashan and passed the news to the British Legation. He was arrested by the gendarmes at Qom and handed over to the British in Tehran, where Sir Percy Cox, his friend from pre-war days at Bushire, was now Minister and highly embarrassed to have him as his prisoner. Refusing to accept his fate, Wassmuss was tied up and escorted by British soldiery on a trip that should have taken him back to Germany via Baku, Batumi and Marseilles. At Qazvin, eighty miles to the west, he escaped and from there made his way back through the mountains to the German Legation at Tehran. After lengthy negotiations he was sent once more under British escort to Batumi and on to Cologne. At Cologne he was interned by the occupying British authorities but escaped again and, a year after the end of the war, the British let the matter drop.

Ever the romantic visionary, Wassmuss returned to Persia to start a mechanized farm behind Bushire. He intended to make enough money to repay what he had borrowed from the tribal chiefs, but his innocent intentions were not believed and he was forced to leave the country. This disappointment broke him and he died shortly afterwards.

Although the Armistice had brought the war in Europe to an end, the situation in Persia was far from resolved. The Persian government was close to collapse, both politically and financially. Most of the Russian forces had melted away after the revolution, leaving only a few Cossacks, and the Bolsheviks were sweeping down from Baku. The British government wanted to find some means of maintaining security in Persia against the new threat of Bolshevism but, not wishing to be saddled with the expense of maintaining the SPR, decided at one point to hand it over to Farman Farma as soon as the Bushire road had been opened. This meant that it could at last become a truly Persian force, as originally intended.

The Persia Committee of the British Cabinet, under Curzon, had decided in January 1918 that the Qajar regime was bound to collapse and that they should now put all their money on the Young Persians and the Democrats and that, since Sykes was so associated in the Persian mind with the old regime, a new face was needed. He might, they thought, be replaced by Major Stokes, the military attaché in Tehran, who had been cultivating the Democrat leaders for years and had very good relations with them. Sir Arthur Hirtzel, Political Secretary of the India Office, who had always been a supporter of Sykes against his detractors, sent a tactfully worded telegram to the Chief of the General Staff at Delhi that the presence of so senior an officer as Sir Percy Sykes was no longer required at Shiraz and that he should be instructed to proceed at once via India to London, where his oral advice regarding the future maintenance of order in South Persia would be welcomed. He added that HM Government had accepted his views on Sykes's conduct of military operations and went so far as to ask him to pass this news on to him.

Sykes set off immediately on his last journey in the country that been his home for nearly twenty-five years, but before he went he received a note from Farman Farma, hastily written in Persian in his own hand on a scrap of his office paper, going round the sides of the sheet after he had got to the bottom, in which he bade farewell to the man who had launched him on the road that had led to his becoming, through his connection with the British, one of the richest and most influential men in the country.[9] In it he said, with informal and touching Persian felicity:

> My dear General,
> Your departure has broken up both our assembly and our hearts. Your going will leave us alone indeed. Your old friend feels that you have done your duty with great honour and respect and

---

[9] Through his thirty-six children out of eight wives he founded something of a dynasty.

have gained a good name and we congratulate you on being
called for consultations at this crucial time. I am writing this
short note in my own hand for Lady Sykes to congratulate her
on regaining her husband and I am sending a few articles made
in Fars as a small present for her, for her to open herself. I wish
long lasting prosperity and honour to your family.

Abdul Hussein Farman Farma, 13th December 1918

On his way to India Sykes passed once more through Kerman,
where he had made so many friends. The SPR put on a parade for
him in the Meidan but this time the crowds did not turn out. The
mood had changed and the nationalists, who could no longer be
branded as pawns of the Germans, were getting stronger. It was
time for him to leave Persia.

Sykes's career was now effectively over and he was officially
retired in the following year, at the age of fifty-two. Although
many had criticized him for his inept military performance, many
also came to defend him. Lancelot Oliphant, who was in charge of
the Persia desk at the Foreign Office, had criticized his 'wild and
undigested ideas' but later wrote that he had 'done exceptionally
well'. Even Clarmont Skrine, when he later came to write his
book on Persia in the war, came round:

The choice of this remarkable man, who had done no sol-
diering since the Boer War, to raise a new corps in hostile
country was a bold one, but it was justified by the result . . . He
cannot be denied the credit for exploiting British prestige,
bluffing enemy agents and Persian hostiles alike and thus, with
quite inadequate resources, keeping South Persia comparatively
quiet during a long and critical phase in the war.

Sir Arnold Wilson, who had been a political officer in
Mesopotamia responsible for paying subsidies to the tribal chiefs
around the oil fields and who had criticized the enormous expense
of the SPR, later generously wrote: 'Sykes had done wonders with
the material at his disposal.'

20

The end of the game?

WITH SYKES GONE, the political dust-up between London and India could settle. Feeling that he had been undeservedly relieved of his duties, Sykes wrote two long articles for *The Times* on 26th and 27th February 1919. As was the tradition, there was no by-line to the articles but his hand was unmistakable. Using language that later reappeared almost word for word in his supplement to the *History of Persia*, he wrote about his role in the establishment of the SPR and referred unblushingly to 'the courage, foresight, skill and intimate knowledge of the Persian character of General Sykes' and described how he had saved Shiraz virtually single-handed from the Qashqai in June 1918. He made no mention of any of his consular or military colleagues. Curzon wrote to Edwin Montague at the India Office to complain of the 'glowing account of the performance of Sir Percy Sykes at Shiraz who gave in many respects a quite one-sided view of the operations'. Both Curzon and Balfour, who was now Prime Minister, were incensed by Sykes's letters and made sure that Sykes, who had few friends in high places to help him, should have no further career.

Appreciation of a kind did, however, come from an unexpected quarter. Shortly after the end of the war Sykes received a letter of thanks from two British officers who had been prisoners of war in the north of Turkey. They wrote to say that, while in prison, they had been sent a copy of his *History of Persia* and that the 'excellent map of Anatolia in the back' had enabled them to escape and find their way down to the Mediterranean, where they had stolen a small boat and sailed to Cyprus.

Whatever Sykes's superiors may have thought about his performance in charge of the SPR – and whatever his personal failings – he had left a worthwhile legacy. Roads had been built in South Persia where wheeled traffic had never been able to pass before and he had created a properly paid and disciplined force for public order, where the Persian government had nothing of the kind. For months after the end of the war a 700-strong robber gang under the famous Naib Hussein Kashani, a gangster so powerful that Tehran at one point tried to make his position official by appointing him Governor of Kashan, had been laying waste to the lands between Kashan and Isfahan, which were outside SPR territory. The Persian government tried and failed several times to arrest him and, in desperation, swallowed its pride and appealed to the SPR, who within forty-eight hours captured the untouchable Naib Hussein and dispersed his gang. This act is still remembered by Iranians today, who will admit of the SPR: 'They were good, but then they had money. If we had only had the money we could have done the same.'

The SPR was now under the command of Colonel Orton but decisions needed to be taken about its future. Influenza had wiped out many of them and the British officers wanted to go home. Consul Gough, who regarded the Fars Brigade as useless and expensive, wanted to disband the whole force and the General Staff agreed. The Kerman Brigade, who had not been infected by the recruitment of the Shiraz gendarmes, were quietly and efficiently maintaining order and preventing robberies in their sector.

Apart from the SPR, there were other British forces still in Persia at the end of the war in Europe. General Dunsterville's force occupied north-west Persia. He had taken a small and inadequate force by sea in an effort to defend the Baku oil fields against a strong Turkish attack, but had been forced to retreat. His force, now taken over by General Ironside, and called 'Norperforce', was holding much of the country between Tehran and Enzeli on the Caspian against the local Jangali guerrillas, who were supported by the Bolsheviks.

In the north-east General Malleson, based at Meshed, had taken over the largely Indian-manned East Persia Cordon force and was fighting a railway war against the Bolsheviks on the north side of the mountain range that formed the border with Russia, along the line between the Caspian port of Krasnovodsk and Bokhara. This bizarre war was conducted between armoured trains, the armour being not of steel but of bales of locally grown cotton.[1]

Those Russian officers of the Persian Cossack Brigade who had remained in Persia after the revolution were by now much reduced in numbers and in morale. They had to be paid for by the British and were of doubtful reliability. Because of the collapse of the Russian market, which had taken two-thirds of Persian exports, foreign trade had broken down, and the Allies had ceased spending on supplies for their troops, so that the merchants were bankrupt. There was famine in the north, where the harvest had failed. The Persian government had lost all sense of purpose and was practically bankrupt. The portly young Ahmad Shah was concerned only with the security of his personal investments in Europe. The state of his country at the time was best described by one of Sykes's Persian friends, who likened Persia to the last act of the *Tazieh* (the passion play performed in the month of Muharram): 'Everyone is hurrying to gather up his shoes, cloak and bag of dried fruit in order to get out before the end. No-one is paying attention to the play.'

The Democrats were now well organized and had a large following. The British had two options. One was to withdraw all their troops from Persia and revert to their old role of political peacemaker between the various factions, while making a separate deal with the Sheikh of Muhammerah for the protection of the oil fields at the head of the Persian Gulf.[2] The other option was to take upon themselves the task of reviving the Persian economy and turning the country into a British protectorate. This was the policy proposed by Curzon.

Curzon, who had been chairing the Persia Committee of the War Cabinet and had become Foreign Secretary in 1919, had

---

[1] See Reginald Teague-Jones, *The Spy who Disappeared*.
[2] For a moving account of the subsequent British betrayal of their old friend the Sheikh of Muhammerah see Gordon Waterfield, *Professional Diplomat: Sir Percy Loraine*.

decided that India needed to be defended against the new threat of Bolshevism by the establishment of a strong Persia, to be run by his own person. As the *Sunday Sun* had written about him in 1892, 'he seems to be under the impression that he discovered Persia and that, having discovered it, in some mysterious way, he owns it'. However, much had changed in Persia since Curzon had 'discovered' it. Oblivious to the fact that since his travels nearly thirty years earlier the country had come of age politically and would no longer stand for overt foreign dominance, by August 1919 he had bulldozed into existence a partially secret agreement with a 'triumvirate' of Persian grandees who would govern the country under his direction. The triumvirate was made up of the Foreign Secretary, Farman Farma's eldest son, Firuz Mirza Nosrat ud-Dowleh, together with the Prime Minister, Vossouq ud-Dowleh, and the Minister of Finance, Sarem ud-Dowleh ('Cutlass of the State'), the son of Zill us-Sultan. Huge sums were paid to these three men to secure the necessary votes in the Persian Majlis for approval of the agreement, together with an agreement that, if they failed and were forced into exile, further funds would be made available to them to maintain their standard of living. The payments were supposed to be secret but word soon got out in Persia, causing considerable jealousy among those who had been omitted from the list of benefactions.

Curzon's Anglo-Persian Agreement of 1919 allowed for the British to take over the management of the Persian finances and also of the army, which would be based on the SPR. Aid and advisers would be provided. All other countries would be excluded from playing any role in post-war Persia, which particularly displeased the French and the Americans, who expressed their view that Persia was not Curzon's private hunting ground. The Agreement was pushed through in the face of much advice to the contrary from the Government of India and from Herman Norman, the new Minister at Tehran, who all pointed out that the three Qajar members of the triumvirate were hardly representative of the new Persia and that public opinion would be opposed to it.

Sykes, although easily caricatured as an old imperialist, was vociferous in his opposition to this folly of Curzon's. Curzon was oblivious to the fact that Persian public opinion even existed and assumed that any local opposition to his superior will could be resolved with cash. Sir Percy Cox who had negotiated the agreement, persuaded him to spend more and more of it on the triumvirs who, without satisfactory inducement and assurances as to their own futures if it blew up in their faces, refused to sign it. Curzon became increasingly enraged by this fruitless expense. Contemporary Persian historians now agree that Persia had little choice at the time but to accept some form of British financial assistance and military advice, but that Curzon could not have made a more unpopular choice of agents for his policy. The Agreement, although it took effect briefly, was never ratified by the Majlis and there was much popular protest against it, some of it organized by those who had missed out on Curzon's largesse. Bolshevik forces began to advance on Tehran from the north-west and 'Norperforce' retreated ignominiously in front of them. This retreat, although intended to be a tactical withdrawal to a stronger position, was seen by the Persians as a defeat for the British. The government in London wrung its hands and Herman Norman wavered. All would have been lost, had not Henry Smyth intervened.

Smyth, who had been military attaché under Sykes at Meshed and who had made Sykes godfather to his son when he was born there, had ended up in Qazvin, eighty miles to the west of Tehran, as second-in-command to General Ironside. He was employed by Army Intelligence and, after Ironside had had to arrange for the dismissal of all the now ineffective Russian officers, was now in effective command of the Persian Cossacks, although they were under the nominal command of Sardar Homayun. Their most efficient officer was Reza Khan, a colonel. Smyth was on very good terms with him and promoted him to command of the brigade.

On 21st February 1921 Reza Khan, at the head of the Persian Cossacks, marched into Tehran, launching the coup that led to his becoming Minister of War and then, in 1923, Prime Minister of a government dominated by the Democrats. In October 1925 the Majlis deposed Ahmad Shah, who had left the country, and declared Reza Khan to be the new Shah. In April 1926 he crowned himself as the founder of the Pahlavi dynasty and decreed that from then on foreigners were to call Persia by its proper name of Iran.

Much speculation still surrounds the coup. Persians have always believed that the British government was behind it and that General Ironside organized it. However, Henry Smyth's private diary, which has only just come to light, shows that neither the British government nor the British Legation was even aware of the final events. Ironside had left the country, as had most of the British forces. The Persian Cossacks in Tehran had become undisciplined and had started looting. To restore order, Smyth, acting on his own initiative, suggested to Reza Khan that he withdraw these Cossacks and replace them with a fresh detachment. Reza Khan, who was in close touch with the Democrat leaders and had been biding his time, needed no further encouragement and did the rest himself. The ineffective Qajars were swept away and Curzon's Agreement was denounced. Shortly afterwards all British forces were withdrawn, with the exception of the SPR. Persia at last had stood up.

Colonel W.A.K. Fraser had been put in command of the SPR in early 1919, with the expectation of a ten-year contract as part of Curzon's Agreement. The object was to maintain a force to balance the Cossack Brigade, whose loyalties were uncertain. By the end of 1919 he had been seconded to the Anglo-Persian Military Mission as adviser and had made a detailed survey of Persia's military potential and an outline scheme of organization for the Persian armed forces. In 1922, some time after Reza Khan's coup, he was ordered to disband the force, which by now, after the desertions and the devastating effect of the influenza epidemic, stood at a strength of six thousand. Although the existence of the SPR had officially come to an end, a large part of it became the nucleus of the new and efficient Persian army, free of the taint of its previous British and Russian associations.

Kal Heidar, with whom this story began outside the barber's shop in Shiraz and who years before had taught marching and musketry to the young Reza Khan, joined the new army. He had been cashiered successively from the Cossack Brigade, the Ottoman army, the Swedish Gendarmerie and the South Persia Rifles. There was now nowhere else to go, so he became an honest soldier for a while.

In his retirement, to keep himself occupied and to earn some much-needed cash, Sykes took to writing and turned out a history of Afghanistan, a life of his benefactor Sir Mortimer Durand, a history of exploration and a history of the discovery of China by the West. He also edited a serial magazine for boys, with stories of exploration and adventure. He was invited to lecture in Canada and America, where he fascinated his audiences with tales of his adventures in Persia, a country of which they had only heard in connection with carpets and fairy tales. He became involved with the Royal Geographical Society, the Central Asia Society and the Royal Asiatic Society and corresponded with explorers and scholars all over Europe about Persian history and archaeology.

Although his career was over, Sykes was still regarded in some quarters as a person of influence. In late 1933, in a hint of the war that was to follow, he was approached by Dr Filchner, a German explorer of Tibet, on behalf of Captain Ernst Röhm, the head of Hitler's storm-troopers. Röhm wished to know whether Sykes could interest the British secret service in co-operating with Germany in the Far East. Sykes sent Filchner packing, 'on the grounds of German maltreatment of [the Bulgarian] Dimitroff and others, who were shortly afterwards released'.

The *History of Persia* was translated into Persian and Sykes involved himself in promoting Persian culture. He worked on a committee which in 1931 organized a magnificent exhibition of Persian art in London, with carpets, miniature paintings, pottery, tiles and prehistoric bronzes lent by private collectors and various museums in Europe and America, including the Tehran museum. Reza Shah himself lent some items from his own recently acquired collection. It was a great occasion and made London aware of the riches of Persian culture. Sykes also maintained good relations with the Muslim community in London, who invited him to a celebration of *Eid* at the London Mosque.

Sykes had never had his own home in England but on his mother's death he inherited the house at Lyndhurst in Hampshire, where he expected to live the life of a country gentleman and bring up his family, from whom he had been parted for so long. The private memoir written by his youngest daughter, Elinor, a remarkable, conventionally unconventional woman, gives a touching picture of Sykes as a family man.

The end of the game?

I did not love my father but at the same time I thought he was all that a father should be, pompous and kind, incapable of talking to any of his six children at any time. We called him 'Father' and rather despised children who had 'Daddies', who romped with them. We later heard from other people that my father was extremely proud of his children. This surprised us as he never paid us a compliment . . . None of the boys was the least interested in the East or in becoming cavalry officers like him. By his standards they were most undistinguished. Of his daughters he expected nothing except that they should marry. My marriage [to 'Sinbad' Sinclair, of Shell Petroleum in India] was considered a mésalliance, but I was already twenty-one and in his eyes any husband was better than none.

My father, who thought and talked and wrote only of Persia, was greatly admired and honoured throughout the British Empire for his works but was considered a bore by his children . . . All his friends seemed to be colonels and generals and retired civil servants, but never a Persian or a businessman among them.

Our mother brought us up in the belief that we were very poor but extremely well born, when in fact we were neither, but we all of us still carry both of these convictions through life . . . Social acceptability for my parents did not include a culti- vated mind or a knowledge of the arts. The touchstone was fitting into a house party. Being able to play bridge and tennis were the chief qualifications for this occupation and rigorous training in these skills was started from earliest childhood. Chess, draughts, backgammon, bezique, cribbage and piquet were played continuously with much quarrelling and frequent tears. My father, when playing chess, never failed to show his feeling of triumph at winning, even though his opponent may not have been more than seven or eight . . . All this competitive sport developed in us aggressive, decisive natures. We became physically brave and strong, with powers of endurance; we were quite intolerant of other families whose tennis or bridge were not up to standard.

My parents were not as unsympathetic as they seemed. They were Victorians, rather ahead of their time, who knew nothing about children and did not seek to find out what was going on in their minds. They left us alone and, apart from commenting on our unkempt appearance and gross table manners, carried on with their own interests, giving us a strong feeling of security by both just being there all the time. They had nothing in common with each other, disagreed on almost every point, but never actually quarrelled.

Within a year my mother, who from now onwards made more and more of the decisions affecting our lives, decided that the money available was not sufficient to live as gentlefolk in the country. Hunting, shooting and entertaining were a necessary part of this, and educating the children at leading boarding schools was equally necessary.

Like many others at the time, Sykes had put his money into South American railways; it was a disaster, and Lyndhurst had to be sold. The 'lifelong prosperity' that Farman Farma had wished him had eluded him. Evelyn moved the family to St Briac, a seaside village in Brittany, where life was cheaper. Elinor describes her father there:

He would sometimes roll up his grey flannels carefully to the knee, put on his panama hat and take us to the Frémur to catch shrimps and dabs. He bought land from his neighbour and built tennis courts. He and Frank used to play all day. When Frank, aged about sixteen, first beat my father in a single, my father gave up tennis and took to golf. Swimming my father taught us patiently. He would stand, stout and serious, in his short-sleeved, short-legged bathing suit with wide black and white bands across it, holding us under our chins and clutching the back of our suits, urging us on, one after the other, and reward-ing us with toy sailing boats when we could swim twenty yards . . . To my father we were always troops from whom courage and endurance was expected, in return for justice and consider-ation. To have shown fear would have been unthinkable.

In 1931 Evelyn decided to move again, this time to Territet, near Montreux on Lake Geneva, where there were good schools and no income tax. Sterling had lost a third of its value and economies had to be made. It was either that or a return to a rather friendless form of shabby gentility in England. They spent nine years in Switzerland. The only paintings in the house were portraits, including a particularly grim one of Sykes in uniform looking like Lord Kitchener. Evelyn always made interiors gracious and pleasing, the foundation being Sykes's collection of Persian carpets and tiles, with some Chinese jade and porcelain that he had brought back from Kashgar. He occupied his time peacefully with his writing and correspondence and they played bridge with the English community and with some White Russian Romanovs. He encouraged young explorers and travellers, including Ella Maillart, who travelled with the unwilling Peter Fleming in Chinese Turkistan. This life lasted them until 1931, when sterling came off the gold standard and they could no longer afford to live abroad and returned to England. Sykes longed for the Central Asian Society and Evelyn longed for country squires who would marry her daughters. He had missed the society of fellow generals from the East and the semi-learned societies who welcomed him on to their committees, for he was both tireless and scrupulous. At the Athenaeum he met T. E. Lawrence, Allenby and Storrs and found a quiet room to write.

Adventurously, they had taken a flat in Olympia, well outside the limits of socially acceptable London, which was then bounded by Gloucester Road, Oxford Street, Regent Street and Sloane Square. Sykes never brought his friends home. Elinor imagined that it was because he felt ashamed of his quarrelsome family, who took so little interest in his beloved East.

With a large family to educate, they constantly felt short of money, which mattered more to Evelyn than to Sykes, who used to say to his son-in-law Sir Patrick Reilly how glad he was that he had never had any. 'If I had,' he said, 'I would never have done anything.' Ella was generous to her brother's family and paid for much of their education and, when she died in 1940, she left them her flat. As each of the children married Sykes gave them as a wedding present a set of his two-volume *History of Persia*, his standard wedding present to all his friends' children.

At the beginning of the Second World War, although on the retired list, Sykes was given a brigadier-general's uniform and sent to lecture to the troops. He was very pleased to be back in uniform but the invitations to lecture soon dried up, presumably because the soldiers found him very dull. Evelyn worked in a canteen through the Blitz until her health deteriorated and her doctor advised her to leave London. They moved to Sunningdale, where Sykes took up golf. He and Evelyn, whom Elinor remembers as 'not liking him very much', lived rather separate existences at this stage of their lives. He adored his youngest daughter but was not particularly affectionate to the rest of his offspring and family gatherings were not occasions of harmony. Most of his family remember him boring them to distraction, banging on interminably about his days of glory in Persia like a gramophone that would not stop. Only after Sykes's death did his son-in-law the late Sir Patrick Reilly, who subsequently became ambassador to Moscow and Paris, remark that he wished he had listened to him more.

After the publication of his *History of Afghanistan* in March 1940 Sykes gave a lecture to the Royal Central Asian Society on 'The Current Position in Afghanistan'. It was obviously a good lecture, because he was asked to repeat it to a combined audience of the RCAS and the more intellectually minded Royal Asiatic Society at the Caxton Hall. It was considered an important occasion and Lord Zetland, the Secretary of State for India, was in the chair. On the stage with him were Lord Lamington and Sir Louis Dane, both retired Indian governors, and Sir Michael O'Dwyer, the ex-Governor of the Punjab. As all were standing to congratulate Sykes, an Indian nationalist named Udham Singh got up from the audience, came up to the platform and fired a number of shots with his revolver. O'Dwyer fell dead and most of those on the platform were wounded, including Lord Zetland. Sykes, aged seventy-three, charged at the Indian and floored him, holding him pinned until he could be arrested. The newspapers of the following day gave glowing tributes to his heroism, but he was mortified that he had been unable to save O'Dwyer.

Two years later Sir Reader Bullard, the Minister at Tehran, wrote in a letter home that Sykes was 'conducting a tremendous correspondence . . . all the letters being in his own very clear handwriting, with Dr Isa Sadeq, the Persian Minister of Education, about the translation of the *History of Persia*'. In 1945, at the age of seventy-nine, he was still playing golf and acting as the Honorary Secretary of the Royal Central Asian Society, spending much of his time at the Athenaeum. On 11th June, a very hot day, he went to London. There were no taxis to be had, so he set off from Waterloo Station for the Athenaeum on foot carrying his suitcase. Half-way across Trafalgar Square he collapsed. He was taken to hospital, from where he telephoned Evelyn to say that he was 'done for', but that he had had a good life and was thankful for it. By the end of the day he was dead. Only the day before he had been playing golf at Sunningdale. Elinor wrote in her memoir:

I heard the news on the wireless at Kasauli [near Simla] and felt truly sorry but, even more, guilty. I had given him no affection, been critical of him and impatient and shown him my boredom when he went on about Persia or Marco Polo, and yet he had been so kind to me always, and embarrassingly proud of my least achievement. I had thought him indestructible.

I wrote affectionately to my mother but tactlessly hinted that perhaps she would be happier now as she and my father had not got on well. My mother denied this reflection on her marriage angrily, saying that she and my father had always been devoted to one another.

Sykes never ceased to profess his admiration for the people, the literature and the art of Persia. In none of his writings, whether private or public, did he ever criticize or disparage the Persians. At a time when Persia was largely unknown to the English he lectured widely about her ancient civilization and praised her native genius, often repeating his view that, in spite of the terrible corruption obtaining in Persia, which Reza Shah's new government was trying to suppress, and despite the lack of education and the absence of progress in the shape of roads and railways, he considered the Persians to be the finest and most gifted race in western Asia. Much as he loved Persia, he entertained no romantic illusions about the country that had given him a home for the best part of twenty-five years and had made him what he was.

Many Englishmen have come and gone and been forgotten in Persia. To keep Sir Percy's name alive, his family endowed the

Sykes Medal to be awarded by the Royal Central Asian Society. It shows Sykes, with the inscription *Author, Traveller, Statesman*, and is awarded to those who have added to the knowledge and understanding of Persia and Central Asia. Among those recently honoured are Sir Denis Wright, Peter Hopkirk and Sir Mark Tully. Outside the small circle of Persophiles in England Sir Percy has now been largely forgotten but to this day his name is remembered in Iran, if not with affection, then with respect, fascination and not a little awe – as the embodiment of 'the hand of the English' that controlled so much of their country.

Postscriptum

MANY PERCYS HAVE appeared in Persia and there was often confusion between them. Sir Percy Cox was Resident in Bushire and Minister at Tehran and Sir Percy Loraine became Minister at Tehran in 1921. There were also unrelated Sykeses in the area. Sir Mark Sykes involved himself in the Near East and was responsible for the Sykes–Picot Agreement, while Christopher Sykes travelled in Persia with Robert Byron between the wars. When Sir Percy Loraine was appointed Minister, his friend Andrew Barstow of the Anglo–Persian Oil Company penned him the following:

> PERCII PERSORUM
> Three Percys have, for better or for worse,
> Filled from Great Britain's coffers Persia's purse.
> The first who propped her 'gainst external shocks
> With British gold was Percy Cox.
> Next, squandering gold as floods that burst their dykes
> On Southern Persian Rifles – Percy Sykes.
> Shrewd Cox! Brave Sykes! Their efforts still were vain,
> Yet may the third redeem the other twain,
> And luck attend Sir Percy of Loraine.

Chronology

1888	Joins 16th Lancers (India), then transferred to 2nd Dragoon Guards 'Queen's Bays'.	
1889		Conservative government under Lord Salisbury. Curzon travelling in Persia.
1892	Spying mission to Samarqand.	Curzon Parliamentary Under-Secretary of State for India. Conservatives defeated in July. Liberal government under Gladstone.
1893	First journey in Persia. Reconnaissance in Baluchistan.	
1894	Founds Consulate of Kerman and Baluchistan.	
1895	Assistant-Commissioner Perso–Baluch boundary.	Conservative government under Salisbury. Curzon Parliamentary Under-Secretary of State for Foreign Affairs.
1896	Mission to Karun Valley.	Nasir ud-Din Shah assassinated, succeeded by Muzaffar ud-Din Shah.
1897	Escort to Nasir ul-Molk, Persian Ambassador to St James'. Investigates gun-running in Persian Gulf.	
1898	Founds Sistan Consulate. Returns to Kerman.	Curzon appointed Viceroy.
1901	South Africa: Intelligence Department, then in command of Montgomeryshire Imperial Yeomanry.	
1902	Marries Evelyn Seton.	Balfour succeeds Salisbury as Prime Minister.

1903	Resumes post as Consul at Kerman.	
1905	Appointed Consul-General at Meshed.	Curzon resigns as Viceroy.
1906		Liberal Government wins election. Persian Constitutional Revolution. Muzaffar ud-Din Shah dies, succeeded by Muhammad Ali Shah.
1907		Anglo-Russian Convention divides Persia into zones of influence.
1909		Muhammad Ali Shah forced to abdicate. Ahmad Shah succeeds as a minor.
1912		Russians bombard the Shrine at Meshed.
1913	Leaves Meshed.	
1914	City Commandant, Southampton, then posted as interpreter to Lahore Division in France.	Outbreak of First World War.
1915	Acting Consul-General, Kashgar, with Ella. Knighted (KCIE).	
1916	Raises South Persia Rifles. GOC South Persia to 1918.	
1919		Curzon, now Foreign Secretary, forces through the Anglo-Persian Agreement to turn Persia into a British protectorate.
1920	Retires.	
1921		Reza Khan's *coup d'état* in Tehran.
1932–42	Honorary Secretary of Royal Central Asian Society.	

Glossary of Persian terms

Alachik	Turkoman felt tent, yurt
Alaman	Turkoman raid, *also* raiding party
Anderun	Private quarters of a house
Anjuman	(Secret) society esp. of the Constitutionalists. Some *anjumans* were official.
Arg	Citadel
Bandobast	Preparations for a journey
Bast	Sanctuary
Bughala, buggalow	Small sailing boat of the Persian Gulf
Dragoman	Interpreter and guide (from Turkish *terjuman*)
Farangi	European
Farrash	Footman
Fedayeen	Those prepared to sacrifice themselves for a cause
Ghazi	Warrior for the faith
Gholam	Legation messenger, courier
Hamam	Public bath
Istiqbal	Official reception outside a town
Kajaveh	Pair of panniers slung either side of a mule to carry women or children
Karguzar	Liaison official between foreigners and local Governors
Khabar	News
Luti	Larrikin, but with a code of honour among thieves
Majlis	Parliament. During the Constitution each large city had its own separate *majlis*.
Mujahid	Volunteer for a cause
Mujtahid	Doctor of Islamic (Shia) law
Nulla (Indian)	Dried-up river valley
Pish-khedmat	Head servant
Qajar	Persian ruling dynasty (1787–1921)

Glossary of Persian terms

Qalyan	Water pipe, hubble-bubble
Qanat	Line of wells joined at the bottom, bringing irrigation water from the mountains
Sardar	Chief
Sartip	Brigadier, tribal chief
Seyyid	Descendant of the Prophet (frequently impostors)
Shamianeh	Open-sided tent
Sharia	Islamic law
Shikar	Hunting, or big game
Sigheh	Temporary marriage (among the Shia Muslims)
Sowar	Horseman, cavalryman
Syce	Groom
Takhte-ravan	Ladies' travelling sedan, slung between two mules
Toman	Unit of currency, made up of 10 *qrans*. Over this period sterling varied between four and five tomans to the pound.
Vaqf	Endowment held in trust by the Shrine
Zakuska (Russian)	Hors d'oeuvres

Persian names and transliteration

THERE ARE MANY conventions for transliterating Persian names into English, not one of which is entirely satisfactory. I have used a combination of the system commonly used by the India Office at the time, with some adaptations for modern usage. The English referred to Bushehr as Bushire, Mashhad as Meshed, Yazd as Yezd, Ashqabad as Askhabad or Ashgabad, etc. If you cannot find a place name on the map, you should be able to find something close to it which will be correct. Similarly, Nasir ud-Din is often spelt Nasser ed-Din.

Persian titles under the Qajar dynasty were sonorous and lengthy. Some of them were inherited and others came with the job – and the jobs were bought. There was no hierarchy or gradation to the titles. By the end of the dynasty so many 'ud-Dowlehs' and 'ul-Molks' had been created that the titles had lost most of their value. The full style of a Persian nobleman would start with his name and be followed by the title, as in Ali Ashraf Khan, Ihtisham ul-Vizarah. If a prince, 'Mirza' would follow his name. 'Mirza' before his name signified only that he was a man of education. The English found these names indigestible and frequently shortened them, referring, for example, to Rukn ud-Dowleh as 'The Rukn', which no Persian would ever do. Nevertheless, to make it easier for the reader not familiar with Persian names, I have followed this bad practice and make due apology to Persian readers for this lack of courtesy.

Acknowledgements

THE UNATTRIBUTED QUOTATIONS are from the published works of Sir Percy Sykes or his sister Ella: *Ten Thousand Miles in Persia, The Glory of the Shia World, History of Persia, Through Persia on a Sidesaddle, Through Deserts and Oases of Central Asia* or from his official consular diaries.

Extensive use has been made of the consular diaries. The originals were sent to the Foreign Office in London with copies to the Government of India. They are now in the Public Record Office at Kew and in the Oriental and India Office Collection at the British Library (previously known as the India Office Library). To the distress of historians, in 1946 the Foreign Office, suffocating under the weight of paper, ceased the practice of keeping these diaries. It would be tedious to list all the documents referred to. The PRO documents are to be found in the series of FO/60,65,248,371. The OIOC documents are in the Political & Secret series L/PS/7,10,11,18. The illustrated reports of Sykes's tours in Khorasan are in L/PS/7/232 and L/PS/11/76. Illustrations of his travels in the Pamirs are in L/PS/20/A119 (re-archived as Photos 1042). The letters of Captain Keyes and Clarmont Skrine are also in the OIOC. The Imperial War Museum houses the war diaries of Major W.A.K. Fraser and the letters of Captain Sherwood.

Sir Percy's son-in-law the late Sir Patrick Reilly sent the most important of Sir Percy's papers, as well as copies of his own writings on Sir Percy, to the Middle East Centre at St Antony's College, Oxford. Colonel T.W. Haig's memoirs are also at St Antony's.

The photographs, nearly all of which were taken by Sir Percy or his cousin Herbert Sykes, were supplied by the Imperial War Museum, the Department of Oriental Antiquities of the British Museum, the Oriental and India Office Collection of the British Library and the Royal Geographical Society. The British Museum has Sir Percy's and Herbert's early photographs and the RGS has Sir Percy's later photographs which, one day, somebody might be inspired to publish as a superb architectural and ethnographic record of Persia and Turkistan as they were a hundred years ago. The cartoon of the Russian bombardment of Meshed was supplied by St Antony's College, Oxford, which also has a large collection of Sir Percy's photographs. Other illustrations were lent by Sir Percy's family.

Select bibliography

Balfour, J.M., *Recent Happenings in Persia* (Edinburgh, 1922)

Bast, Oliver, *Les Allemands en Perse durant la Première Guerre Mondiale* (Paris, 1997)

Bayat, Mangol, *Mysticism and Dissent: Socioreligious thought in Qajar Iran* (New York, 1982)

———, *Iran's First Revolution: Shiism and the Constitutional Revolution of 1905–1909* (Oxford, 1991)

Browne, E.G., *A Year amongst the Persians* (London, 1893)

———, *The Persian Revolution of 1905–1909* (Cambridge, 1910)

Cronin, Stephanie, *The Army and the Creation of the Pahlavi State in Iran, 1910–1926* (London, 1997)

Curzon, George, *Persia and the Persian Question* (London, 1892)

Dickson, W.E.R., *East Persia: A Backwater of the Great War* (London, 1924)

Dunsterville, L.C., *The Adventures of Dunsterforce* (London, 1920)

Dyer, R.E.H., *The Raiders of the Sarhad* (London, 1921)

Farman Farma, Manuchehr, *Blood and Oil* (New York, 1997)

Fraser, David, *Persia and Turkey in Revolt* (London, 1910)

Ghani, Cyrus, *Iran and the Rise of Reza Shah* (London, 1998)

Greaves, Rose L., *Persia and the Defence of India, 1884–1892* (London, 1959)

Grey, Sir Edward, *Twenty-Five Years, 1892–1916* (London, 1925)

Griesinger, Walter, *German Intrigues in Persia: The Niedermayer Expedition* (London, 1918)

Hardinge, Sir Arthur, *A Diplomatist in the East* (London, 1928)

Hardinge, Charles (Lord Hardinge of Penshurst), *Old Diplomacy* (London, 1947)

Hopkirk Peter, *The Great Game* (London, 1990)

———, *On Secret Service East of Constantinople* (London, 1994)

Jones, Geoffrey, *Banking and Empire in Iran* (Cambridge, 1986)

Katouzian, Homa, *State and Society in Iran* (London, 2000)

Kazemzadeh, Firouz, *Russia and Britain in Persia, 1864–1914* (New Haven, 1968)

Keddie, Nikki, *Qajar Iran and the Rise of Reza Khan, 1796–1925* (Costa Mesa, California, 1999)

Kennion, R.L., *By Mountain, Lake and Plain* (London, 1911)

Select Bibliography

Keyes, Terence, Private letters in the OIOC, MSS Eur. F131

Korff, Baron, S.A., *Russia's Foreign Relations during the Last Half Century* (London, 1922)

Lieven, D.C.B., *Russia and the Origins of the First World War* (New York, 1983)

Lorimer, J.G., *Gazetteer of the Persian Gulf, Oman and Central Arabia* (Calcutta, 1915)

Macartney, Lady, *An English Lady in Chinese Turkistan* (Oxford, 1985)

McLean, David, *Britain and her Buffer State* (London, 1979)

Moberly, F.J., *Official History of the War: Operations in South Persia 1914–1919* (London, 1987)

Morgan, Gerald, *Ney Elias, Explorer and Envoy Extraordinary in High Asia* (London, 1971)

Nevill, Ralph, *Unconventional Memoirs* (London, 1923)

O'Connor, Frederick, *On the Frontiers and Beyond: A Record Of Thirty Years' Service* (London, 1931)

Savill, M., *Daybreak in Iran: A Story of German Intelligence Service* (London, 1954)

Shuster, W. Morgan, *The Strangling of Persia* (New York, 1912)

Siegel, Jennifer, *Endgame* (London and New York, 2002)

Skrine, Clarmont, *World War in Iran* (London, 1962)

——, *Macartney in Kashgar* (Oxford, 1987)

Sykes, Ella, *Through Persia on a Sidesaddle* (London, 1901)

Sykes, Herbert, *Wanderings in Persia* (private, n.d.)

Sykes, P.M., *Ten Thousand Miles in Persia* (London, 1901)

——, *The Glory of the Shia World* (London, 1920)

——, *History of Persia*, 2nd edn (London, 1921)

——, *Sir Mortimer Durand* (London, 1926)

Sykes, P.M., and Sykes, Ella, *Through Deserts and Oases of Central Asia* (London, 1920)

Sykes, Christopher, *Wassmuss* (London, 1936)

Teague-Jones, Reginald, *The Spy who Disappeared* (London, 1990)

Waterfield, Gordon, *Professional Diplomat: Sir Percy Loraine* (London, 1973)

Wilson, Sir Arnold, *Loyalties, Mesopotamia 1914–1917* (London, 1930)

——, *South-West Persia, A Political Officer's Diary* (Oxford, 1941)

Wright, Sir Denis, *The English amongst the Persians* (London, 1977)

Yate, C.E., *Khurasan and Sistan* (London, 1900)

Index

Index